ORIGINS OF
EUROPEAN CIVILIZATION

ARTHUR COTTERELL

MICHAEL JOSEPH / RAINBIRD

TO MY WIFE AND SON

First published in 1985 by Michael Joseph Ltd,
44 Bedford Square, London WC1B 3DU
and The Rainbird Publishing Group
40 Park Street, London W1Y 4DE

This book was designed and produced by
The Rainbird Publishing Group,
40 Park Street, London W1Y 4DE

ISBN: 07181 2634 3

ILLUSTRATION ACKNOWLEDGMENTS
Between pages 96–7 (pp. i–viii)

J. Allan Cash: i, iii (below), vi (above), viii (above); Sonia
Halliday: iii (above); Robert Harding: viii (left); Hirmer Fo-
toarchiv: v (below), vii (top); Rainbird Archives: ii (right), ii
(below), iv (above), v (top right), v (top left), vii (below);
Ronald Sheridan: iv (below), vi (below).

Printed and bound by
Butler & Tanner Ltd, Frome, Somerset

ORIGINS OF
EUROPEAN CIVILIZATION

CONTENTS

ILLUSTRATIONS

PREFACE

This volume was conceived as an attempt to answer one question: what was the significance of the Greek repulse of the Persian invasion of Europe? The event itself remained so surprising to the following generation that Herodotus may be said to have invented western historiography to explain it. Like his younger contemporary Thucydides, who sought to understand the subsequent struggle between Sparta and Athens, Herodotus was prepared to delve into the mists of the distant past when he considered that the ultimate cause of an historical action lay there. For both writers, however, European antiquity reached back only to the shadowy figure of Minos, who ruled the waters of the Aegean from his palace on the island of Crete. Not only did they lack an awareness of the splendid achievements of pre-Greek peoples in the Aegean, but more, they had no inkling of the collapse of civilization which occurred at the end of the Bronze Age, following the destruction of the Mycenaean citadels on the Greek mainland.

Our perspective on the period down to 479 BC is a longer one. Modern archaeology has revealed the origins of European civilization among the Minoans and traced its antecedents through a succession of neolithic sites to such settlements as Nea Nikomedia in Macedonia. This village is dated by radiocarbon method to about 6200 BC. Excavation has also shed light on the Dark Age, the four centuries of decline, stagnation and recovery, starting in 1100 BC. The evidence of the spade has encouraged the author to widen the scope of the question initially posed and consider the development of European civilization until the confrontation with the Persians. As a result, the reader is offered a survey of our cultural origins in the Aegean, the cradle of Europe. Having treated the emergence of settled life in the Neolithic Age, the narrative reviews the progress made by the Minoans and the Mycenaeans, their palace-based civilizations spanning the entire Bronze Age; then it endeavours to chart the beginnings of a new form of social organization in the city-state, essentially a legacy of the disappearance of the palace; and finally, after describing the remarkable cultural renascence and physical expansion of the Greek world in the Archaic Age, the account ends with the desperate struggle of the Persian Wars.

In translating from the Greek I should like to acknowledge the invaluable assistance given by Clifford Cope. Nevertheless, I must bear full responsibility for the opinions expressed in the text.

Thames Ditton
June 1984

PART ONE

THE EMERGENCE OF CIVILIZATION

Chapter One

THE AEGEAN: TRANSITION FROM THE NEOLITHIC

When in 400 BC the Athenian author Xenophon was bringing up the rear of a retreating column of Greek mercenaries in Asia Minor, he was dismayed to hear loud shouts ahead, thinking that yet another attack was being mounted by the local hillsmen. With his comrades-in-arms he had marched northwards from Mesopotamia after the death of Cyrus, the younger son of Darius II, whose claim to the Persian throne they almost secured on the battlefield at Cunaxa, sixty kilometres from Babylon. Undaunted by their distance from Greece, the thirteen thousand infantrymen had fought a passageway through the bitterly cold mountains of Kurdestan and Armenia. The inhospitable terrain and the fierce inhabitants placed a great strain on the Greeks, and Xenophon as one of the elected generals was only too aware of how close they all were to despair. With tears of joy therefore he learned that those in the vanguard were shouting because they could see the Black Sea. Mounting the rise and looking towards the shore there near Trapezus, Xenophon knew that his men were saved. They were as good as home already – all the waters in the ancient world led to Greece.

The association of the Greeks with ships was based on longstanding historical experience. As we shall see, the invading Persians under Xerxes found to their cost at Salamis in 480 BC that the decision in most of the wars in Greece came not by land but by sea. Geography dictated the importance of naval power: no other area in the Mediterranean was so open to the sea, so reliant upon sail and oar for communication. While the Greek mainland is almost closed to the European continent its shoreline offers access to the rugged interior, especially where inlets and gulfs push between mountain ranges. The Greek islands themselves are really no more than the peaks of other submerged chains. From early prehistoric times the Aegean was a sea familiar to voyagers from the coasts of Europe, Asia and Africa. On the large island of Crete, which lies across the southern entrance to the basin, there arose about 2000 BC the first civilization in Europe comparable with the more ancient traditions of Egypt and West Asia. That Greek legend regarded the Cretan ruler Minos as the first king of the sea only serves to underline the crucial role maritime transport played in the development of Bronze Age civilization on the island. Midway between the Greek mainland, south-western Asia Minor and Libya, Crete was able to enjoy contact with more advanced cultures and to avoid for several centuries the attentions of aggressive neighbours.

10

Here, we trace the events of the Neolithic and early Bronze Ages, the prehistoric conditions from which European civilization eventually emerged.

After 6000 BC the era of foodgatherers and hunters living in caves was followed, even before the invention of pottery, by a definite transition to a way of life based on agriculture. An early neolithic farming settlement was planted at this time on the hill later to bear the great Palace of Minos at Knossos. Excavation of the site has detected ten successive building levels, the mound being some seven metres thick. The first houses were merely huts of wood, but in level nine, where pottery is first attested, the settlers used mud or mud bricks and thatch for construction purposes. Eventually mud bricks rested on solid foundations as stone came into use. A typical middle neolithic house on the Knossos hill, built around 4500 BC, comprised a large rectangular room with one or two doors; inside were a number of storage bins, a firehole, and a bed platform. At its various stages of development, the settlement remained an agglomeration of houses, a labyrinth of rooms and passages which foreshadowed the layout of the Minoan palaces themselves. Minoans was the name given to the ancient Cretans by Sir Arthur Evans, the excavator of Knossos, after the legendary Minos.

The neolithic villagers at Knossos raised a variety of crops, including wheat, barley and pulses, and kept goats, cattle and pigs. Present evidence of the distribution of the wild prototypes for these domesticated plants and animals suggests that they must have been brought by sea from either Asia Minor or another part of West Asia, but we cannot be certain that the farmers were also immigrants to Crete. Archeology tells us nothing of any earlier occupants of the island and indicates that Knossos was the only farming settlement to be established there near the start of the New Stone Age.

Elsewhere in Greece the archeological record for early farming is richer. At the cave of Franchthi, an undisturbed sequence of deposits from about 5800 BC reveals the advent of stockbreeders who were still using old types of flint tools. Situated near Koilada in the Argolid, this cave provided shelter initially for a group of hunters, then a group of pastoralists who were possibly once hunters; a century or more later, the cave housed a group with knowledge of cereal production and the manufacture of pottery. While the greatest concentration of early farming sites is on the fertile plain of Thessaly, the oldest village we know is Nea Nikomedia in Macedonia, at the head of the Aegean. Some fifty kilometres west of Salonika, Nea Nikomedia dates from before the end of the seventh millennium BC, a surprisingly early radiocarbon date of around 6200 BC which compares with the spectacular discoveries made since World War II in southern Turkey at Çatal Hüyük and Hacilar. At these sites in Asia

11

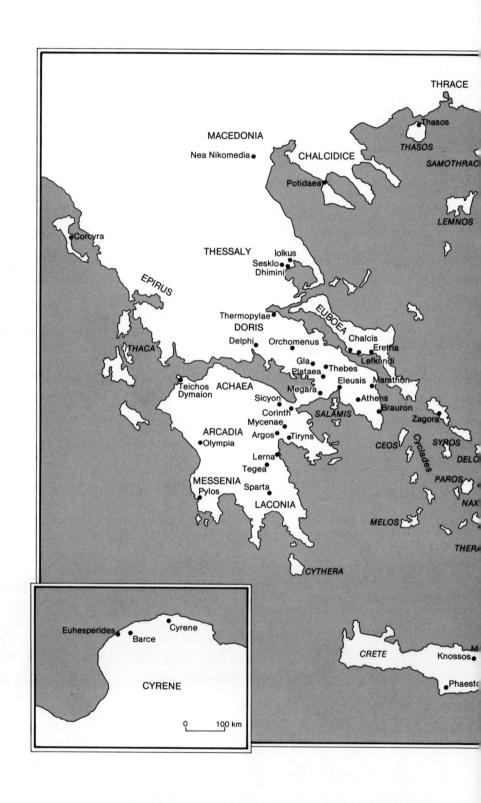

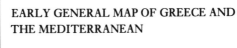

EARLY GENERAL MAP OF GREECE AND
THE MEDITERRANEAN

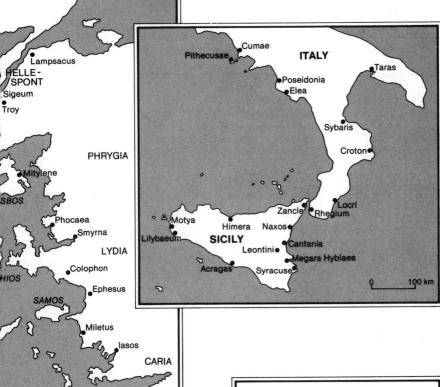

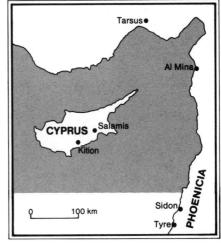

Minor, there flourished from about 6250 BC two sizeable towns, the former boasting elegant houses, shrines with elaborate wallpaintings and plaster relief sculpture, and advanced skills in the crafts of weaving, woodwork, metallurgy and stone cutting. As with the Minoans, the bull was revered as a symbol of strength and fertility; its size, powerful grace and potency inspired the inhabitants of Çatal Hüyük to set plaster reliefs of bulls' heads in niches as well as to incorporate the actual horns in benches within shrines. Their use of horns to represent the bull, or a bull deity, may incidentally resolve uncertainties over the significance of the so-called Minoan horns of consecration. It reveals at least the existence of an organized religion complete with symbolism and mythology.

The low mound at Nea Nikomedia provides a humbler picture of neolithic life, though pottery was present from the beginning. A scattering of timber-framed huts, with rectangular or curved walls, comprised the village, and one of them seems to have acted as a communal building or shrine, judging from its clay statuettes of fertile women. The villagers grew cereals, maintained livestock, and supplemented their diet with wild game, fish, shellfish, and frogs from a nearby lake. Their pottery ranges from large storage jars to tiny pieces such as figures and ornaments which probably had a religious function. The dead were buried in pits outside their houses, in one case three children being crowded together in a partly filled refuse pit.

A clearer view of neolithic religion on the Greek mainland can be gained from the finds at Sesklo in southern Thessaly. At its height, after 4800 BC this compact village had between 150 and 180 inhabitants. Although the idols these people made in clay and stone are less fine than the figurines unearthed at Hacilar in Asia Minor, they reach an impressive level of competence and originality. Examples in the National Museum in Athens testify to the profound worship given to the earth goddess, the Great Mother. She is shown with ballooning breasts, thighs and buttocks. One damaged figurine includes a well-marked fold on her belly, that mysterious source of plenty. The import is plain: the overriding need of a farming village for the repeated fertility of its women, animals and crops. Another terracotta at Sesklo portrays the earth goddess fondling a child, the only male figure to appear until late neolithic times. The adding of a few males to cult groups may reflect a change in religious emphasis, since it would correspond with West Asian notions concerning the young consort of the mother and later religious traditions in the Aegean itself. Devotion for the earth goddess, however, was general among the first farming communities in Europe and West Asia, and survived in various guises well after the life of Christ.

A further advance evident at Sesklo is the diversification of agriculture. In addition to planting wheat, barley and millet the Sesklo farmers cultivated peas, vetch, almonds, figs, pears and acorns. They also took advantage of the wild vines and olives growing in the neighbourhood. Their tools remained chipped stone and sharpened bone, but obsidian, a dark volcanic glass, was replacing flint as a cutter because it flakes more readily. There was widespread trade in the material, the best veins being on the island of Melos. From the safe distance of modern travel it is easy to underestimate the difficulties which faced neolithic sea traders. Their enterprise is all the more remarkable when we remember the laborious task of building rafts or log ships with stone tools and the actual dangers involved in acquiring navigational skills on the changeable Aegean waters. If Melos was settled, satisfactory arrangements had to be made with the islanders who would barter lumps of obsidian for things in scarce supply locally. If the island was still unsettled, then the crew would have to mine the rock itself. Trade and manufacture, however rudimentary they may appear to be in neolithic times, presuppose a considerable degree of organization as well as an acceptance by communities of the need for hazardous expeditions. This gradual quickening of the neolithic economy must have been accompanied by the beginnings of craft specialization. Initially there would have been few specialists because the skills of a community had not yet passed out of the reach of the individual member. Tillage, cattle rearing, tanning, building, flint making, pottery, spinning and weaving: these activities every household could manage. Only a reliable surplus of foodstuffs would have freed the most able exponent from the tasks of agricultural production and permitted the emergence of the craftsman. Such a person may have been responsible for the highly finished pottery unearthed at Sesklo. If the brightly painted vases did come from the hands of a professional, there is a strong possibility that carpenters, tool makers, basket weavers and others were also about to attain semi-independent status.

Social distinctions are even stronger at adjacent Dhimini, a settlement belonging to a new people who invaded Thessaly from the north in the fourth millennium BC. The invaders burned some of the unfortified villages they encountered, occupied others, and built their own settlements with defensive walls. Dhimini was surrounded by several. At first three walls sufficed, then fear drove the inhabitants to add outer stone walls topped by bricks. Probably they were not very high and were intended to provide cover for defending archers. The bow would seem to have been the basis of Dhimini's superiority, for the newcomers were not numerous. Though only a small village, its principal building, the dwelling of the ruling family, was placed carefully within the inner defences. This double-roomed house with a central hearth is not unlike the later megaron, or great room, which formed the core of Mycenaean palaces. There may even have been an open-air altar in the centre of the courtyard before the chieftain's house, just as there was later opposite the entrance to the royal apartments at Tiryns.

Architecturally Dhimini has much in common with the first fortified level of settlement at Troy, where a large hall with a vestibule probably acted as the ceremonial suite of the king. The origins of the Dhimini people are obscure, though it has been suggested that they crossed the Bosporus from Asia Minor. At this period of historical development, such a question has little relevance because small bands of neolithic farmers were constantly on the move in Europe, West Asia and Africa. From archeological evidence, it would appear that various groups arrived in Thessaly from both Anatolia and the Balkans, so that the inhabitants consisted of a mixture of peoples from the start. A similar situation would have prevailed elsewhere. Writing in the fifth century BC, Herodotus was aware of the survival of older languages in parts of Greece. He calls them Pelasgian and informs us that the people of Attica were Pelasgians who had changed their speech to Greek. A tradition recorded in the following century by Andron of Halikarnassus says that the homeland of the Pelasgians was Thessaly.

Until the last few decades hardly anything was known about the Neolithic of the Cyclades, whose strangely irregular forms stud the southern Aegean. The oldest site investigated is on the islet of Saliagos which was once part of an isthmus linking Paros with Antiparos. At the very centre of the archipelago, this fishing village stood within an enclosure wall, flourishing according to radiocarbon dating between 4200 and 3700 BC. Most of its protein came from the sea, domestic animals being mainly sheep, but as at other southern settlements barley was becoming the dominant crop; this shift in cereal production may mirror either a change to a drier climate or some exhaustion of the soil. It is not impossible that a small circular building there represents the first built granary so far discovered which dates from neolithic times. Of equal interest is the excavation of a stylized marble figurine, a precursor of the slender statuettes of goddesses and musicians now recognized as the triumph of early Cycladic art. A rather poorly preserved settlement at Kephala, situated on a headland on Ceos, off the coast of Attica, has also yielded a few grave goods including a marble vase. The cist-graves themselves were circular or rectangular in shape, consisting of small flat stones, and containing several burials each. In the cemetery, too, were found a number of interments of children in pithoi, large storage jars which are still made in the Aegean. Elsewhere in the Cyclades stonelined graves have preserved numerous examples of marble figurines and vases, which remained undisturbed until modern collectors took an interest in their contents. But the chief cultural developments in the islands did not take place until after 3000 BC, six centuries later than the radiocarbon date for Kephala.

The advent of the third millennium BC was a turning-point in European prehistory. It signified the tentative start of the Bronze Age and a southward shift of population and prosperity. Central Greece, the Peloponnese, the Cyclades and, above all, Crete began to employ the new metal technology to lay the foundations of our civilization. The southward move can be seen as a reflection of an underlying economic change, a shift towards a more truly Mediterranean agriculture. The corn and livestock farming of Thessaly was supplemented by the cultivation of the olive and the vine. The slow growth of the former – some thirty years are required for the attainment of full productivity – and its uneven yield from season to season imply ordered social conditions, for few men would have lived long enough to benefit from the trees they planted. Not without reason did the Greeks choose the olive branch as a symbol of peace and name the goddess Athena, patron of patient craftsmen, as the tree's protecting genius. Olive oil soon became a staple commodity, its three chief uses being for cooking, for cleaning the body, and for lighting. Its importance can be gauged in the palace accounts of later Mycenaean princes where there are meticulous entries denoting the rations of oil awarded to staff. One entry even refers to the preparation of a luxury cleanser made from olive oil and sweet-smelling herbs. The domestication of the olive was a decisive step, for it radically altered the pattern of land use. Because the olive as well as the vine require only a little seasonal attention and can be cultivated in areas where cereals and pulses will not grow, and also in cornfields, their introduction brought about an overall increase in output, without disrupting the existing arrangements for tillage and animal husbandry. Between cereals and arboriculture there was conflict neither for land nor labour. An estimate of the likely increase in agricultural productivity for Messenia and Crete is as high as forty per cent.

A consequence of the move away from cereal self-sufficiency was that local variations in landscape, where valley bottoms favoured arable farming and hillsides allowed viniculture and olive production, led to a local surplus of various commodities, and to their exchange. At the so-called House of Tiles in Lerna, on the southern coast of the Argolid, intricate stamped sealings point to the evolution of some system of redistribution prior to 2200 BC. Exchange would have encouraged specialization, especially when metal became an item of more extended trade. Those communities which were unable to make their own bronze tools either had to produce surplus food to buy them or struggle on with traditional stone implements. Those which could cope with the new metallurgy developed a commercial way of life quite beyond the simple organization of the neolithic farmers. Although in Europe this transformation did not create the great city cultures of West Asia, which as early as 3000 BC were fully established in the river valleys of Mesopotamia, it prepared conditions

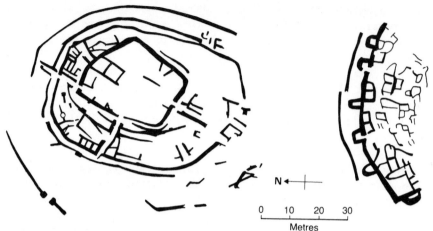

Plans of neolithic Dhimini (*left*) and Chalandriani (*right*). Note the massive bastions of the latter site.

for the palace economies of Minoan and Mycenaean rulers, whose starting dates are 2000 and 1700 BC respectively. The Bronze Age in the Aegean can be said to have lasted the best part of two millennia, from about 2800 to about 1100 BC.

Even before the Bronze Age occupation at Lerna around 2500 BC there were defensive works, but these hardly compare with the massive walls and bastions thrown up by the users of metal. Two large towers have been excavated as well as long sections of a stone wall topped by mud bricks. Fortification of settlements on the Greek mainland and on the Aegean islands, with the notable exception of Crete, testifies to a growing militarism and the concentration of wealth in the hands of a few princes. The culmination of this tendency can be seen in the second millennium BC in the massive fortress that housed the Mycenaean palace at Tiryns. Only Crete was lacking fortifications in the prehistoric period: neither the early Bronze Age settlements before 2000 BC nor the palaces and mansions after that date reveal clear traces of any defences. The apparent peacefulness of Minoan Crete cannot be entirely attributed to the development of a powerful navy, though its vessels would have had a salutary influence on the activities of pirates. A quiet sea does not necessarily mean a quiet island. Yet it would seem that the Cretans were able to devote far fewer resources to defence than their neighbours, and in the process be the first European people to achieve civilization. Quite possibly the distinct agglomerate plan of Minoan buildings reflects a social organization which was capable of ensuring the minimum of conflict. Nothing on Crete remotely parallels the elaborate defences of Chalandriani on the island of Syros. Chalandriani was protected by a line of six semicircular towers, which projected from a thick stone wall. There are also traces of what may have been a second circuit wall five metres outside the first. Access to the rather poor dwellings in the settlement was deliberately restricted to a few narrow gaps in the defences, placed either in a tower or midway between two of them. Despite the obvious preoccupation with safety, the inhabitants of Chalandriani seem to have fled in haste because they left behind a substantial quantity of storage jars and valuables, including a silver diadem on which are punched a collared animal and a bird deity.

At Lerna, which is contemporary with Chalandriani, the long neolithic period is unconnected with subsequent occupation levels. After a gap in time, newcomers reshaped the settlement mound, flattening the top and filling up the hollows; then they built their first houses with thick foundations of stone, laid in a herringbone pattern. The rectangular walls were made of mud brick and doorways opened onto courtyards or gravelled streets. In the centre of the houses stood a more imposing structure, an indication that a stronger sense of social organization was coming into existence. Constructed beneath its more famous successor, the House of Tiles, the building consisted of large rooms with surrounding corridors and a schist roof. Its burning down along with most of the houses within the defensive wall was a setback for the inhabitants, but they rallied their strength and rebuilt the settlement, the focus of which was then the House of Tiles. Whether or not this well-planned building, measuring twenty-five by twelve metres, acted as a small palace we cannot be certain, but such a purpose would seem reasonable. On the ground floor, two large rooms were divided and flanked by corridors and storage spaces. The area immediately outside and the ground floor itself was covered with a layer of smooth yellow clay, while the interior walls were

Plan of the House of Tiles, Lerna. This small palatial building was probably used as a redistributive centre for agricultural produce, until its destruction about 2100 BC.

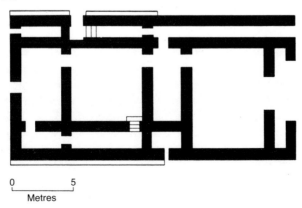

0   5
Metres

plastered in red lime. Clay benches ran along the outer sides of the long north-south walls, possibly for people who had business to transact. Wooden stairs encased in clay led to an upper floor and a gabled roof of stone and terracotta tiles. When it was burned too, between 2200 and 2100 BC, the House of Tiles was empty save for a few jars and seal impressions.

Well over 100 clay sealings have been unearthed at Lerna, showing that at least seventy different seals were in common use. They must have guaranteed the contents of wooden boxes, wicker baskets and terracotta jars. They may have indicated ownership and, as elsewhere in the Bronze Age, their charms could have deterred thieves. Their presence in the House of Tiles supports the view that a ruling family oversaw there the storage and redistribution of agricultural produce. Besides maintaining the royal family, the dues paid in kind by the people would probably have been employed for religious ceremonies and for trade in such essential materials as metals. The actual seal designs are more primitive than those cut on contemporary Crete, but they indicate the presence of a local school of Argive seal makers, whose preference for geometrical forms is pleasing to the modern eye. At both Lerna and pre-palatial Tiryns, evidence of another kind of seal has been found. This is the cylinder, or roller, seal of a specialist potter, whose trademark was an incised design rolled across wet clay. The sign was a hound and its quarry. Itinerant craftsmen like this one help to explain the diffusion of discoveries and techniques in the pre-palatial era, while the concentration of skilled workmen in Minoan and Mycenaean palaces accounts for the take-off of the economy in the favourable conditions for wider trade created by Minos' navy.

Details of daily life are not easily reconstructed from a series of building levels, which is virtually all the data we possess for Lerna because as yet no graves furnished with personal belongings have come to light. Our ignorance of the people who erected the House of Tiles is more than disappointing when it is realized that its destroyers were from an entirely different stock. The little we can deduce from the extant remains suggests a certain cultural vigour, sustained by economic advance. The remarkable new method of roofing, despite its advantages over traditional thatch or flat plaster, was not repeated for over 1,600 years. At nearby Tiryns similar tiles used on a circular building fourteen metres in diameter only emphasizes the prosperity of the Argolid down to 2100 BC. The distinctive piece of pottery at this period in Lerna looks like a sauceboat. Found widely in the Peloponnese, the vessel may have been a spouted drinking cup, the spout being shaped to fit the mouth. A rare example recovered from Arcadia is hammered of pure, thin gold. On pottery forms, however, the existence of marks denoting either the potter or the owner indicate a

Some of the seal-impressions found in the House of Tiles at Lerna, dating from 2200 BC.

growing sophistication, if not the remote beginnings of a sign language. The concept of expressing meaning through a symbol was, of course, already implicit in the use of seals, but the intellectual jump from simple pot marks or abstract seal designs to the hieroglyphs and linear script first encountered on Crete in the second millennium BC was a large one. Not until after 1450 BC, the end of the Minoan period, would Mycenaean princes have the use of a linear writing system on mainland Greece.

The destroyers of the House of Tiles used pot marks but no seals. Their grey-surfaced vases, which imitate in appearance metal vessels, have connections with types of pottery found both in Greece and north-west Asia Minor. It is ancestral to the burnished Minyan ware, so named as its first discovery occurred at Orchomenos in Boeotia, the seat of legendary king Minyas. A fabulously rich monarch, he was the ancestor of the Argonauts, whose exploits under the leadership of Jason form the subject of one of the earliest Greek sagas. Although a reminder of the epic importance of Mycenaean Orchomenos, the term should not beguile us into assuming that the intruders at Lerna, or elsewhere, were Greeks. We have no idea as to what they called themselves.

One argument advanced from the arrival of the so-called Minyans is an invasion of Anatolians who spoke Luvian, a language related to Hittite. This would mean that Luvian settlement preceded settlement of the mainland by the Greeks. Cited as proof are the wheel-made grey vases, the survival of pre-Greek word terminations such as -nthos and -ssos, and the appearance of a new kind of house, a megaron-type structure reminiscent of the chieftain's house at Dhimini. The spread of pre-Greek forms is impressive: towns like Tirynthos, or Tiryns, Korinthos, or Corinth; mountains such as Parnassos, Lykabettos and Hymettos; and for rivers Kephissos and Ilossos. Yet they are also evident in place names throughout the Aegean, with Apeiranthos on Naxos in the Cyclades, Lindos on Rhodes, and on Crete Tylissos and Knossos. The conclusion perhaps should favour something not unlike the situation we noticed in the Neolithic Age, with a variety of peoples living side by side. It is possible that the destruction at Lerna was part of a violent invasion, or it might have been simply an event in a whole series of migrations. The Aegean was probably settled in the late third millennium BC by several language groups, among whom Indo-European speakers were predominant. Culturally Central Greece had affinities with Thessaly and the region around Troy, the Peloponnese had a likeness to Crete, and Attica was linked with the Cyclades.

Equally suspect must be the counter argument which regards the Minyans as Greeks. Until further discoveries provide conclusive evidence, the honour of being the first Greek speakers remains with the Mycenaeans, on the decipherment of whose palace records the identification rests. It can even be considered rash to call the Mycenaeans the ancestors of the Greeks of classical times. The course of ancient European history was never smooth, its upheavals causing any number of uncertainties. Better from an historical point of view is the acceptance of the Minyans, and even the Mycenaeans, as an element in the ancestral stock of the Greek people. The Minyans themselves appear to have absorbed some of the previous inhabitants of Lerna as they treated with deep respect the ruins of the House of Tiles. Instead of rebuilding on the desecrated site, they piled up earth to make a low tumulus, marking its perimeter with a circle of stones. Their awe of the ruined monument is unusual; it left in the centre of their own settlement an untouched mound. For the Greeks, Lerna was also associated with an awful destruction, though in this instance it was Heracles slaying in the surrounding marshes the terrible Hydra, a nine-headed dragon sacred to Hera, the earth goddess of Argos. Blame for the destruction of Lerna has been indeed attributed recently as much to the weakening effect of the malarial marshes as to the superior arms of the invaders.

The sack of Lerna and other settlements in the Argolid, after five centuries of growth, interrupted the advance of material culture on the mainland. Whoever the attackers were, they were barbarous and backward compared with the peoples whose dwelling-places they burned prior to 2100 BC. The comparative scarcity of metal finds in their graves is singular. It means that in spite of the skill displayed in pottery, the Minyans had only recently emerged from the Neolithic and at this point were still behind in other techniques of civilization. Although they learned from those they supplanted, economic and social recovery was slow. Until 1750 BC most towns remained unwalled and unplanned, the population of Lerna only reaching 800 by this date. The return to a uniform culture had to await the rise of the Mycenaean princes, who held sway over the surrounding countryside from powerful strongholds. Even then, the Greek mainland and the Aegean islands were coming increasingly under Cretan influence, as can be seen unequivocally in the contents of the royal shaft graves in the citadel at Mycenae.

Some of the Aegean islands may have become tributary to Crete. Before 2000 BC a Minoan colony was founded at Kastri on the island of Cythera between the western tip of Crete and the Peloponnese. The site was continuously occupied until 1450 BC and at its end was a vigorous outpost, possibly trading with the Mycenaean palace of Pylos in Messenia. Excavation of a rubbish pit close to Kastri has revealed numerous objects of mainland origin. A similar find of Minoan goods at Phylakopi, the capital of nearby Melos, tells us that obsidian remained an important cargo for a time during the Bronze Age. Phylakopi is one of the few major habitations in the Cyclades to be properly dug. On the top of an extensive initial settlement, two fortified towns grew up: they contained neatly rectangular houses of three or four rooms; a sensible network of streets and alleys; and what may have been a small royal residence. Like other Cycladic sites, Phylakopi was situated on a low hill overlooking the sea. From one of its rock-cut tombs must have come the well-known stone model of a granary. Really a composite vase, formed of seven circular hollows and a central irregular one, the arrangement resembles the silos at the Mallia palace on Crete. Storage was always a prime concern of Bronze Age rulers, the storage jars and lined cists in the magazines of the Palace of Minos at Knossos having a capacity of as much as half a million litres.

The growing maritime trade in the Aegean marked a Bronze Age revolution in communications. The dependence of the neolithic people on just their feet and hands would seem remote in the first half of the second millennium BC, when there were ox-carts, chariots drawn by horses, and seagoing ships. On land, pack animals may have been employed throughout the Bronze Age, though the first direct evidence we have comes from a late Minoan figurine unearthed at the Phaestos palace. It is a terracotta model of an ass carrying two water jars. Whilst the horse is not documented on the island of Crete till the fifteenth century BC, it was already known at both Troy and Mycenae; a stele at the later dating from the previous century gives us the first representation in Europe of a horse and a chariot. Wagons and carts were, of course, available for the transport of bulky goods, as a fine model of a painted wagon from the Minoan settlement of Palaikastro proves. Mycenaean rulers and dignitaries later took special delight in riding in the two-wheeled chariot, which was introduced from either Asia Minor or Egypt. The size and weight of such a vehicle had to be kept to a minimum. Bronze chisels and gouges assisted in the manufacture of spoked wheels – the technique of using heat to bend wood was early understood in West Asia – but the chariot maker sought every means to increase speed. A chariot discovered in the tomb of the pharaoh Tutankhamen (1352–1344 BC) even has a featherlight floor of interlaced leather thongs. The palace records at Knossos draw attention to the importance of the chariot to the Mycenaean conquerors there after 1450 BC: more than 400 vehicles are listed.

Because of the geography of the Aegean, neither the wagon nor the chariot were of economic significance, nor were they a great aid to communication when compared to the ship. The key innovation in transport was the longship. Representations of this new vessel are found incised on the back of Cycladic 'frying-pans', curious pottery dishes of unknown function. Along with a lead model of a long, slender craft from a grave on Naxos, they provide a picture of shipping in the Cyclades during the late third millennium BC. The typical ship looks very long for its beam, with a high stern post and a low, blunt prow. A projecting beak could have acted as a probe in shallow waters or a ram in sea battles. Another interpretation would see the higher end as the prow and the projection at the lower end to be a fixed rudder. None of the vessels on the 'frying-pans' have masts, but a drawing of a similar ship on a fragment of a vase from mainland Orchomenos does include two masts. The sail may have had only a minor role because the safest method of navigation would have been to find a quick anchorage whenever a sudden Aegean storm blew up. Nevertheless, a variant of the Greek legend of the flight of Daedalus and his son Icarus from Minos' court tells how Daedalus invented sails, not wings, as a means of outstripping the pursuing galleys. The death of Icarus is said to have happened when the boy's careless steering caused their boat to capsize. Perhaps in the story there is a memory of the Minoan development of sailing vessels.

The little we know about the ships of Minos' navy came until lately from tiny engravings on seal stones. The discovery in the early 1970s of naval scenes in frescoes excavated on Santorini, the ancient island of Thera, has added considerably to our still limited knowledge. Strongly under Minoan influence, the Theran frescoes reveal that Cretan shipwrights favoured rounded hulls and not the angular-ended types common in the Cyclades. The vessels shown are slender and rounded; they possess unornamented prows and sterns and fixed rudders, and are often propelled by sail as well as oars. Merchantmen are decked and those carrying passengers have a shelter on the deck too. These graceful craft of about 1500 BC evolved from the longship, which in turn was an advance in construction made possible by improvements in metallurgy. For the first time then the shipwright had at his disposal bronze bolts as well as bronze tools.

On Crete a cave find gives a radiocarbon date of 2550 BC for the last phase of the Neolithic, but this could be no more than a backward contemporary of what Evans termed Early Minoan I. The threefold division of Minoan history he proposed was based on changing pottery styles. There was the Early Minoan period, represented by dark-surfaced and burnished wares found in southern and eastern parts of the island; the Middle Minoan period, when pottery with polychrome decoration on a dark ground was fashionable; and the Late Minoan period, character-ized by elaborate vases and naturalist styles of decoration. The further subdivision of these periods has only served to make this chronology into something of a straitjacket, even on such a politically stable island as Crete. Where similar arrangements were devised for other parts of the Aegean – Helladic for mainland Greece and Cycladic for the islands – they have become an unnecessarily complicated method of approaching the Bronze Age. For this reason we have discarded them here in favour of radiocarbon determinations.

Recognition of the need for a less confined perspective on Minoan Crete has led to the invention of a new system by Nicolas Platon, who commenced digging the small palace at Zakro on the eastern end of the island in 1962. Platon distinguishes four periods relating to architectural and cultural developments. They are Pre-palatial (2600–2000 BC), the period before the palace economies, corresponding to Early Minoan; First-palatial (2000–1700 BC), the age of the old palaces which ended through earthquake, and representing Middle Minoan I and II; Second-palatial (1700–1400 BC), the age of the new palaces which replaced the first ones, that is Middle Minoan III and Late Minoan I and II; and Post-palatial (1400–1100 BC), the period following the destruction of the surviving palace at Knossos, or Late Minoan III. But it should be noted that the date for the final conflagration of the Palace of Minos is still not generally agreed.

Most of the finds for the early pre-palatial period come from burials. The first settlers seem to have abandoned the neolithic habit of burying their dead inside their houses before they arrived on Crete, the remains of only seven children having been discovered in the lowest levels of the Knossos mound. Inhumation in caves or rock shelters was the normal practice before the appearance of the rock-built tomb. On the Messara plain, the broad southern valley which the Phaestos palace overlooks, there are numerous circular tombs dating from the fourth millennia BC onwards. Although referred to rather grandly as tholoi, the name given to the stone beehive-shaped tombs favoured by the late Mycenaeans, their small dimensions and rough masonry suggest that roofs may have been finished in thatch or rafters covered with clay. A mud-brick vault, however, is not an impossibility. It is even argued that a tomb at Kamilari, west of Phaestos, had a stone vault from the way in which certain large wedge-shaped stones were placed. The Kamilari tomb comprised a circular burial chamber, several anterooms for offerings, and an enclosure with an altar stone. Grave goods taken from the tomb include stone vases, terracotta ware, statuettes and beads. Specially interesting are two dramatic clay models dating from about 1600 BC: one shows four deified ancestors or deities with tables or altars in front of them upon which offerings of food and drink are being placed by two worshippers; the other represents four dancers holding hands in a ring, inside the horns of consecration, their dance perhaps relating to Minoan reverence of the mother goddess as the divine dancer.

The custom of communal burial in caves or rock-built ossuaries persisted into the Bronze Age. Near the Mallia palace, to the east of Knossos, a large rectangular building with a colonnade along the east side and a maze of rooms within functioned down to 1450 BC as a tomb for the local royal clan. Its popular name, the Gold Hole, suggests what grave-robbers may have found there prior to archeological investigation. Quite likely the treasure of gold jewellery acquired by the British Museum in 1892 from sponge-fishers on the island of Aegina came ultimately from the burial house. The pieces are very similar to the beautiful bee pendant unearthed in it. Continuity of population is one of the strongest impressions which arise from the study of Minoan tombs, for though later Bronze Age burials tended to be individual or family affairs, they represent no sudden break in tradition. None of them abandoned the prehistoric Mediterranean idea of a cavelike sepulchre, which found its most impressive form in the palatial architecture of the Temple Tomb, south of the Palace of Minos. This royal burial place covered a large area with several rooms and had a rock-cut chamber for interments; it is thought to be of second-palatial date.

From about 2400 BC there was an increase in the value of grave goods, as metal artifacts were left for the benefit of the deceased. These bronze daggers and gold jewellery point to a dynamic expansion and development in the life of prehistoric Crete. Of the fifty or so settlement sites identified in the pre-palatial era, however, only a few have been thoroughly explored. Most remarkable is the mansion, or great house, at Vasiliki, situated on a hilltop to the south of the later Minoan town of Gournia. It is a carefully laid-out complex, over thirty metres long, built of timber, mud brick and plaster. The hard red plaster on the interior walls has been indeed compared with that found in the House of Tiles at Lerna. Although it is not possible to reconstruct the original plan, there is reason to believe that the various wings of the mansion were grouped round a central open courtyard. If this were the case, then Vasiliki may parallel the pre-palatial buildings which stood on the site of the Palace of Minos. The levelling of the settlement mound at Knossos, as at Phaestos, on the construction of the first palace, destroyed the final neolithic phases and with it much of the evidence for understanding the transition to the Bronze Age.

At Vasiliki, the rectangular rooms of various shapes and sizes, the irregular placing of the doorways, and above all the long passageways and corridors prefigure the labyrinthine style of design typical of the Minoan palaces. The orientation of the building, with its corners towards the cardinal points of the compass, has been cited as evidence that its owners were of West Asian or Anatolian descent. Debate as to the genesis of Minoan civilization continues unabated, with one side proposing a fresh wave of settlers around 3000 BC, or even as late as 1700 BC, and the other regarding its growth as the consequence of greater prosperity on the island rather than foreign invasion. Outside influences cannot be denied, though they may have operated solely through the medium of trade. Two Egyptian stone bowls found in a late neolithic house at Knossos bear witness to early contacts overseas. While the question of the debt owed by the Minoans to other lands must remain open, Vasiliki demonstrates the material progress achieved on Crete at the close of the third millennium BC.

Craft specialization is perhaps the obvious indicator of this advance.

Two Cretan plans compared: a late neolithic house at Knossos (*left*) and the mansion at Vasiliki (*right*).

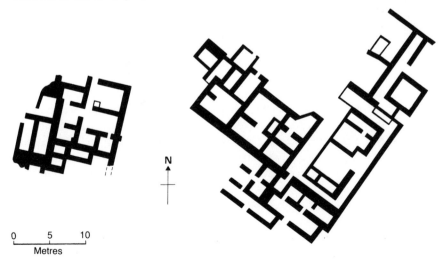

N

0   5   10
Metres

In Vasiliki, the two-piece moulds used for bronze allowed, for instance, the casting-to-shape of both surfaces of a double axe. The new range of metal equipment that gradually became available through the development of the smith's art encouraged the growth of other crafts. Besides aiding the farmer and the forester, bronze tools were invaluable to the carpenter, shipwright, cartwright, stonemason and gem cutter. Axes, axe-adzes, sickles, knives, chisels, hammers, saws, gouges, borers, awls, crowbars, gravers and tweezers transformed prehistoric Minoan society and provided the means of establishing the palace economies. That the Minoans were fully aware of their dependence on metal is shown not only in the religious significance accorded to the double axe itself but even more in the copper ingots they later sent as presents to the Egyptian pharaoh. On the walls of the tomb of Rekhmire, vizier under Thotmes III (1504-1450 BC), 'men of Keftiu and the Islands', in other words Minoan visitors, are shown bearing tribute in the form of vases, jewellery and ingots. Copper was one of the staples of Bronze Age international trade, the island of Cyprus possessing the richest mines. The Minoans had their own sources of copper ore, but for tin, the other constituent of bronze, they probably relied on supplies coming from as far afield as Bulgaria and Romania. No tin sources have been located in the Aegean.

The increase in population and craft specialization is also discernible at another settlement to the south of Vasiliki. This site is known as Myrtos, though the actual Minoan village is on the summit of a nearby hill called Phourou Koriphi, sixty-six metres above the beach. Because of the steep slope the plan of the village is much less regular than at Vasiliki. The foundations of the walls are of stone, their upper parts of mud brick, and inside some of the houses are traces of red plaster. The overall plan is reminiscent of the agglomerate one we noticed in the neolithic levels of Knossos. A set of rooms was clearly set aside for the fulling and dyeing of textiles; they contain a large spouted tub and channels for drainage. Over 250 complete vases have been found, together with a number of stone tools, but metal finds are restricted to a copper dagger.

The inhabitants of Myrtos grew barley and wheat, cultivated the vine and the olive, and kept sheeps, goats, pigs and cattle. The agglomerate plan of their village can be looked upon as the correlative of the rock-built tomb, which in eastern Crete tended to be rectangular, not round. Both in the compactness of settlement plan and the communal use of ossuaries we can discern perhaps a society as yet undifferentiated into individual families. There may have been some kind of chieftain in Myrtos, but the authority of this person is not expressed in the archeological remains. Evidence does exist, nonetheless, for religious practices which point forward to the great palaces. One room anticipates the arrangement of the Shrine of the Double Axes at Knossos; it has a similar low bench against a wall, on which a terracotta goddess once reposed, and on the floor are a number of good-sized pots intended for offerings. It is thus the earliest example we have of the Minoan household shrine. A preference for unaffected surroundings was a feature of Minoan religion, the cult rooms in the palaces themselves being in effect enlarged household shrines. Even at Gournia, where untypically a separate building was erected for a town shrine, we find that it consists merely of a porchless room. Its late date may well reflect foreign taste.

The Myrtos figurine of a goddess carries a jug. She may be the protectress of water – there are no wells on the hilltop itself – or she could be connected with those crafts which rely on water. From Mochlos, a site facing the Gulf of Mirabello to the east of Gournia, comes a clay statue of the mother goddess in characteristic pose; she is shown as the embodiment of fecundity, purposefully cradling her full breasts. On Crete the mother goddess adopted the distinctive Minoan dress of ample skirt and bare-bosomed corset. This was probably invented for the goddess and was a ritual dress long before it became a costume of palace ceremony.

The outstanding representations of this attire are the two famous second-palatial faience statuettes of goddesses, or priestesses with snakes, from Knossos. One of them has three serpents coiled around the figure. The head of one she holds in her right hand, its body curls up the arm, goes behind her shoulders and then descends her left arm. About her hips and breasts two more serpents coil. The other statuette holds out a small snake, tail upwards: the missing left arm most likely ended in a second snake. Here we encounter a familiarity with reptiles that undoubtedly goes back to prehistoric times, for in the ancient Aegean birds and snakes were the creatures most favoured as cult objects. In 1969 at Mycenae a bricked-up storeroom was discovered jammed with clay objects, including lamps, vases, human figures, and snakes with heads raised, coiled up in naturalist manner.

The radiocarbon dates for Myrtos run from 2800 to 2200 BC, when the village was destroyed by fire. The burning of the mansion at Vasiliki about the same time should not lead us to link these disasters with the widespread destruction in the Argolid, since other pre-palatial sites on the island continued to be occupied without interruption. In general, the archeological record suggests that the construction of the great palaces at Knossos, Mallia and Phaestos resulted from the increasing wealth of Crete down to 2000 BC. The upsurge in agricultural productivity is reflected in the construction of a massive silo at Knossos just before the first palace arose. Referred to as a 'dungeon' by Evans, the dome-shaped, underground chamber was ten metres in diameter and fifteen metres in height; a staircase wound down from the top for easy access. This granary stands on a watershed – one side looks back to the slow transition from the Neolithic, the other forward to the revolutionary progress in material life brought about by the inception of the palace economy. Above all, it emphasizes continuity of development on Bronze Age Crete.

PART TWO

THE BRONZE AGE

Chapter Two

THE MINOAN PALACES

Discovery of Minoan civilization had to await the end of Turkish rule on the island of Crete. Not until the spring of 1900 could Arthur Evans sink a spade in the Knossos mound and commence an excavation there that, except for the period of World War I, only ceased in 1932. His original intention in travelling to Crete was to track down the source of engraved jewellery he had first seen in Athens several years earlier. In 1882 Heinrich Schliemann, the pioneer excavator of Troy, showed Evans engraved beads and signet rings which were unearthed in Mycenae, the stronghold of Agamemnon. These artifacts caused him to ponder the antecedents of Mycenaean civilization, which Schliemann was revealing not only at the chief site of Mycenae but also at the major centres of Tiryns and Orchomenus. Whilst their design seemed to recall Mesopotamian and Egyptian gemstones, some of the subjects engraved, like the octopus, suggested an Aegean provenance. When Evans came across similar designs on small lens-shaped stones in an Athens antique shop and learned from the proprietor that they were worn by Cretan women as charms, he realized that they were seals belonging to an early form of writing which must have been used in remote times on the island. He records that he felt 'the golden age of Crete lies far beyond the limits of the historical period'. It was an intuition proved correct by the initial week's digging at Knossos. 'Nothing Greek – nothing Roman', runs an entry in his diary. 'Nay, its great period goes at least well back to the pre-Mycenaean period.' What Evans had located in his quest for an unknown writing system was the capital of Europe's earliest civilization, which flourished for nearly 600 years after 2000 BC.

Quite soon the excavation uncovered a hoard of clay documents and by the end of the first season there were available for study over a thousand inscribed tablets, hardened during the burning down of the palace buildings. We know today that they formed part of the archives of the Mycenaean princes who occupied the Palace of Minos from 1450 BC. Although Evans was still interested in the ancient scripts of Crete when he published his *Scripta Minoa* in 1909, he had already decided to make his life's work the description and preservation of the labyrinthine ruins daily being unearthed by his workmen at Knossos. In consequence, he resigned as Keeper of the Ashmolean Museum at Oxford and invested £250,000 of his own money on the project.

Critics of Evans' 'reconstitutions' of sections of the Knossos palace tend to overlook the difficulties of a sloping site, and especially the problem he had in salvaging the Grand Staircase, whose original timber framework

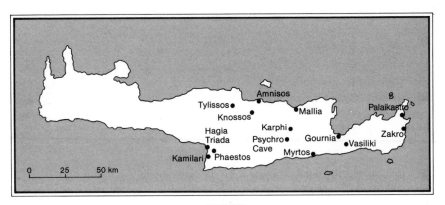

CRETE

of huge posts gave access to no fewer than five floor levels. Perhaps it may be said that there was too much enthusiasm for reinforced concrete restoration but at least a modern visitor to the Palace of Minos is spared the baffling horizontality of so many other ancient ruins. The overall impression remains that of a building in harmony with its natural surroundings; the inhabitants of Europe's first elaborate pile were contented with the simple companionship of low surrounding hills. Their architecture exalted the female spirit, just as in Minoan religion a dominant role seems to have been accorded to goddesses. At Knossos, the only surrounding wall of any size is the retaining one for the West Court. Cretan palaces, unlike Mycenaean, bear no resemblance to castles.

Knossos, though the largest of the palaces with more than 1,500 rooms, was only one of several on the island. Just after 2000 BC palaces were also constructed at Mallia and Phaestos, while following the earthquake of 1700 BC entirely new ones arose at Zakro in the east and at Hagia Triada near Phaestos. Because of the extensive rebuilding necessary at the older sites after the natural calamity, the ruins we see today are those of the new palaces. Only the Phaestos site provides an idea of what the oldest buildings were like, since later reconstruction was not always on top of existing remains. In many places the outlines of first-palatial rooms are discernible, except on the eastern and southern sides of the central courtyard, where erosion has altered the slope of the hill. There is strong reason to believe that the Palace of Minos was the model followed here, not least because the name of Phaestos occurs in inscriptions found at Knossos and the general similarity of the ground-plans. It is thought likely that another palace will be discovered in the vicinity of Khania, the ancient Kydonia, which Greek tradition ranked alongside Knossos and Phaestos. The fertile north-western coastal plain of Crete should have been able to sustain a large palace and a number of mansions.

33

In the design of the Palace of Minos is evident a preference for habitations of human proportion. The use of flat roofs and terraces on the hillside site created a palatial complex that was both elegant and charming. Ingenious architectural arrangements, such as the grouping of main living rooms around rectangular light-wells and the employment of folding wooden doors between stone piers to respond to varying climatic conditions, allowed its residents to maintain the closest links with the natural world. They were able to live unseparated from the earth and the sky; through a gap in the hills they could also see the sea, five kilometres away to the north. An almost conscious attempt to avoid symmetry in the layout of buildings and façades not only added to the overall variety of the great palace but more gave rise in Greek legend to the idea of the labyrinth, the abode of the fearsome Minotaur in the story of Theseus.

So different was Knossos from later European cities that its intricate ruins were misinterpreted by the Greeks as a place of horror. Nothing could of course be further from the truth. The atmosphere of the Palace of Minos appears to have been easy and friendly, with nothing there akin to the overwhelming presence of the pharaohs, whose contemporary statues topped hundreds of tonnes in weight. Neither the oppressive divinity of Egyptian monarchs nor the military prowess of Mesopotamian rulers are echoed in Minoan civilization.

There are even significant differences between the apparent function of the palace in Crete and in West Asia during the Bronze Age. With the possible exception of the palace at Ugarit in northern Syria, where Platon believes there were Minoan influences at work, the unusual feature of structures such as the Palace of Minos is the agglomerate plan. Whereas the basic principle of palatial building in West Asia was the placing of units within a strong enclosure wall, Minoan palaces spread out organically from a central open area. This synthetic system must reflect the continuing influence of the collective form of social organization we have noticed already in neolithic times. The layout of the Knossos palace suggests the survival of a large, closeknit household, reminiscent of the divine families of Mesopotamia, but in contrast with Sumer and Babylonia the cities on Minoan Crete were not dominated by temples. Nor was there any corresponding reduction of village settlement. Furthermore, the craftsmen who laboured in the palace workshops do not seem to have suffered the loss of independence and prestige which befell their colleagues elsewhere.

It is doubtful whether the Minoans would have understood the Sumerian notion of the city deity as the owner of the city. While Minos was supposedly the son of Zeus, he was probably never regarded as a farm bailiff managing the god's estate. Perhaps in the simplicity of Minoan worship, which at Knossos took the form primarily of the Pillar

Crypts, we should recognize a religion not yet fixed on anthropomorphic deities but still close to the elemental powers and processes we now call Nature. Such an interpretation would go some way in accounting for the semi-rural tranquillity of the Palace of Minos and its surrounding city.

The modern visitor to Knossos approaches the palace via the West Court, a broad area paved with irregular slabs of stone and crossed by three raised walkways, one of which leads directly to the West Porch, the entry to the main reception rooms. A distinctive feature of the West Court are three large circular pits, known as koulouras. These appear to have been constructed as granaries rather than repositories for ritual

Palace of Minos at Knossos. 1. West Court. 2. West Porch. 3. Corridor of the Procession. 4. South Propylon. 5. Central Court. 6. West Magazine. 7. Pillar Crypts. 8. Throne Room. 9. Grand Staircase. 10. Hall of the Double Axes. 11. Queen's Room. 12. Court of Distaffs and Toilet. 13. Workshops. 14. North Entrance. 15. Lustral Basin. 16. Theatral Area. 17. Royal Road. 18. Koulouras. 19. Shrine of the Double Axes.

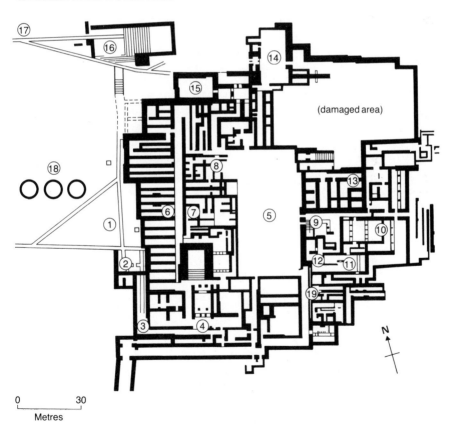

0 _____ 30

Metres

35

offerings because the eight smaller examples at Mallia retain some of their central pillars and suggest that each pit was domed. The prototype of the koulouras, a Greek work Evans took up meaning round and hollow, may have been the storehouse underlying the southern edge of the palace. This granary, as we have seen, is of late pre-palatial date. All Minoan palaces set aside extensive areas on the ground floors for the storage of foodstuffs, as did the small 'palaces' or mansions dotted about the countryside. At Knossos the West Magazine, a long row of rooms opening off a north-south corridor adjacent to the West Porch, contained the largest of all facilities yet discovered. Evans argued that the pithoi and cists contained oil, since no trace of grain was discovered in them, but from evidence of other sites it can be assumed that the Minoan palaces stored oil, grain, and wine. The curious Greek legend of Glaukos reveals another treasured commodity. When this tiny son of Minos disappeared at play in the palace, the Delphic oracle was consulted and the child traced to a storage jar full of honey. Minos insisted that his discoverer raise him up from the dead, or be shut in the magazine with the drowned prince. After the latter course of action was adopted, the reluctant companion noticed a snake approaching the boy's corpse and, seizing his sword, he killed it. Presently another snake crept along to its dead mate with a herb in its mouth which it laid on the lifeless scales. Slowly the snake revived and, seeing this miracle, the incarcerated man applied the incredible herb to Glaukos with the same result. The resurrection of Minos' son may be connected with the practice of embalming, for which we are aware the Babylonians found honey useful. Interestingly, the Glaukos story parallels one of the adventures of Gilgamesh, the semi-legendary ruler of Uruk, the greatest of the Sumerian city-states. A snake is said to have stolen the herb of deathlessness from an exhausted Gilgamesh when the king was resting at a waterhole on his journey home. Magazines and workshops, however, occupy a relatively larger area in Minoan palaces than in any of the temple complexes of Mesopotamia.

Honey and wine acquired a religious significance during the era of the palaces. In the Tomb of the Tripod Hearth at Zapher Papoura, north of Knossos, there are fourteen bronze vessels to heat food and beverages: cups, basins, jugs, plates, ladles, a tripod cauldron and a lamp. The tripod hearth itself is made of plaster. These elaborate grave goods, buried about 1550 BC, hint at the rituals involved with the Minoan cult of the dead. They suggest that the rites performed were connected with fermentation, a natural process full of meaning for those concerned with the renewal of life. Intoxicating drink prepared from honey, or strong wine, was probably taken by the participants of religious ceremonies too. No doubt these beverages were amongst the gifts offered to the deity when Minos, according to the *Odyssey*, once every nine years 'held converse with mighty Zeus'. Homer does not mention the place of the meetings. The fact that the Minoans built no great temples and carved no large statues of their deities indicates that worship occurred in small sanctuaries, and initially in caves. Although Evans identified as the sacred cave of Knossos the largest cave on the Skotieno plateau, about ten kilometres north-east of the Palace of Minos, better preserved in the Psychro Cave on the heights of Lasithi is an altar of roughly squared stones about one metre high. Nearby this unadorned place of offering were discovered pieces of libation tables and cups dating from throughout the Bronze Age.

The cult rooms between the West Magazine and the Central Court at Knossos actually reproduce the subterranean world of caves. The Pillar Crypts, with their stone pillars marked with the sacred symbol of the double axe and their stone libation trays set in the floor, patently recall the stalactites and stalagmites which were widely reverenced on the island. A cave at Amnisos, the port of Knossos, survived in the Greek period as a sanctuary of Eileithyia, goddess of childbirth, its unusual double stalagmite having been originally associated by the Minoans with twin goddesses. Even the so-called Throne Room next to the Pillar Crypts is deliberately left without direct sunlight. Its sunken lustral chamber could have been used for rites of purification, though who the chief participant was in the palace rituals remains a mystery.

It is likely that as priest-king the ruler of Knossos performed the sacred tasks. An alternative view would make the occupant of the throne a high priestess who impersonated the Minoan mother goddess, the Lady of the Labyrinth. In this case the king might have approached her as a divine consort, just as at the time of the New Year festival the Sumerians celebrated a holy marriage between the ruler and the goddess of a city, represented by a priestess. The Sumerian texts regard the sacral coupling as the source of good government, plentiful harvests, victory and success. They state that the king, by uniting with the life-giving goddess of love, ensured life and fertility to his land. Although Evans thought that the Throne Room was inserted into the palace by Mycenaean dynasts shortly before 1400 BC, the purpose of the previous room, if this were correct, would still have been of a ritual nature. Not only were there more spacious rooms available for ceremonial gatherings on the floor above, but also the Hall of the Double Axes in the eastern wing was better suited for courtly affairs. Little is known of the rooms on the upper floor of the west wing, but we can see today the remains of magnificent staircases leading from the Central Court and the main entrance passage on the south – the columned South Propylon is one of the original triumphs of Minoan architecture.

Another characteristic advance was the application of a thin veneer of alabaster to conceal an inferior wall. Bronze saws and chisels allowed the Minoans to surface their important buildings with this sparkling stone, thereby obtaining a fine effect with a minimum consumption of high-quality material. The next people in Europe to hit on this economical device were the Romans, who surfaced their immense structures of brick and concrete with a thin revetment of marble or other fine stone. Interior decoration, on the other hand, gave rise to the magnificent frescoes for which Bronze Age Crete and, more recently, Thera are justly acclaimed. One fresco in particular fascinated Evans at Knossos; the scene of the bull-leaping. In it Evans marvelled:

> The girl acrobat in front seizes the horns of a coursing bull at full gallop, one of which seems to run under her left armpit. The object of her grip clearly seems to be to gain purchase for a backward somersault over the animal's back, such as is being performed by the boy. The second female performer behind stretches out both of her hands as if to catch the flying figure or at least to steady him when he comes to earth the right way up.

Of all known illustrations of the bull games this is the only one showing all parts of the contest. What is so striking is the dramatic contrast between the unbridled power of the beast and the vulnerable suppleness of the unarmed toreadors, whose safety depended on a rare combination of personal bravery and athletic prowess. In this amazing ritual may be the germ of the story of the Athenian tribute of youths and maidens to be sacrificed annually to the Minotaur. Objection has been made to the feasibility of the Minoan bull-leap, though an agate seal in the Ashmolean Museum shows an acrobat starting to somersault over the head of a bull whose forefeet are resting on an elaborately decorated stone. Quite possibly the bull-leaper was taking advantage of an altar, the stone base for which has survived in the central courts in both Mallia and Zakro. Evans could not imagine the sport taking place in the Palace of Minos because in the poorly preserved boundaries of the Central Court he saw no signs of precautions to prevent an enraged bull from careering into surrounding passages and porticoes. But post holes at Mallia suggest that fences were put up for the event; the barrier was not adequate to keep people out of the court, but it was sufficiently narrow to keep a large animal in. Whatever the status of the toreadors, free or slave, it would seem that they assisted in a sacred rite that began with the capture of a wild bull by hunters and ended with its slaughter on the altar stone of a palace courtyard.

Across the Central Court, which at Knossos measures fifty by twenty-five metres, stands the Domestic Quarter, whose Grand Staircase Evans called 'the most daring exhibition of Minoan architecture'. Constructed around a light-well, this great stair had two flights for each of the five storeys it served, the wide steps of dressed gypsum being let into the flanking walls and the structure resting on huge pillars of cypress wood. Here the typically downward-tapering column, bright red in the reflected sunlight, transcends the present-day reconstruction and reminds us of Minoan reverence for the sacred post as the symbol of life rising from the earth, that inviolable source of fertility and shrouded abode of the dead. More than in any other monumental building in antiquity, this section speaks of human pleasures and domestic comforts rather than of courtly formalities and political intrigue.

The private apartments of the royal family comprise a set of well-drained and well-lit rooms which end in a terrace looking out over the valley to the east. Hygiene was cared for by a toilet which flushed into the main drainage system of the palace. A plug prevented odours from escaping upwards, though during the winter months the rain that fell would have been sufficient to clear out refuse. Storm water was drawn off eastwards in a carved runnel designed to precipitate the water into a

The Domestic Quarter of the Palace of Minos. 1. Grand Staircase. 2. Hall of the Colonnades. 3. Corridor to the Northeast. 4. Hall of the Double Axes. 5. Queen's Room. 6. Toilet. 7. Court of the Distaffs. 8. Service Staircase.

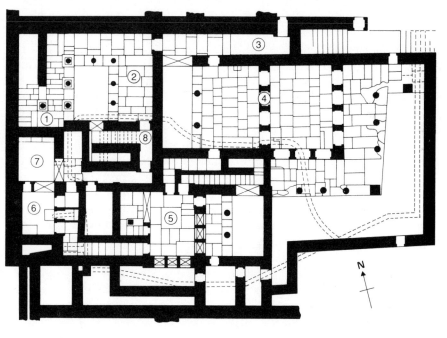

series of small settling basins from which mud could be readily scooped. The chief room, called by Evans the Hall of the Double Axes because of the numerous double axe symbols incised on the walls, is a delightful double room measuring eight by twelve metres, and divided by the characteristically Minoan pier-and-door partition. The Hall of the Double Axes could have been the king's own room, as a private corridor from the inner part connects with the Queen's Room, where there are beautiful frescoes of marine life and figures of dancing girls. A small garden may have been laid out in its light-well for the benefit of the court ladies.

The south wing of the Palace of Minos has suffered from erosion, but it includes a well-preserved sanctuary in the Shrine of the Double Axes, which in 1902 was found as left at the beginning of the fourteenth century BC. It consists of a small room with a plastered bench at the back on which stood clay figurines of a goddess, a god, and their attendants, together with two pairs of horns of consecration with holes in the top to receive cult objects such as double axes and leafy boughs. Pebbles were strewn on the bench and the floor, where clay vases and a plaster tripod once held offerings of food and drink. The goddess of the shrine has her arms raised in the customary Minoan manner, and wears a full skirt, copious jewellery, and on each wrist a seal stone. The only creature associated with her is a dove, even before Aphrodite the emblem of love and fertility: it rests gracefully on her head. Another terracotta from Knossos which also includes the dove is a small shrine comprising three pillars with beam-end capitals, each surmounted by a bird. The column oval in cross-section was a favourite Minoan motif and, like the horns of consecration and the double axe, may have had a religious connotation. Bird epiphanies usually seem to relate to the mother goddess, though in some instances they may refer to the presence of a household deity.

In the contrast between the quiet indication of the divine spirit in Minoan art and the grandiose monuments of Egypt and West Asia lies perhaps the essence of the Cretan Bronze Age achievement. The Minoans were unmoved by cosmological speculation and unpreoccupied by the world of the dead; their singular disregard for time was the corollary of a joyous acceptance of life, a delight in the everyday world that expressed itself as a feeling of grace, a love of movement, and a taste for elegance. As islanders, the Minoans were apt to absorb cultural influences from more technically advanced neighbours but, throughout the palatial period, they showed an ability to absorb these influences in such a way as to enhance their own unique civilization. The stability of prolonged development in the late Neolithic and early Bronze Ages ensured that the palaces rested on a firm economic base. Crete was densely populated and agriculturally productive, the large surpluses stored in the palace magazines supporting the courts, religious observances, arts, crafts and overseas trade.

A cache of over 150 cups, all silver except for one made from gold, discovered at Tôd in Egypt and dating from the reign of pharaoh Amenemhet II (1938–1904 BC), is a sign of early Minoan trading links with other countries. Many of the vessels appear to be of Cretan origin, though they may have come into Egyptian hands as tribute from states in Syria and Palestine. Since the Aegean islands were comparatively rich in silver, the Minoans were able to manufacture and export such luxury items to markets in the eastern Mediterranean. The reason so few metal vases have survived is the age-old tendency to melt them down in order to reuse the metal. International confidence in Cretan skills became apparent in 1467 BC, when pharaoh Thotmes III commissioned Minoan, and possibly Cycladic, merchant ships to transport a valuable consignment of cedarwood from Phoenicia. Trade in the palatial era explains the increasing diversity of specialist production and the continued social prestige enjoyed by craftsmen. We can hardly say artists because the only name to come down to us is that of Daedalus, the legendary epitome of the Minoan genius. According to Greek mythology, he was the first person to carve statues and to construct buildings that were beautiful as well as habitable. Daedalus was not originally a personal name; it had connections with the labyrinth, as one of its meanings could have been 'a skilful thing'. However, the presence of this towering craftsman in Minos' court is a recollection of the value attached to the arts and crafts by the palace authorities.

At Knossos the workshops and stores are situated in the north-east portion of the palace. Unfortunately, this area has been subject to considerable damage, the processes of erosion being exacerbated by the decision of the Venetians to quarry stone from it for defences against the Turks. Once the craftsmen working here included carpenters, sculptors, lapidaries, glass makers, potters, faience makers, smiths, armourers, tanners, weavers, painters, and all the other specialists necessary to service the palace organization. Their activities were carefully supervised, with scribes keeping detailed records of materials disbursed and of items made.

The need to account for all the transactions involved in the palace economies caused the evolution of a linear script, which before 1700 BC had superseded a hieroglyphic form not far removed from sealing signs. The script termed by Evans Linear A was in use over most of Crete by 1600 BC, though tablets inscribed with it are rare outside Hagia Triada. But at no other site than Knossos, and then only after 1450 BC, is found the rather similar script Evans called Linear B. Although some Linear A signs occur in Linear B inscriptions, a circumstance implying a degree of debt, there are sufficient differences in the 3,000 tablets recovered to make it clear that another language is represented. Today it is generally accepted to be Mycenaean Greek. Nevertheless, no archive room has been discovered at Knossos, clay tablets turning up at widely scattered points in the palace and its environs. Yet there is one instance of records being located along with the objects listed on them. In the north wing Evans uncovered two piles of bronze arrowheads, with the ash of the wooden shafts, and a broken clay tablet listing two lots of arrows in Linear B script.

The North Entrance, which leads directly up a sloping passage to the Central Court, is one of the least understood sections of the palace. A small lobby with double doors each side opened onto an imposing hall with ten freestanding pillars, whose sturdy proportions indicate that they were designed to support a large room above, possibly a banqueting hall. Double axes are carved on the blocks of the pillars, just as they are on those of a pillar crypt in a separate building, twenty metres north of the North Entrance. Evans thought the external crypt may have been a shrine that people visited before approaching the palace. He strengthened this argument by pointing out that the sunken bathroom, which he restored to the west of the North Entrance, could have been used for the purification of visitors before they gained admission. This bath, or lustral basin according to Evans, is deeper and bigger than most, with sixteen steps going round three sides instead of the usual two. Moreover, it was very well built; six pillars held up the ceiling and a high gypsum dado covered the lower walls.

Although pottery found in the bathroom might be reckoned to have had a ritual purpose, the presence nearby of a fragment of an alabaster jar inscribed with the name of the Hyksos king Khyan hints at another possible use for the north-west wing. The broken lid was unearthed with Minoan ware of the early second-palatial era, suggesting that this section

One of the baked-clay tablets with Linear A script found at Hagia Triada, southern Crete. By 1600 BC Minoan scribes were employing this script over a large part of the island.

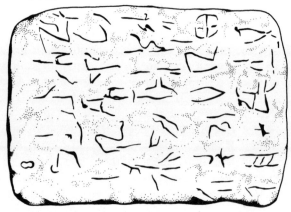

was constructed shortly after earthquakes levelled the old palace. If the bathroom had been furnished with a clay bathtub, like the one in the Domestic Quarter, then servants could have filled and emptied it by hand at the request of distinguished visitors, even foreign guests. In other words, the facility might have formed part of an elaborate suite for the entertainment of envoys, fellow princes or leading members of the aristocracy. At the almost contemporary palace of Mari on the middle Euphrates a virtually self-contained suite of rooms, including a bathroom, court and kitchen, near the main palace entrance, was put at the disposal of high-ranking guests. The limited communication of the north-west wing of Knossos with other parts of the palace might therefore be seen as a means of allowing visitors some privacy. Arrangements in both the west and east wings of the Phaestos palace can also be recognized as guest quarters.

Raised walkways from the North Entrance and the West Porch meet at what Evans named the Theatral Area, a flagged courtyard with terraces of low steps on the east and south sides, and at the junction of these terraces a platform capable of taking a wooden royal box. The Theatral Area would have acted as a terminus for processions along the Royal Road, another raised stone walk coming westwards from the Little Palace. Spectators crowding the shallow steps could have witnessed other spectacles because the layout is reminiscent of Homer's description of the 'dancing place that at Knossos Daedalus wrought for Ariadne of the lovely tresses'. As the poet confers the ornamental epithet 'of the lovely tresses' more on goddesses than mortals, the dancing place might have been prepared for a goddess who was impersonated by Minos' daughter.

There is the Kamilari model of dancers whirling within a circle of horns of consecration to remind us of the religious significance that dance held for the Minoans. In Greek legend, too, it is Ariadne who gave to Theseus the famous thread by means of which he negotiated the labyrinth. She ensured the hero's safe passage through the lair of the bull-headed, man-eating Minotaur, a monster conceivably related to the Egyptian hippopotamus-god Ammut, the eater of unsaved souls. For the Minoans, Ariadne's intricate steps may have symbolized the journey of the deceased soul through a perilous place. In her dance, as a leader of souls, the Lady of the Labyrinth would have revealed the dual aspects of the mother goddess: light and darkness, life and death, the antithetical, paradoxical nature of divinity. The mystery of the labyrinth Evans believed he had solved, lay in the discovery of the remains of a complex meander pattern which ran in one direction only, towards a small courtyard framed by seven columns. All we can be sure of today is that the maze was fundamental to Minoan thought.

Whatever the precise meaning of Ariadne's dance or of her death on the island of Dia, opposite Amnisos, the restraint shown in the burial of the royal dead is remarkable, considering the funeral megalomania of other Bronze Age rulers. The only certain royal or princely tomb of the palatial period is the Temple Tomb, discovered by Evans in 1931 nearly six hundred metres south of Knossos. Originally this tomb had an upper storey and was entered from an enclosed open court at the east. An inner pillar crypt built against a low cliff led to a rock-cut burial chamber. The whole complex recalls the tomb of Minos in Sicily described by the historian Diodorus Siculus, who lived shortly before the life of Christ, as a concealed tomb below the earth and a temple to the goddess Aphrodite above. Greek tradition says that the king died at the city of Kamikos, on the western end of the island, when he sailed there to apprehend the fugitive Daedalus.

The Temple Tomb is one of the few structures excavated in the neighbourhood of the Palace of Minos, because so far the surrounding city has been hardly explored. Other known buildings are substantial houses, two of which were linked with the palace itself. The first is the Little Palace, a residence built on an artificial terrace facing the Theatral Area. It possesses spacious main rooms and a peristyle hall very similar to the one in the Phaestos palace. A late addition is a small shrine inserted into a bathroom some time after the destruction of Knossos. The Royal Villa, the second-palatial building, is situated on the opposite side of the valley and is joined to the North Entrance by a paved road. The most interesting features here are a recessed seat or throne; a staircase which branches unusually into two wings at the first landing; and a crypt whose pillars were cut from the trunks of huge trees.

The cities and towns near the great palaces were well populated. While an estimate puts the inhabitants of Knossos at 5,000, the actual figure could have been higher, because the territory under the direct rule of the palace had living in it at least 50,000 persons. From the Linear B tablets we know that the Mycenaean conquerors were able to maintain plenty of sheep and goats, the traditional livestock of the Aegean islands. Records number over 1,000 for single flocks of sheep. Today with a population of 425,000 Crete is self-sufficient in basic foodstuffs and exports a surplus of fruit, wine and oil. By comparison the estimated population of 256,000 in the second-palatial period would not have overburdened a Bronze Age economy. The prosperity of Crete was indeed famous: it was Homer's 'rich and lovely land ... boasting ninety cities'. But until there has been far more detailed investigation of the numerous Minoan settlements, it is incautious to state other than that the island was the most populous part of the Aegean.

Half the size of the Palace of Minos, the Phaestos palace is spectacularly sited on the end of a ridge that declines into the Mesara plain. The dramatic view northwards, towards the austere outline of the Psiloriti or Mount Ida range, must account for the placing of the Residential Quarter, the private rooms of the royal family, in the northern wing. The veranda used for this breathcatching sight adjoins a three-chambered room divided by piers and doors like the Hall of the Double Axes at Knossos. A dogleg corridor from it provides access to a bath, a toilet, and another small room, which have been cut into the hillside, perhaps so as not to obstruct the outlook of a gallery built above the fine Peristyle Court behind. The latter has four columns on each side and may have been laid out as a secluded garden for the royal family.

The main approach to the Phaestos palace was from a paved court on the west as at Knossos, though the wide stairway, the massive columns, and the large light-well belonging to the entrance were extraordinary. Unrivalled in the Bronze Age was the Grand Stairway, a flight of twelve limestone steps whose gently sloping treads were calculated to impress the visitor with the splendour of the king of Phaestos. The upward curvature of each step towards the centre, to produce a certain feeling of elasticity and life, as well as to offset any tendency for long horizontal lines to appear to sag in the middle due to an optical illusion, exhibits an architectural subtlety not repeated in Europe until the classical period of Greece. At the head of the Grand Stairway stood a platform and a portal over nine metres wide, framed by projecting walls on either side and supported in the centre by a single oval column. Immediately behind were a pair of large doorways opening into an anteroom, split by three more oval columns and illuminated by a light-well. Typically Minoan are the three small doorways out of the anteroom, though the absence of a grand inner door after such a magnificent entrance has promoted some scholars to wonder if the ruler sat in state there to receive important visitors. No trace, however, of a throne or throne base has been located. One of the small doorways led by a zigzag passage to the open space of the Peristyle Court; another took the visitor near the storerooms in the west wing and on to the Central Court; the last was for the guardroom. The lack of an impressive door is reminiscent of the indirectness used in the design of Knossos, where the Corridor of the Procession heads south after the West Porch and turns east only at the south-west corner of the palace, so as to align itself reluctantly with the South Propylon, an inner entrance which fronts a staircase to the first storey and a way on to the Central Court. This oblique method of bringing an outsider into the inner sections of a palace was a favourite conceit of Minoan architects: a circuitousness that must have fostered the later notion of the labyrinth as a bewildering trap.

The ground plan of Phaestos seems more ordered and more simple than that of the Palace of Minos. This is specially true of the new palace

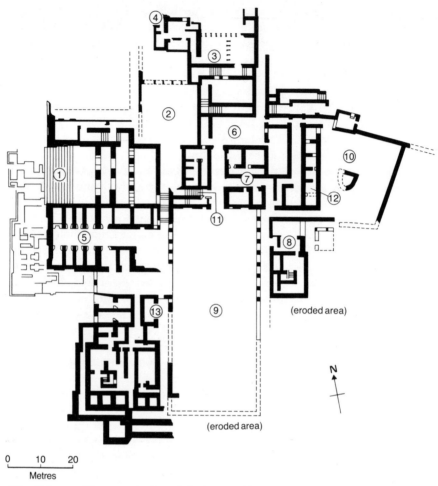

The Palace at Phaestos. 1. Grand Stairway of Main Entrance. 2. Peristyle Court.
3. Residential Quarter. 4. Toilet. 5. Magazines. 6. North Court. 7. Kitchens. 8.
Guest Quarters. 9. Central Court. 10. Court of the Oven. 11. Stairway to East
Hall. 12. Stores and Workshops. 13. Cult Rooms (?).

built after 1700 BC; its layout of areas and rooms is meticulous, though
the complete plan cannot be envisaged, because whatever rooms there
may have been along the south end and southern half of the east side of
the Central Court have disappeared over the eroded edge of the hill.
Besides the usual open space in the centre of the palace, there were three
good-sized courtyards, one of which, the Peristyle Court, finds its only
Minoan parallel on the monumental scale in the Little Palace of Knossos.
The other two, the North Court and the Court of the Oven, were prob-

ably used mostly by the palace staff. The North Court, a small paved space next to a set of half a dozen rooms situated below the East Hall, is connected to the Central Court and the Court of the Oven by two wide passageways. The former has a broad stairway rising to the East Hall, which appears to have been the chief banqueting room. It also possesses a sentry box to guard the foot of the stairs. From pottery finds and cupboards in the rooms below the East Hall we can safely identify the section as the palace kitchens. A similar arrangement existed at the north end of the Central Court of the Mallia palace. This identification would make the unroofed area, with its single door opening onto the North Court, a pen where animals were kept for meat and milk by the royal chefs. Off the passageway leading to the Court of the Oven are further storage rooms, one below ground level acting as a kind of cold cellar. To the north of these long rooms were several cisterns. The palace entrance at the end of the passageway comprises a small room with doorways to the north, east, and west, and with benches against the walls. Through these portals must have been carried the daily food supplies into the palace. The Court of the Oven itself, with the remains of an oven or furnace in the middle, faces a line of stores or workshops.

South of this busy part of the palace, beyond a passageway, is found a self-contained suite, with its own columned veranda abutting onto rocks and facing the distant Lasithi mountains to the east. A bench outside the single door to the Central Court might have been used by people awaiting admission to these guest rooms, or perhaps it offered a resting place for servants accompanying the visitors within. Remains of a wall and a small passage in the main room show that there were once steps to another floor. Across the Central Court from this residential quarter were, on the ground floor, the palace magazines and above them, as at Knossos, the state apartments. It is likely that the very thick walls of the magazine block were designed to carry here at least two upper storeys. Leading off the Central Court is what might have been an office, a large room paved with gypsum and divided down the middle with column bases. Heavy doors protected the office and the storerooms on either side of the passage behind it. The magazine complex is similar to the one in the west wing of the Palace of Minos except that there are no cists let into the floor. A terracotta stool next to one of the pithoi reminds us of the difficulties encountered by palace servants when they came to remove the last dregs from the bottoms of the enormous jars. The pride of their makers is equally evident in the elaborate patterns decorating the pottery – rows of small handles, loops of imitation rope, impressed circles, even plants in relief. Another notable sight on the walls is the scorch marks of the conflagration which in 1450 BC brought about the abandonment of the site. The stored olive oil must have fuelled the raging flames.

The harm sustained by the rooms south of the magazines makes their purpose not easy to comprehend. Two of them with wide openings to the Central Court had gypsum benches along the inside walls. They may have acted as rest rooms, but it is more than possible that they related to the palace cult. Behind them and reached by a long bottle-shaped corridor from the wide entrance way next to the magazine complex, were two suites of rooms each with a private bath, and with one middle room in common; they too could have been for visitors. The entry itself was securely shut at the outer wall of the palace by stout double doors. Close by are openings to a pair of double rooms, which have the appearance of tiny shrines. If they were, then people could have entered them from the western court and worshipped without needing to enter the palace. A similarly accessible shrine previously stood at the foot of the Grand Stairway in the time of the first Phaestos palace. The outline of this older building can be seen clearly today as one approaches from the west.

Perhaps the most fascinating find on the site is the so-called Phaestos Disc. It is a disc of fired clay, about fifteen centimetres in diameter, impressed on both sides with a spiral inscription of picture writing. Ever since its discovery in 1909, the disc has been the centre of academic controversy, including a number of unconvincing attempts at decipherment. In the next chapter we shall consider its place in the writing systems of Bronze Age Crete.

Though less elegant than either Knossos or Phaestos, the Mallia palace was in its overall plan much the same, apart from one or two individual peculiarities. Few buildings were placed on the south and east sides of the Central Court, which measures forty-eight by twenty-two metres and is not completely paved. The bulk of the palace lay in the west wing, but to the north there were a number of important service rooms also fronting onto an internal North Court. These included the kitchen and, on the floor above, the dining hall. At the later palace of Zakro, a similar cooking facility in another large six-pillared room was found behind a portico in this position. The survival of animal bones and cooking pots can leave us in no uncertainty as to the purpose of the adjacent storerooms. The porticoes of the Mallia Central Court ran down the north and west sides, a balustrade in the spaces between the columns providing a safety screen for spectators of the bull games. In the middle of the Central Court there stood an altar stone, but the most interesting religious find is a kernos, a large disc-shaped stone with a circular depression in the centre and a series of smaller depressions round the rim. Situated by the south-west corner where a paved passageway from the South Entrance meets the Central Court, the limestone kernos rests on a raised platform before a small anteroom which was probably connected with the ritual. Either offerings were made here of the first fruits, or handfuls of seeds were sprinkled into the hollow in order to be blessed and made fertile. Another significant find is the so-called Harvester Vase, a beautifully carved jar of black stone unearthed at Hagia Triada and dating from 1550 to 1500 BC, whose design illustrates the festivities which accompanied sowing. A procession of farmworkers carrying on their shoulders hoes with willow-shoots attached to the ends is shown being led by an older, long-haired man with a cloak and a stick. Midway in the group comes a singer

The Palace at Mallia. 1. Magazines. 2. Entrances. 3. Kitchen, with Dining Room above. 4. Royal Apartments. 5. Cult Rooms. 6. Altar. 7. Portico and Balustrade. 8. Central Court. 9. Kernos. 10. Guest Quarters. 11. Garden (?). 12. Workshop. 13. North Court. 14. Staircase for Upper Floor.

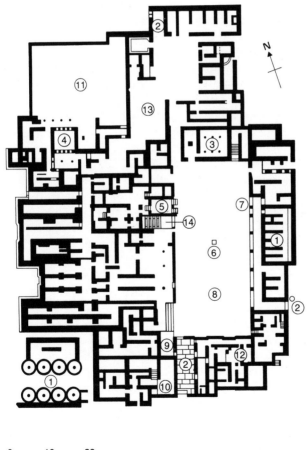

brandishing a sacred rattle, who is followed by a choir of three. Even without the evidence of this festive scene, the siting of the Mallia kernos would serve to emphasize the spiritual and material leadership exercised by the palace authorities. At Zakro, this interconnection of the economy and religion is admirably demonstrated in the south-west corner of the palace, where in close proximity stood a shrine, an archive, a storeroom, a workshop and a treasury. The nine mud-brick and plaster chests of the Zakro treasury were crammed with valuable cups, vases, statues and ornaments.

The main magazines of the Mallia palace are concentrated in three areas. Both the west and east wings contained a storeroom complex though the one in the east was used solely for processing and storing oil. Outside the palace proper, in the south-west corner, were constructed eight koulouras to enhance the storage capacity for grain. Four surviving central pillars indicate that each of these circular pits once possessed a beehive roof, but they were never as deep as those in the West Court at Knossos. The surprising number of storerooms and small associated workshops dotted about other sections of the palace too, gives to Mallia the agrarian character of a great country mansion. Its rural air is further reinforced by the comparative homeliness of the building materials themselves. No gypsum or alabaster has turned up on the site: the semi-urban splendour of the Palace of Minos, with its sparkling façades, seems far distant from this seaside residence, built of red standstone blocks, small grey pieces of limestone, large mud bricks, heavy wooden beams and lime plaster. The site itself, on a low hillock at the end of a northern spur of the Lasithi mountains, is only a few minutes' walk from the sea. A palace, however modest, so close to a beach must be proof that for centuries the peace the Minoans enjoyed was secured by a navy. The only known wall of any thickness on the outskirts of a Minoan town is at Mallia, but this stretch of second-palatial stonework does not appear to be more than a boundary marker. If it were a late defence wall of the town, it would be the exception to the rule on Minoan Crete.

In spite of its unadorned style and its size – about 8,000 square metres or half that of Phaestos – the Mallia palace was the seat of a ruler. The west wing has cult rooms not unlike those found at Knossos and the arrangement of the royal apartments near the north-west corner of the palace strikingly resembles the Residential Quarter at Phaestos. Confirmation of princely status is available in the regalia discovered in one of the cult room stores. The cache is made up of several highly prized objects: a bronze bracelet, a bronze dagger, a ceremonial bronze sword with a pommel of rock crystal, and a sceptre of brown schist in the form of a panther straining on a leash, and covered with an elaborate design of interlocking spirals reminiscent of stone vase patterns. These symbols of power are the equivalent of the impressively carved stone throne which Evans dug from the ground almost at the start of the Knossos excavations. Although the ancient name for Mallia remains unknown, a strong contender is Milatos, since its colony of Miletus on the Carian shore of Asia Minor was established not later than 1600 BC. According to Greek legend, Sarpedon the king of Mallia quarrelled with Minos and had to flee Crete in order to escape his brother's wrath. The expulsion of a 'brother' monarch could be seen as part of the creation of Knossian hegemony, since Minos needed to assert his kingship of the island before he was recognized as king of the sea. The implication of the tale is that once Sarpedon was of equal rank with the king of Knossos.

The first Mallia palace was put up about 2000 BC and badly damaged three centuries later by an earthquake: its successor was consumed by fire in 1450 BC. The palace at Zakro, built shortly after 1700 BC, also ended in flames, but unlike most of the other palatial sites it was never reoccupied. Because looting seems to have been minimal, the current investigation under Platon holds much promise for our understanding of Minoan life. A Minoan site was identified and partially explored at Zakro just after the turn of the century by D.G. Hogarth, director of the British School in Athens. In 1894 Evans had told him of the natural port of Zakro, 'the last on the directest route from the Aegean to the Cyrenaic shore', but the excavation uncovered only part of the town and missed the foundations of the palace by a few metres.

In its main essentials, the small but fine Zakro palace is not unusual. It has its cult and ceremonial rooms as well as its storage facilities situated in the west wing, while the royal suite was placed across the courtyard in the east wing. To the north of the private rooms of the royal family there was a large bathroom or lustral basin. The royal suite itself opened eastwards on to a colonnade flanking the side of a court, in the middle of which stood a circular spring chamber which may have been roofed. Immediately adjacent, a second spring chamber appears to have been accessible only from the outside of the palace; a well also in the eastern wing certainly received offerings of olives in the final days of the palace. Possibly we have here at Zakro a palace incorporating a sacred spring or even a couple of sacred springs. The water table is fairly close to the surface of the site, causing the palace waterworks to be among the best achieved by Minoan architects. The northern wing had the kitchens on the ground floor and a dining room above; the southern was a two-storey block which appears to have housed the workshops.

The other site with a palatial foundation commencing after 1700 BC is Hagia Triada, whose un-Minoan name is derived from the neighbouring church of Holy Trinity. A half hour's walk from Phaestos, the palace remains something of an enigma because there were two periods of habitation, the second one after 1450 BC being accompanied by much re-building and remodelling. It is commonly supposed that the first palatial villa built at Hagia Triada around 1550 BC was a seasonal residence for the rulers of Phaestos, in the same manner as the Little Palace at Knossos. An aspect of the ancient site was the presence of the sea, which then came right up to the villa ridge. The house was constructed on the grand scale; the lavish gypsum veneering alone would mark it off from Mallia and Zakro, even if the renowned frescoes did not exist. The ground plan forms an irregular L, rather like half a palace, the open area so enclosed being partly flagged and resting on the crest of the ridge into whose slopes the first-floor rooms were terraced. The long northern wing held the living quarters of the royal family, while the short western wing was filled with workshops, storerooms, and accommodation for servants. From one of the rooms at the junction of the L came an archive inscribed in Linear A, the oldest form of Cretan linear script.

The villa and the large village to the north were destroyed in 1450 BC. Shortly afterwards the village rose again from the cinders, but not until 1200 BC was anything erected on the ruins of the royal residence. This new building took the form of a Mycenaean megaron, a hall that probably served a religious purpose in connection with an open-air sanctuary from the innumerable votive offerings of terracotta bulls unearthed there.

The last building with palatial features is a poorly preserved house in the town of Gournia, midway between Mallia and Zakro. It is smaller than Zakro and could have been the residence of the governor of this busy town. Perched on the north end of a small ridge above the sea, Gournia was inhabited as early as 3000 BC, though no settlement of any size existed until about 1650 BC, when a 'governor's palace' ten times smaller than Knossos was constructed. It possessed a tiny western court-yard, a magazine complex, a main west entrance, small cult rooms, and to the south a wide, open space. This could have been the scene of less spectacular bull games, as a huge flat slab nearly three metres square and pierced by a large hole from top to bottom might be an altar stone. The town shrine, to the north of the palace, consisted of a single room without a porch. Inside was found a figurine of a snake-entwined goddess with raised hands, together with fragments of other clay statues.

It has been plausibly argued that such shrines were first introduced to Crete in the final stage of Minoan civilization. Compared with the sub-stantial town houses of Mallia, the dwellings of the people living in Gournia were workaday and poor. The general impression is of a com-mercial centre rather than a small palace city. The diminutive palace of the governor might have had a role to play in the town's manufacturing trade, both local and overseas. Quite obviously it was very different from that of the country mansions at Sklavokampo and Tylissos, to the west

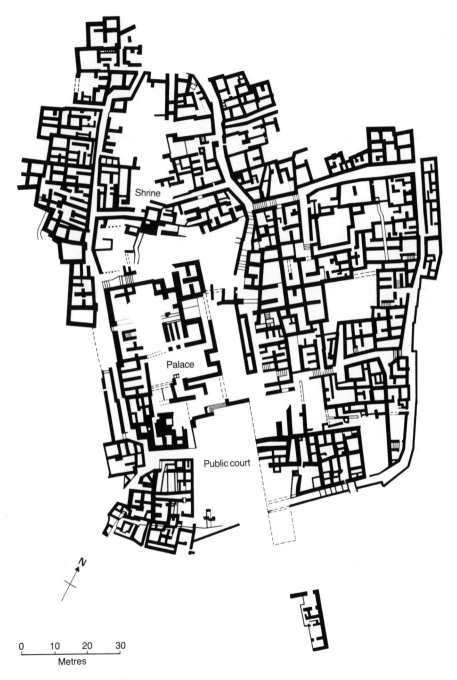

Plan of Gournia which shows the compact nature of this Minoan settlement.

of Knossos, where senior members of the aristocracy oversaw village life. Commodity production in the Bronze Age was mainly of luxury goods and on Minoan Crete workshops tended to be kept firmly under princely control. Even in hieroglyphic inscriptions – the earliest form of writing known – it is transparent we have detailed accounts of foodstuffs and materials received, stored and disbursed. At the core of Minoan civilization was the palace household with its storage rooms, workshops and land. But it must not be forgotten that the ruler was sacred and the palace as much a temple as a place of residence, since clay tablets record the payments made to the divinities as well as men.

Chapter Three

MINOS, KING OF THE SEA

Greek legend is ambivalent about Minos, the ruler of Knossos appearing both as a just lawgiver and a cruel oppressor. The first aspect of his character presumably derived from traditions concerning the sacerdotal line of kings which sat on the 'oldest throne of Europe', the handsome stone chair excavated in 1900 by Evans within the first month of digging at Knossos. As Minos seems to have been a title rather than a personal name, the ancient Greeks remembered the great days of Minoan civilization by a single nameless king. Plato was certain, however, that the source of Minos' reputation as a wise ruler and a great judge was the meeting he had with Zeus once every nine years. Since Zeus is a relative latecomer on the Aegean scene, at least under that name, the Minoan ruler of Knossos may have held tenure of office subject to a periodically renewed mandate, from the Cretan mother goddess. It is also likely that the nine-year cycle was connected with the calendar, which took fully eight years to adjust the annual number of days. Acceptance of a calendar was part and parcel of Bronze Age kingship, especially when the palace economy depended on agricultural resources, and there is some evidence in support of the view that the lunisolar calendar of antiquity goes back to the Minoan period. The second aspect of Minos' legendary character, autocracy, in all probability refers to an actual king, the last Mycenaean ruler at Knossos, whose harsh rule over the island was a means of acquiring sufficient wealth to extend his power beyond the shores of Crete. The Linear B tablets unearthed by Evans reveal the un-Minoan extent of the military preparations he made. His thalassocracy, as we shall see, may have been the reign of fear which Homer termed overbearing in book eleven of the *Odyssey*.

Nonetheless, Greek historical tradition names Minos as the first ruler of the Aegean waters. Herodotus and Thucydides agree that the Minoans possessed a navy and territories overseas, but whereas, according to Thucydides, Minos drove the piratical islanders out of the Cyclades, according to Herodotus he used them to man his ships. Herodotus writes:

The Carians, now a mainland people, were once islanders. Long ago, when they lived on the islands, they were known as Leleges and were subjects of Minos; but as far as I have been able to discover, they never paid tribute in money but manned his ships whenever he had need of them. In this way, through the military success and widespread conquests of Minos, they became in his day by far the most famous of all nations. The Greeks are indebted to them for three inventions: fitting crests on helmets, putting devices on shields, and making shields with handles. Before, everyone who used a shield had managed it, not by a handle, but by means of a leather thong slung round the neck and left shoulder.

Though we should discount because of lack of proof the important invention of the round shield, later to be the distinctive piece of armour of the Greek infantryman, there is archeological testimony of cooperation among the inhabitants of the Aegean islands under the suzerainty of Minoan kings. It would appear that the Cyclades were infiltrated gradually from Crete rather than swiftly colonized. No doubt Herodotus and Thucydides interpreted the story of Minoan settlement overseas in terms of Greek experience, where colonies were usually founded as a result of unrest or scarcity at home. The general absence of fortifications for towns and weapons for grave goods, coupled with the agricultural self-sufficiency of the island of Crete, suggests that in Minoan society there was little impetus to send out colonizing expeditions. Therefore, the idea of a Minoan empire as originally proposed by Evans needs to be modified into something less warlike and aggressive. Recent excavations in the Cyclades themselves disclose rather an economic control effected by long-distance trading with the assistance of these islanders. There are few signs of a direct relation between Crete and mainland Greece prior to 1500 BC, so that the spread of Minoan cultural influence to the Peloponnese may stem from the rise of the Mycenaeans, whose increasing prosperity would have allowed the purchase of luxury goods carried by Cycladic and Minoan traders. If we include the period of Mycenaean rule at Knossos, the Cretan supremacy at sea may be said to have lasted from about 1600 BC until 1400 BC, or shortly afterwards.

Investigation of Akrotiri, the Pompeii of the ancient Aegean, is shedding light at the moment on the nature of this thalassocracy. There seems to have been no great body of settlers in what was a flourishing port, but more a Minoan influence exercised over an indigenous population with its own developed culture. When Spyridon Marinatos discovered the site on Thera, in 1967, he started to bring to life again a city that had lain undisturbed beneath its volcanic ashfall since 1500 BC. Today it is possible to walk between three-storeyed houses, treading on flagstones placed over a sewage system which runs down the centre of the streets and is connected with domestic toilets via clay pipes incorporated in house walls. There is no standard house-plan apparent in the small area already excavated, nor is there any structure of palatial proportions.

With one exception, called Xeste 3, the buildings appear to be the homes of affluent families who commissioned artists to paint lively murals on the walls of their upper floors. These marvellous frescoes – some of which are now in the National Museum in Athens – are full of vitality as well as astonishing detail. While they use Minoan technique, they are free from the conventions of the palaces and draw much of their strength from local folk art. In contrast with the ladies wearing formal Minoan dress in the wallpaintings from the House of the Ladies, stands in naked splendour the Fisherman fresco of the West House. Two panels were decorated with young fishermen holding bunches of fish, the best preserved one being found detached from the wall, a circumstance perhaps linked with the flight from Akrotiri on the eve of the eruption. Quite likely the panel was never fixed in position at all. Apart from the striking effect of the silhouette, the work is remarkable in that, as Marinatos pointed out, here for the first time classical nudity has been applied to an ordinary man.

Xeste 3 has produced the largest number of wallpaintings so far. A large building with at least fourteen rooms at ground level, a well-preserved second floor and traces of another above, it exhibits features which imply ritual purposes, not least a lustral basin decorated with a painting of several women gathering saffron. These pickers of crocus stamens each wear different garments in the Minoan style and are shown filling a large

Plan of Xeste 3, Akrotiri. It possesses the largest number of frescoes of any building so far excavated on the site.

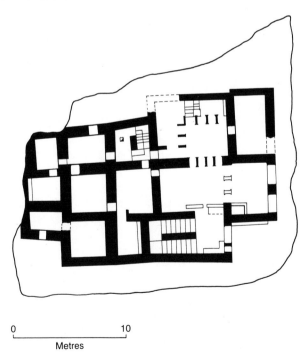

0   10

Metres

basket next to a female divinity, who is flanked by a blue monkey on her right and a griffin on her left. When the fresco is completely restored, we should have a unique picture of an Akrotiri goddess as well as choice examples of coiffure, jewellery and clothes. Like other buildings, Xeste 3 owes a great deal to methods of construction pioneered by the Minoans. Besides semi-rigid timber framing to strengthen rubble walls and yet provide enough elasticity to absorb and resist the shock of earth tremors, the building makes extensive use of the pier-and-door partition between ground-floor rooms, and has a paved vestibule furnished with benches.

The most exciting frescoes in terms of originality and narrative content come from the West House, so-called because on the occasion of its discovery this building was at the westernmost edge of the excavated area. Once it possessed two or even three storeys. The wallpaintings are concentrated in two rooms on the second floor, a large well-lit square room and an L-shaped room adjacent to a small bathroom and toilet. The walls of the L-shaped room are decorated with a single motif, a kind of elaborate screen comprising three upright poles topped by Egyptian lilies, hanging garlands, and stretched ox-hide. In one of the corners of the room 'as by a miracle', Marinatos noted, was 'an intact figure of a young priestess, over one metre high'. As the dimensions of this wall-painting are the same as those of a jamb of the door connecting the L-shaped room and the large square one, it is now thought to have been intended for such a position, despite Marinatos' own placement of it among the screens. The portrait was identified by him as a 'young priestess' because of her long heavy garment and the fact that she 'holds with her right hand a metal vase, to be understood as made of gold and silver, fluted and bearing a long, straight handle'.

Since the discovery of the fresco, the excavators have recovered a number of clay and bronze braziers, which are similar to the one into which the young woman is shown sprinkling incense or some aromatic substance. Whether we should accord the subject a religious significance or simply look upon it as a domestic scene, the purification of the air hard by the toilet, is unimportant when compared with the exquisite work of the artist. Like the Fisherman fresco, which was located not far away, there is in the composition a delicacy, an appreciation of the human figure that immediately marks it out as a work of art.

The layout of the large room in itself put to the test the ingenuity of the artists working in Akrotiri, but they were neither daunted by the four windows in each of the two external walls nor the doorways and niches punctuating the two internal walls. They painted continuous landscapes above the windows, niches and doors, filled with figure portraits the spaces between windows and doorways, and decorated the area beneath the windows as imitation marble slabs. They seem to have been in the process of completing the decoration of this room when the volcano erupted.

The completed wallpaintings directly appeal to our curiosity, as the two friezes with ships reveal a wealth of information about ancient Aegean life and customs. Least easy to understand because of its fragmentary condition is the fresco entitled 'Sea Battle', of which two separate sections have been reassembled. The first could show a gathering at a mountain sanctuary; men in assorted garments and youths wearing Minoan loin-cloths are approaching the top of a hill. The second section, much better preserved, consists of three scenes painted close together. In the fore-ground, near a rocky seashore lie several craft; the prow of the leading vessel is apparently shattered and in the sea are the bodies of three drowned men along with their ox-hide shields. A hooked instrument also in the water might be a grapnel or a boathook – interpretation of its purpose turns the episode depicted into either a seabattle or a shipwreck. Above this marine disaster, almost at the water's edge, stands a single-storey building with four openings. A man clad in dark clothes and carrying a pole on his shoulder is passing one of the entrances. Some distance to his front, a detachment of warriors, equipped with boar's-tusk helmets, swords, spears and big rectangular ox-hide shields slung from their necks, is on the march. From the helmets, Marinatos concluded that the soldiers were Mycenaeans conducting a raid on Libya, the identi-fication of their target coming from an African sheep shown in the last scene above.

Although Marinatos was probably too ready to introduce a Mycenaean presence on Thera, the warlike spirit of the 'Sea Battle' fresco is Mycen-aean rather than Minoan. Perhaps there were people from mainland Greece living in Akrotiri, just as on Melos the Minoans seem to have tolerated Mycenaean traders, but it is rash on the data presently available to claim that Mycenaeans occupied leading positions in Theran society before 1500 BC. Even more extravagant is the notion that a Mycenaean adventurer 'was the admiral of the fleet' whom Marinatos considered to be the owner of the West House. The basis of Minoan policy in the Cyclades was always indirect influence, the maintenance of a strong buffer against enemies attacking from the north. The arrival of Mycenaeans in the island is of great significance, whether they ventured there as traders or soldiers, and reflects a change in the balance of Aegean power; but the mural under discussion cannot be taken to signal Mycenaean domination of Thera, if only for the reason that the soldiers are shown to be depen-dent on Cretan or Cycladic ships: 1500 BC is too soon for the inhabitants of mainland Greece to have acquired comparable skills in shipbuilding and seafaring. The advancing Mycenaean warriors may instead be the mercenaries of an island power.

The final scene of the 'Sea Battle' is pastoral. Two shepherds drive their flock towards a pen, besides which is a brick well. Women are shown carrying away jars filled with water, balanced on their heads, while men loiter and talk as they do today in village squares. There is nothing dangerous in sight. The ordinariness of the episode has led to questioning the fresco's title and the suggestion that it depicts a sea festival in which armed men act as a guard of honour and sailors swim in the sea. Whether or not this is correct, we should resist Marinatos' own enthusiastic interpretation of events.

Uncontroversial is a narrow frieze painted above two doors and three niches on the east wall of the room. It depicts a riverscape; on both banks of a meandering watercourse dotted with palm trees and bushes there are wild creatures including a griffin, a panther, a deer and a group of ducks. Although Marinatos thought both the flora and the fauna supported his Libyan theory, the wallpainting was probably intended to be no more than a piece of exotic decoration.

The third and last frieze, the 'Flotilla', on the south wall is the most impressive and informative painting in Akrotiri. It shows a voyage from one harbour town to another. Of the eight vessels forming the flotilla, only one is in full sail, the rest having stowed their sheets and fallen back on oars; the largest craft possess up to twenty-two oarsmen each side. The superior speed of the sailing vessel is cleverly shown by the two steersmen required to guide it on its course and a line of birds flying alongside. A garlanded ship in the centre of the composition may well be the flagship and its commander 'the admiral of the fleet'. At the stern of all the ships, except a small one trailing behind the flotilla, there is a special structure which looks like a cabin and shelters a seated figure, probably the captain. Since they are identical with the screens painted on the walls of the L-shaped room, and not part of the superstructure of the vessels, they may be palanquins or banners. Some boar's-tusk helmets can be seen hanging from poles supporting lowered sails too.

The town from which the flotilla departs lies at the foot of a well-weathered mountain, on whose upper slopes there is a lion pursuing a herd of deer. The inhabitants bid the ships farewell from the flat roofs of multi-storeyed houses as well as from the quayside. The port of destination, a more extensive settlement with Minoan characteristics, is thronged with people watching the oncoming vessels. Small boats are anchored near the shore and one rowing boat, with a crew of two, moves towards the flotilla. On a headland is situated a watchtower, to which some men are running to obtain a better view. The gaiety evident at both harbour towns presupposes a peaceful visit, either of friends or allies, and lends nothing to interpretation of the fresco as the return of a fleet following a successful mission abroad. The sporting dolphins, recalling those of the wallpainting in the Queen's Room at Knossos, only add to the joy of the spectacle, which for us is a privileged glimpse of ancient Aegean seamanship. Nor can the ferocious lion be cited as a North African phenomenon at this period. The last time the animal was mentioned as wild in Europe was in 480 BC, when Macedonian lions attacked Xerxes' baggage train. *En route* to Therma, Herodotus records the Persian king's 'pack-camels were savaged by lions, which came down from their haunts at night and never molested either men or any other of the animals, but only the camels'. The historian concludes that the unusualness of the desert beasts of burden must have aroused the lions to wrath: the camel, not the lion, was obviously the marvel.

Akrotiri is a site rich in finds. In a single room have been unearthed several hundred items consisting of pottery, stone vases, stone tools and implements. The scarcity of metal objects can be ascribed to their luxury status, the inhabitants of the town carefully removing finished pieces and ingots during its evacuation. The geographical position of Thera at the southern extremity of Cyclades – on a clear day the Cretan coastline is visible ninety kilometres distant – would have favoured Akrotiri as an entrepôt for the metal trade, since Crete and Cyprus were the chief centres of production during the Bronze Age. This commercial activity, in fact, was within the Minoan economic sphere of influence, as can be seen from the Cretan lead weights used by Akrotiri merchants. More Minoan pottery has been recovered from the still partially dug site than any other, with the notable exception of Knossos. A broken jar containing snail shells may have been part of the imports of foodstuffs which Akrotiri obtained from Crete; other items imported were oil, wine and corn. From the large number of animal bones found, the diet of the inhabitants appears to have relied upon sheep and goats, and to a lesser extent pigs, supplemented with seafood and snails.

The busy port of Akrotiri paid for its imports by means of trade and manufacture, the huge quantities of obsidian from Melos being useful for both, since the suitability of local rock encouraged a stone industry to continue into the late Bronze Age. Workshops turned out grinders, pestles, polishers, hammers, anvils, millstones and anchors, besides the biggest stone jar known in the Aegean, a pithoi made from grey-black lava over a metre in height.

Minoan influence at Akrotiri was pervasive. The local population of several thousand persons lived under the Cretan thalassocracy. As tributaries they may have had to row in Minos' navy, but to date the excavation has uncovered no instance of oppression. Even though so many features of the artifacts already discovered echo Minoan achievements, there was scope enough for an artistic independence that must be attri-

buted to a fair degree of cultural and political autonomy. As a consequence, the colonies which Thucydides reports were planted in the
Aegean islands by Minos may be better understood as trade or diplomatic
missions dispatched from Crete to secure the goodwill and assistance of
the islanders.

Other than Kastri, a pre-first-palatial foundation on Kythera, and Miletus, Sarpedon's second-palatial refuge in Caria, the only site of an un-
doubted Minoan colony is at Triandha on Rhodes. One of the oldest
names for the island of Rhodes was Telchines, after the semi-divine
experts in metalwork and magic who, Greek legend says, arrived there
from Crete via Cyprus, and it could allude to the arts of civilization the
Minoan settlers introduced. Cretan connections were very strong with
south-western Asia Minor, where the Termilians of Lycia in Herodotus'
lifetime still believed themselves to be the descendants of the colonists
who had accompanied Sarpedon. Elsewhere in the Aegean the archeological record does not indicate permanent Minoan occupation, though for
a period Cretan traders may have lived at Phylakopi on Melos and Ayia
Irini on Kea. The 'Minoa' of antiquity were probably seasonal trading
posts, open to merchants from the Greek mainland and the islands. Such
a role would account for the siting of one on the Laconian coast at
present-day Monevasia and a second on an islet off Megara in the Saronic
gulf. Minos' own reported depredations in the Megarid and Attica square
badly with the general tenor of Minoan relations in the Aegean and seem
to be stories more appropriate to a Mycenaean dynasty established at
Knossos. Moreover, they jar with the archeological testimony of the
Cretan palaces themselves, geared as they were to a far greater extent
than their counterparts in West Asia and Egypt to the needs of commerce.

For this reason the renowned exploit of Theseus needs to be placed in
the context of Mycenaean rivalry. The Theseus legend of the slaying of
the Minotaur is sometimes invoked as an explanation for the end of the
Cretan thalossocracy, but the narrative does not credit the Athenian hero
with the destruction of Knossos, not even in the most favourable Attic
versions. The death of the Minotaur removed from Athens a human
tribute, the seven youths and seven maidens sent every ninth year to feed
the monster as a punishment for the murder of Androgeos, Minos' son,
who was ambushed after he had won all the contests in the All-Athenian
Games.

The legend is best read as a memory of the assertion of Athenian
independence against the last Mycenaean ruler of Knossos, whose house
had seized control over Crete in 1450 BC. With a Mycenaean Minos, the
thread given to Theseus by Ariadne as a means of escaping from the
labyrinth can be taken to symbolize Cretan aid against an alien ruler.
The eclipse of maritime supremacy actually occurred in Sicily, whither

Minos is said to have chased the fugitive Daedalus, after he had escaped from his imprisonment in the labyrinth for helping Pasiphae to conceive the Minotaur. When the sea god Poseidon caused the queen to fall in love with a bull because of Minos' refusal to make a proper sacrifice of the creature, Daedalus had made a hollow wooden cow upholstered with hide so that Pasiphae could deceive the bull and attain her pleasure. Whatever the method of flight Daedalus and his son employed – wings or sails – its superiority over Minos' ships would have been sufficient cause to give chase. No ruler could afford to lose the technical abilities of such a skilled architect and engineer to a competitor. Not only was Daedalus capable of building splendid palaces, an important measure of prestige for a monarch in the Bronze Age, but more he could construct warships and fortresses. The task of remodelling Knossos for a usurping dynasty just may not have been to Daedalus' taste. According to Diodorus Siculus:

> Minos raised a great fleet, and set out in search of Daedalus. He brought with him a shell, and wherever he went promised to reward anyone who could pass a string through it – a problem which no one but Daedalus would be able to solve. Landing in Sicily, Minos offered the shell to Kokalos, king of Kamikos, who undertook to have it threaded. This Daedalus did ... and, when Kokalos claimed the reward, Minos demanded the fugitive's surrender. But the daughters of Kokalos were unwilling to lose Daedalus, who made them beautiful toys, and with his help they plotted Minos' death. Daedalus led a pipe through the roof of the bathroom, down which they poured boiling water, or oil, upon Minos, while he was washing himself.

Kokalos handed over the corpse to the Cretans, who buried the dead king 'with great pomp' in a tomb occupying the centre of Aphrodite's temple at Kamikos. There the bones of Minos lay till in the fifth century BC they were returned to Crete by Theron, the tyrant of Acragas.

The description of the tomb corresponds so closely to the Temple Tomb south of Knossos that some kind of royal burial had certainly been known in Sicily, despite the fact that excavation of burial chambers around ancient Acragas reveals the dominant influence to be that of the Mycenaean tholos-tomb. On the Isopata ridge to the north of Knossos, however, there were built shortly after 1450 BC two chamber tombs for the Mycenaean lords ruling there, a tholos-tomb with a circular chamber sunk deep into the ground at Kepfala, and closer to the sea the Royal Isopata Tomb, which consists of a large rectangular chamber with a high stone vault approached by long passage from the east. It would thus appear that the Sicilian tradition recorded by Diodorus and the Cretan

63

tradition recorded by Herodotus of Minos' violent end in Sicily have an historical basis.

The Sicilian expedition dispatched to wreak vengeance on Kamikos was a disaster, a forerunner of the Athenian expedition at Syracuse in 413 BC. 'Unable to capture the city', Herodotus informs us, 'or to continue the five-year siege through lack of provisions, they finally gave up and went away. In the course of their voyage they were caught by a tremendous storm off Iapygia and driven ashore, and, as their vessels were broken to pieces and they had no apparent means of getting back to Crete, they founded the town of Hyria' on the Italian mainland. Another tradition relates that the Cretans were thrown into disarray because their fleet was burned by the Sicilians. Whatever caused the loss of maritime supremacy, the vulnerability of the island afterwards was notorious. The final conflagration at Knossos, if a date between 1400 BC and 1370 BC is accepted, would fit into an historical sequence of events that left its pugnacious occupants so weakened that they were unable to resist either an internal revolt or an external attack. There is some indication of a fall in population about this period in central and southern Crete. It conforms, furthermore, with the local tradition that people dwelling at the eastern end and the western end of the island did not participate in the ill-fated expedition to Sicily. Herodotus continues to recount that:

> men from various nations, but especially Greeks, came to settle in Crete after it was depopulated by the Sicilian venture. Then, in the third generation after the death of Minos came the war with Troy, in which the Cretans were not the least distinguished of the supporters of Menelaus. Their reward for this service on returning home was famine and pestilence which destroyed men and cattle, so that for the second time Crete was stripped of people. The present population of the island is formed from the remnant of the former inhabitants plus new settlers, the third people to live there.

By the second wave of settlers Herodotus meant further Mycenaeans, by the third presumably he had the Dorians in mind. The unsettled conditions towards the close of the second millennium BC are dramatically reflected in the development of mountain-top settlements. Over a thousand metres above sea-level, a main site like Karphi was merely a small town with two public buildings, a Mycenaean-style megaron and a temple with terracotta goddesses. This refuge was founded about 1150 BC.

While Herodotus specifically states that the original inhabitants of Crete were 'entirely non-Greek peoples', Greek mythology points to the eastern shores of the Mediterranean as their first homeland. The Minoan Minos was regarded as a son of Zeus by Europa, the daughter of the king of Tyre. Her own father Agenor, the offspring of Libya and Poseidon, had left Egypt in order to take up residence in Palestine with his five sons, Kadmos, Phoenix, Kilix, Thasus and Phineas. These young princes were sent out to look for their sister, after Zeus disguised as a bull swam to Crete with Europa on his back. On the island she bore the god three sons, Minos, Rhadamanthys and Sarpedon. It is plausibly argued that Europa, was a goddess of the night, since her name relates to the Semitic verb 'to set'. A text from Syrian Ugarit, a thriving commercial centre until its destruction about 1190 BC, speaks of 'our Lady, the goddess, the veiled bride ... entering the sunset'. In essence, this is the myth of Europa, who was carried away far westward to be married.

After bearing Zeus' three sons, she wed Asterius, king of Crete, who received in recompense from the god a miraculous bronze man to defend his realm called Talos. Perhaps a memory of Minoan skills in metallurgy, Talos is said to have warded off unwanted strangers by hurling stones or fire, or scorching them in his own red-hot clasp. This, and other divine gifts, descended to Minos on his accession to the throne. That Greek legend ascribes a West Asian parentage to Europa must mean that the rulers of the ancient Cretans, the line of Minos, were definitely known to the Greeks as non-Greek, if not Asian, kings. There are references to Phoenician activity in the Aegean: Herodotus writes that the shrine of Aphrodite on the island of Cythera was erected by Phoenicians after the model of that goddess' temple at Ashkalon. He adds that Kadmos, the brother of Europa, searched the islands for her and left behind on Thera 'either because the land was pleasant, or for some other reason ... among other Phoenicians, his kinsman Membliaros'. Later Kadmos founded Thebes, the principal city of Boeotia, and introduced into Europe from Phoenicia an alphabet of sixteen letters. Whether the house of Minos descended from these seafarers remains a mystery, but in the legendary deeds of Agenor's sons, Phoenix in Phoenicia, Kilix in Cilicia, and Kadmos in central Greece, it is tempting to see parallels of the cultural advances achieved by Minoan civilization.

None of the four surviving scripts of Bronze Age Crete throw a bright light on the problem of Minoan identity. These ancient experiments in writing comprise a hieroglyphic form associated with seal-stones, two linear scripts largely preserved on baked clay tablets, and the picture-like signs impressed with wooden stamps on the spiral inscription of the clay Phaestos Disc. Although the art of seal engraving may have been introduced into the Aegean during the course of the third millennium BC from Syria, where ivory was available till the extinction of elephants in Assyrian times, Evans was firmly of the opinion that the Minoan hieroglyphic system was essentially a Cretan invention. The traces of Egyptian and

Mesopotamian signs can be explained by a widespread acquaintance with writing if not a use of it. Discovery of quasi-Mesopotamian forms on early pottery in the Balkans, the Aegean and Cyprus suggests that the first spread of writing occurred in a religious context, whereby inscriptions were copied for magical purposes without them being necessarily understood. On Crete it does seem that hieroglyphics were derived from seals to provide a writing system for the First-palatial Era. The analysis of the forms in Evans' *Scripta Minoa* shows they were centred on the details of daily life. While agriculture is well to the fore, the only interpretation offered by Evans includes trade: he reckoned that a clay sealing, whose impression was a container, an olive-spray, and a ship, signified 'export-oil'.

Hieroglyphic script was succeeded at Phaestos and Knossos before 1700 BC by a linear script, which evolved from it. Within a century Linear A, as Evans called the new system, was used by scribes over a large part of the island, though the number of examples extant is quite small. Fragments of clay tablets with Linear A writing have also been found at Ayia Irini and at Phylakopi, yet at Akrotiri, the likeliest site in the Cyclades, there is only a single complete inscription on the shoulder of a large ewer. No acceptance of decipherment appears forthcoming. Recommendations of Hittite, Luvian and Semitic languages have been challenged, leaving the sole ground for agreement among scholars the view that Linear A is not, like Linear B, an archaic form of Greek. Although the 1953 identification by Michael Ventris and John Chadwick of Linear B as the tongue of the Mycenaeans did not go undisputed, there is now a consensus that the last dynasty of Knossos was a Greek one. In 1939, C.W. Blegen had unearthed on the Peloponnese at Pylos over 500 Linear B tablets, which he noted were 'strikingly similar to their Knossian counterparts ... In some other respects, too, our deposit of tablets bears a remarkable resemblance to the one found in the Palace of Minos, for in the southern corner of the room lying among tablets on the floor, were

Hieroglyphic seal from Knossos. Evans thought it signified 'export oil'.

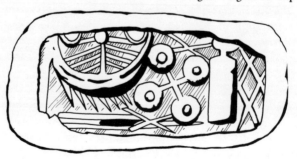

recovered remains of some half-dozen badly corroded small hinges, perhaps the bronze fittings of a wooden box or chest in which the documents were kept.' Blegen was 'almost certain' that the language recorded was Minoan because, like Evans, he thought Pylos, Tiryns and Mycenae provincial in comparison with the amazing ruins of Knossos. They must have been outposts of an empire, 'transmarine offshoots' of the Cretan thalassocracy. Just as the discoveries made on Thera under Marinatos have laid the ghost of Minoan imperialism and shown Aegean relations prior to 1450 BC to be commercial rather than military, so the finding since 1945 of other Linear B tablets at Mycenae, Tiryns and Thebes has proved the independent use of archives by the Mycenaeans. A distinct possibility, of course, is the transfer of Linear B script to mainland Greece, once it had been devised with the aid of Minoan scribes at the behest of the Mycenaean conquerors of Crete. The dispatch likewise of captive craftsmen would have merely intensified a process of absorbing Minoan culture long in train.

The Phaestos Disc is today as enigmatic as it was on the day of its discovery in 1909. Objection to a place of origin outside Crete has been made on the grounds of the disc's fragility. The difficulty of a Cretan provenance, nevertheless, remains the coexistence at Phaestos of an inscription of such underdeveloped syllabary and Linear A script. The argument that the late survival of hieroglyphs on the island, such as those of an axe from the Arkalokhori sacred cave, a stone altar from the Mallia palace, and the Phaestos Disc itself, might be explained by their use as a sacred script long after linear characters had been employed for secular purposes, ignores the non-Minoan features of the stamped picture writing. The feather headdress, which appears a number of times on each side of the disc, was unknown on Crete but worn by some of the peoples who joined the first of the two great sea raids on Egypt in 1218 BC. Later, as we have noticed in Herodotus, the Greeks associated the crested helmet and the round shield with the Carians. It is not impossible that the inscription could be a report of events in Caria, sent to the Phaestos king by a friendly monarch living in south-western Asia Minor.

In 1976 Vladimir Georgiev claimed that the spiral inscriptions on the Phaestos Disc were 'pictographic Luvian writing'. He wrote that, 'it contains many identical or similar signs, including the famous "tail". The difference is that the disc dates from the end of the seventeenth century BC, while the Luvian pictographic inscriptions range from the sixteenth to the eighth centuries BC. They come from different areas of southern Asia Minor or northern Syria, and include many local signs.' Though his decipherment is contested, Georgiev gives us an intriguing insight into what may have been the political rivalries of Anatolian powers. The gist of the communication concerns the aggression of a certain Sarma, whose bellicose ally Wilusa, it is suggested by Georgiev, was none other than the city of Troy.

Another scholar who supports the existence of Luvian speech on Minoan Crete is Leonard Palmer. He would introduce Luvian dynasts at Knossos and Phaestos after the destruction of the old palaces around 1700 BC. It is unlikely that the disaster was brought about by foreign invaders, because new palaces were soon built on a grander scale and on a similar plan; yet even if an earthquake were the culprit, and no influx of outsiders had happened, there is still evidence that some Cretan place-names are apparently Luvian. Tylissos, a town mentioned on the Linear B tablets at Knossos, bears a strong resemblance to tu-li-ya-as-si-is, the adjectival form of the Luvian *tuliya*, 'an assembly'. Tylissos might have been originally called 'a place of assembly'.

Luvian was the tongue of an area called Luviya, which contained the powerful kingdom of Arzawa, centred on the River Meander in southwestern Asia Minor. Closely related to Hittite, the Luvian language may have eventually superseded it as the vernacular in the majority of Hittite territories. King Lubarnas, the 'first' Hittite ruler, is said to have defeated Arzawa about 1670 BC, when 'he destroyed the lands and made them weak, and set his frontiers at the sea'. The palace at Beycesultan, which may have belonged to the Luvian rulers, is the model Palmer unsuccessfully proposed for the late Cretan palaces. Given the widespread worship accorded to bull gods from remote times, witness the seventh millennium BC shrines of Çatal Hüyük, the metre-high horns of consecration at Beycesultan cannot be regarded as the source of the Minoan sacred symbol.

Rejection of an intrusion of Anatolian dynasts does not rule out the presence of Luvian on Minoan Crete. Of the peoples recorded in the *Odyssey* as inhabitants of the island, three were of non-Greek stock: the Kydonians, the Eteocretans, and the Pelasgians. One of these may have well spoken a Luvian dialect. In the Bronze Age, a composite population was not an unusual situation, as the eight different languages in the archive of the Hittite capital testify. If this were true for Crete as well, then the Minoans formed no single nation and their palace civilization was the means of accommodating a diversity of tongues. All that we can do at present is leave the question of Minoan identity open.

Fortunately the archeological record is able to tell us more about the nature of Minoan society and religion. Since there were never fewer than three major palatial sites in use at any time down to 1450 BC, it may be inferred that the government of Minoan Crete was in the hand of princes, their rule combining judicial and priestly duties. The size of the Palace of Minos, even without the tradition of the expulsion of Sarpedon from Mallia, would recommend its pre-eminence though the royal family there could have been seen as spiritual rather than temporal leaders.

The road with the best terraces on the island climbs to a shrine on Mount Juktas, whose conical summit is visible from Knossos. Up this winding roadway the king would have brought sacrificial offerings for dedication to the mother goddess, the supreme deity in the Minoan pantheon. A beautifully engraved seal from Knossos illustrates her epiphany on a mountain peak: the goddess, flanked by two lions, holds out an upright sceptre, or rod, to a male suppliant standing in characteristic pose, his body bent backwards from the waist and his right fist pressed hard against the forehead; to the left of the goddess, a multi-storey shrine displays a double row of horns of consecration. Evans explored the Juktas site in 1909, reporting an extensive enclosure wall as well as a building with a plaster floor.

The list of mountain sites where traces of sanctuaries have been found has grown considerably since then, but Juktas is still the largest and most impressive Minoan shrine. The Greeks were uneasy over the claim that the western slopes of Mount Juktas contained the burial place of 'immortal' Zeus, a piece of lore probably descending from Minoan worship of a dying fertility god, the consort of the mother goddess. The annual death and rebirth of the divine consort, perhaps expressed by the visit of the ruler of Knossos to a cave sanctuary, would correspond with ceremonies elsewhere known to have been undertaken by priest-kings. In Sumer the deceased husband of Inanna, goddess of fertility and love, was reclaimed 'from the river' by the lamentations of his devotees. On a gold ring from Knossos, a woman is depicted greeting with a hand half open a small male apparition which floats down from a country shrine. The scene could conceivably refer to the seasonal rituals of a fertility god, in this instance his return after the budding of the leaves or the ripening of the fruit.

The sacerdotal role of Minoan kingship is evident in the lack of palace defences. Nothing compares with the military preoccupation of Mycenaean rulers, the palaces before the seizure of Knossos fulfilling primarily economic distributive functions. Their numerous magazines and the vast amounts of agricultural produce they so effectively stored not only provided the reliable basis of court life but, through the skilled craftsmen also supported, did much to stimulate manufacture and trade of luxury goods.

As in other Bronze Age economies, the Minoan rulers maintained a monopoly over metallurgy. The sanctity of the double axe underlines the esteem they accorded to metal, Evans arguing that this sacred symbol signified the mother goddess because the double axe is never seen in the hands of a god. Another interpretation would make it the symbol of the thunder god, the Minoan Zeus. Though it is almost positive that Zeus Labraundos was a Hellenized version of the Hittite weather god, who carried a double axe in one hand and a lightning bolt in the other, there is nothing to substantiate the claim of a Minoan connection, notwithstanding the chance of Luvian influence on Crete. We have to be very careful not to assume that every double axe had a religious significance. Besides ritual axes found in shrines and sacred caves, archeologists have recovered a number of strong double axes in association with tools like chisels and saws. Yet the widespread distribution of the double axe, as a sacred symbol, implement and weapon, does serve to remind us of the dependence of Minoan civilization on bronze. Without bronze saws and chisels the stonemasons would have been unable to construct the alabaster-veneered Palace of Minos. Even the brilliant Daedalus, in Greek legend, was moved by a fit of jealousy to kill his nephew on learning that the young man had invented the saw by copying the jaw of a serpent. Possibly the double axe was reverenced by the Minoans as a divine gift, just as the Sumerians saw the pickaxe as the chief blessing of Enlil, their god of the earth and the air. Enlil is supposed to have given the Sumerians the implement to assist in the construction of cities, including his own residence of Nippur.

The unpronounced character of Minoan kingship has ensured that no royal portraits now exist, unless the Young Prince fresco from Knossos is taken as a youthful Minos sauntering in a garden filled with lilies and butterflies. Ecstatic Minoan religion was neither concerned to bestow immortality on the king himself by means of a portrait, as was the case in Egypt, nor to emphasize his descent from the gods, as was the case in Mesopotamia. The Minoans built no pyramids, no ziggurats; their civilization was epitomized in the unobtrusive architecture of the palaces themselves.

If the Minoan kings were advised by a council of elders, or even wider groups of people, no archeological testimony is available to prove it. Recent evidence of a gathering place, an agora, independent of the palace of Mallia is ambiguous. From the general pattern of remains, it would seem that the rulers exercised their power with the aid of an aristocracy. Clear traces of this class are located in the areas immediately surrounding the palaces as well as in the countryside. The two large residences at Tylissos must have been the homes of members of the nobility, even close relations of the ruling house at Knossos, ten kilometres distant. One of them, labelled House A, was furnished with an entrance hall in the middle of the east side; a northern service quarter with food storage and cooking facilities; a southern residential wing containing a lustral basin, a pillar crypt, a bath, a toilet, a light-well, a balcony, and rooms for the family. Drainage passed from room to room in stone conduits. Of the bronze cauldrons stored in the house, one is the biggest ever found. The whole structure eloquently indicates the wealth and social status of its owners, who lived prior to 1450 BC with no measures for defence at all.

House A was fired during the Mycenaean takeover and subsequently reoccupied by an invading chieftain.

We cannot tell whether the Minoan residents governed the country folk in the name of the king or as independent lords possessing their own local estates and owing only certain services to the court, though the minute palace in the busy town of Gournia may be the clue. Its size relative to the settlement itself suggests that the aristocrats living there could have discharged their duties only with the backing of royal authority.

A court nobility is most in evidence after the destruction of the old palaces in 1700 BC. At Knossos substantial private houses started to intrude on the palace precinct; at Mallia a new emphasis on personal comfort led to the building of numerous private residences in the town, such as House Da. This fine upperclass home had two storeys with flagged floors downstairs, ample storage facilities, big living rooms, a bathroom and a toilet, besides a dignified single entrance. The calamitous earthquake of 1700 BC may well have called into question the effectiveness of the king's relations with the divine and inaugurated a period of government in which the ruling hierarchy was enlarged to embrace semi-independent landowners. A strongly centralized monarchy, if the Greek tale of Minos' assertion of Knossian hegemony is correct, should therefore be seen as a reassertion of the royal prerogative against aristocratic encroachment.

The second-palatial trend away from the communalism we recognized as the original binding force of Minoan society in the third millennium BC parallels development among the ancient Hittites, Egyptians and Mycenaeans. The new palaces became the focal points of a highly stratified society, which rested on the labour of an increasingly dependent mass of tithe-paying cultivators. Where the Minoans profoundly differed from their Bronze Age contemporaries was in their lack of interest in war, despite an overwhelming expertise for making weapons. They were not tempted to extend a sphere of direct control beyond the shores of their well-endowed island: instead of seeking to acquire further agricultural resources elsewhere, as did Mycenaean princes, the Minoan rulers were contented with the extra benefits brought by trade.

The peasantry was hardly advanced beyond the Stone Age. Where they were attached to estates or operations under the direction of the palaces and great houses, it is likely that they had the advantage of bronze tools and draught animals. Most village families would have possessed a piece of land on which they grew food for themselves, unpaid labour being due on royal or aristocratic lands and a rent in kind on their own crops. There does not, however, appear to have been a slave class of any significant size, as in classical Greece and Rome. The absence of this

71

degrading institution, undoubtedly the corollary of an unmartial society, is one of the notable features of Minoan civilization.

Life in the settlements that clustered round the palaces and the small towns, especially in eastern Crete, was more complicated. Hagia Triada, the harbour town of Phaestos and the site of an impressive summer palace, had a spacious colonnade of shops and offices. Though the palaces organized the greatest share of trade internally and overseas, there must have been scope for the enterprising trader. The merchant class fostered by the peaceful conditions created by the Minoan thalassocracy can be discerned in the growth of Palaikastro, a humble neighbour of Zakro. Originally a rural agglomeration, little more than a large, self-sufficient village, Palaikastro turned more and more to the sea, becoming in second-palatial times a prosperous community trading with Cyprus and Egypt. The main thoroughfare, which was paved and drained, boasted houses with as many as twenty rooms. But in comparison with Palaikastro, the town of Gournia appears positively industrial, since the ground floors of its tightly packed dwellings are entirely given over to workshops and storerooms. Here on the Gulf of Mirabello was the most important centre of manufacture outside the palace workshops: Gournia may be reasonably called the Manchester of Minoan Crete.

The position of women in the Minoan community has been much discussed, and it is generally agreed that the leading part played by women in art is characteristic of Minoan life in general. Their appearance in cult scenes – the paintings on the sides of the famous Hagia Triada sarcophagus are a superb, though rather late, example – matches the dominance of female deities. In the continuation of priestesses in the cults of goddesses descended from the Bronze Age during the classical period, we have further proof of the high position enjoyed by Minoan women in religious offices. They fully participated in the bull games as well as ceremonies held in household shrines, and one of their number as high priestess, and perhaps also queen, may have been superior in status to everyone but her own husband, the reigning Minos. Impersonating the mother goddess, she would have celebrated a holy marriage with the king each New Year festival in order to secure the renewed fertility of the land. Although Evans considered it appropriate to connect Minoan respect for the female principle with a matriarchal stage of society, we lack conclusive proof, and indeed the predominance of priestesses seems to have been in decline at the height of Cretan sea power.

Herodotus claimed that Lycia was the only place near the Aegean where children were regularly named after their mothers, not their fathers. While he draws attention to the Cretan customs of the Termilians of Lycia, he nowhere proposes that matriarchy had come from Crete. If matrilinear succession ever existed there, it was long forgotten.

Archeology has three things to add in favour of some form of matriarchy. First, it might be argued that the agglomerate plan of Minoan settlements, already present in lower levels of the Knossos mound, and the long practice of communal burial reflects a society closely tied to household cults administered by its womenfolk. Pre-palatial Myrtos shows no differentiation into family units, the clan still acting as the basis of social order. Second, the absence of the martial domination of the male is patently obvious before the arrival of the Mycenaeans. The last evidence comprises the women represented by Minoan artists, though the difficulties experienced over the two snake-entwined faience statuettes unearthed from the Palace of Minos are not untypical. They are taken either as goddesses or priestesses, the conclusion being perhaps that second-palatial religion continued to be shaped by a matriarchal heritage. Whatever the answer, the homeliness of the palaces themselves appears to have owed a great deal to women's love of nature, and in particular gardens.

Identification problems in Minoan religion are acute because we lack a text. The only inscription so far translated from Linear A is an inscription on a libation table found at Knossos, which Palmer asserts to be Luvian, and which reads: 'This altar is erected for My Lady. No one shall take offerings from it.' The absorption of many Minoan beliefs in Greek religion, one of the consequences of the Mycenaean conquest of a more advanced culture, does allow a degree of comparison, but there are dangers in interpretation by analogy, as several scholars have discovered. Fundamentally, the religious beliefs of the Minoans were bound up with natural processes, whose workings they thought were the action of the spirit world. The gratitude felt for an abundant harvest can be readily seen at Knossos in the proximity of the West Magazine and the Pillar Crypts. No shadow seems to have been cast over Minoan religion by the prevalence of earthquakes, nor by the inevitability of death. As Platon remarked of the splendid exhibits in the Archeological Museum at Iraklion, 'a hymn to Nature as a Goddess seems to be heard from everywhere, a hymn of joy and life'.

A large gold ring, titled the Great Goddess Ring, from the treasure of a destroyed shaft grave at Mycenae, may show the generosity of the Great Mother. Probably of Cretan workmanship, the ring has cut on its bezel a scene of the first fruits, or at least a celebration of divine fecundity. The mother goddess sits beside a cairn of stones under a tree, holding with one hand a bunch of poppies, with the other her own full breasts; three female worshippers acknowledge her authority in front of a double axe, two of them carrying lilies, the third receiving or presenting the poppies in the goddess' right hand; a fourth woman raises her arms either in adoration or to touch the luxuriant foliage of the tree. In the back-

Two cult scenes relating to the worship of the mother goddess. The seal on the left shows the goddess on a mountain peak; it was unearthed at Knossos. On the right is the Great Goddess Ring from Mycenae, which according to Hooker incorporates both Minoan and Mycenaen religious elements.

ground stand a figure with a huge figure-of-eight shield and a row of six animal heads without horns, while above the sun and moon shine next to a rainbow. If the animal heads are meant to be nailed on a wall, then that wall would be the one enclosing the sacred tree. Though the seated figure has been called a tree goddess, in the care of the Minoan mother goddess was the whole cycle of vegetation, so that worship of trees would be merely reverence accorded to an aspect of her divinity. The pride of place awarded in the composition to the poppies could refer to the ritual use of opium, as the three heads crowning a bell-shaped statuette of a goddess from the shrine at Gazi, a site contemporary with mountainous Karphi, reveal the incisions necessary for extracting the drug. Whilst Linear B tablets from Pylos and Knossos inform us that poppies were extensively cultivated both in Crete and Messenia, the eating of poppy-seed cakes is not the same as partaking of a narcotic for religious purposes. If the Minoans did use opium, and there seems no valid reason to rule out the possibility altogether, then it is certain that the habit died out well before the end of the second millennium BC.

It was the consort of the mother goddess, the Cretan Zeus, who gave the Greeks most cause for anxiety, because a dying and rising deity was very different from the Zeus of the Greek pantheon, 'the father of gods and men, under whose thunder the broad earth quivers'. The Cretan Zeus was more akin to Dionysus, whom the Greeks knew as a bull god and a dying god. Carl Kerényi has in fact demonstrated the debt that the Dionysus cult owed to the Minoans and argued that they worshipped the same god under an unknown name. The chthonic aspect of Dionysus is quite plain in the Greek legend of his birth, where serpentine Zeus coiling with Rhea, who had transformed herself into a snake to avoid her son's advances, begot Persephone, the wife of the underworld god Hades.

74

Upon his newly born daughter Persephone the writhing sky god then fathered Dionysus, who was born on Crete. A variant interestingly points to a Phoenician link, for it makes the god son of Zeus and Semele, the daughter of Kadmos.

Archaic tales of sacred snakes recur in Greek mythology – even in Olympia Zeus took the place of a serpent – but the most celebrated account of a Greek god supplanting an indigenous snake god concerns the oracle of Delphi. From this shrine Apollo, son of Zeus and Leto, expelled Python, slaying the creature next to the sacred chasm of the earth mother. In the *Hymn to Apollo*, which was probably composed in the eighth century BC, the task of founding the shrine is given to sailors from Knossos, who placed it on Mount Parnassos, a name thought to be Luvian for 'shrine'. Minoan reverence of snakes and bulls undoubtedly carried over into Mycenaean religion, as did a good many articles used in their rites, the most conspicuous of these being the familiar horns of consecration. Such a transfer would have been not entirely straight-forward, given the destruction of the Minoan palaces, and it may explain the legend of the Minotaur as a garbled version of a bull sacrifice in honour of a suffering, dismembered deity.

The sudden collapse of Minoan civilization can be attributed to both the Thera eruption of 1500 BC and the Mycenaean attack of 1450 BC. Four times greater than the Krakatoa eruption of 1883 off Sumatra, an event heard in Australia over 3,000 kilometres away, the eruption of Thera destroyed Akrotiri, caused sea floods among the Cyclades, and spread ash across eastern Crete, Karpathos, Rhodes and south-western Asia Minor. Deep-sea sediment cores establish an ash-fall five centimetres thick, half the amount required on Iceland to cause the abandonment of modern farms. It is suggested that this setback for Bronze Age agriculture on Crete was sufficient to cause economic dislocation, if not a permanent reduction in the area under cultivation. Perhaps it also unbalanced Minoan society and prepared conditions suited to a Mycenaean invasion. If internal economic and social problems weakened Crete for the fifty years prior to 1450 BC, and assistance in building up a navy was available to the Mycenaeans from the Cycladic islands, then we have the stage properly set for Minoan disaster. In the event, the invaders spared only Knossos, because the city and the palace were turned into the capital of a Mycenaean dynasty. Without the palaces Minoan culture could not exist, and so it was that the destruction of 1450 BC extinguished such a genial and artistically original civilization on the very threshold of European history.

Chapter Four

MYCENAEAN SUPREMACY

For Homer the earliest ancestors of the Greeks were the Achaeans or Danaans, even the Argives. One of their chief centres was 'golden Mycenae', the seat of Agamemnon, commander-in-chief of the great expedition against Troy, and it was the discovery of royal burials in this citadel during the autumn of 1876 that led to the adoption of the term Mycenaean to designate the civilization revealed. By careful reading of Pausanias, whose *Guidebook to Greece* was composed about 170, Heinrich Schliemann uncovered just inside the Lion Gate a circular enclosure, some twenty-four metres in diameter, containing six shaft-graves with stone markers showing scenes of chariots at full gallop. Because Pausanias had written that 'in the ruins there … lie Agamemnon and those who were murdered with him', and because the grave goods included impressive gold breast plates, necklaces and face masks, Schliemann believed he had found the resting place of Homeric heroes. Modern archeology has fixed the last interment at about 1500 BC, nearly three centuries before the traditional date of the Trojan War. The epoch-making find established beyond doubt the existence of a mature Bronze Age culture on the

Mycenae. 1. Granary. 2. Grave Circle A. 3. Lion Gate. 4. Cult Centre. 5. Tsountas' House. 6. Staircase. 7. Megaron. 8. House of Columns. 9. Tower. 10, 11. Sally-ports. 12. Underground stair to cistern. 13. Postern Gate. 14. Grave Circle B. 15. Tomb of Cytemnestra.

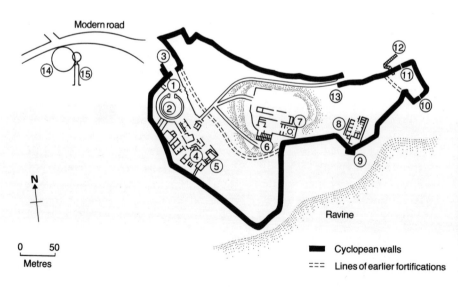

Greek mainland, but the name now used for it must not be taken to imply any centralized political authority. Mycenae was one of several palace-strongholds in central and southern Greece; it never ruled a Mycenaean empire.

There is little to prepare us for the sudden outburst of power and luxury which is displayed by the shaft-graves. The 500 years down to 1600 BC were comparatively poverty stricken, the inhabitants of mainland Greece subsisting with meagre bronze tools in small, huddled communities, usually unfortified and entirely lacking palatial buildings. Nothing approached the level of construction belonging to the House of Tiles. Although this building was destroyed in the violent assault suffered by Lerna prior to 2100 BC, the break elsewhere in cultural traditions only occurred about 1900 BC. Roughly at this date, but earlier at Lerna, grey Minyan ware began to appear alongside a new burial practice. The dead were buried in cist-graves, shallow boxes made of four slabs set vertically in the ground; the floor was strewn with pebbles, and the cover consisted of one or two slabs. Their small dimensions at first necessitated the contraction of the bodies laid in them and discouraged the leaving of grave goods. Gradually the cist-graves were enlarged to take family burials, the extra space being employed to lay out the dead fully and place about them humble offerings such as cups. Another cultural trait was the burial of children, and occasionally of adults, under the floors of houses or behind walls.

The changes in pottery and funerary practice obviously imply some alteration in the population but, as we have seen in Chapter One, the movement of prehistoric peoples was a commonplace event. Newcomers tended to come to terms with their predecessors, especially when they encountered more advanced societies, as at Lerna, where the tumulus raised over the ruined House of Tiles may have been a monument to such an accommodation: hence our reluctance to name the Minyans as Greeks. Instead of imagining Greek-speaking people entering the mainland between 2200 BC and 1900 BC, as some scholars propose, we prefer to believe that the Greek language did not exist before 2000 BC, but was formed in Greece by the mixture of the indigenous population with invaders who spoke another Indo-European language. A further hypothesis of John Chadwick, which goes a long way to account for the upsurge of economic and political activity in the sixteenth century BC, argues that the decisive cultural influence on mainland Greece was Crete, albeit through the indirect agency of trade. This view avoids connecting the improvements apparent archeologically with yet another migration.

At the beginning of the Mycenaean period, which lasted approximately from 1600 BC to 1100 or 1050 BC, the Achaean kingdoms described in the *Iliad* start to take shape. In Thessaly there was Iolkos, the modern Volos, sheltered by Mount Pelion, the home of the Centaurs. From Iolkos Neleus fled after a conflict with his brother Pelias to Pylos, where he became king and father of Nestor, 'the master of the courteous word, the clear-voiced orator'. Thebes and Orchomenus were in Boeotia, as was Gla, a citadel unmentioned in traditional literature. Situated on a small hill in the middle of a lake – an ancient dyke suggests that, as today, it may have been drained – Gla seems to have acted as a refuge from enemy attack for people of a considerable area. In Attica, a minor kingdom based on the acropolis at Athens, though insignificant in mainland politics, alone of the Mycenaean strongholds held out against the disastrous attacks at the end of the age.

The greatest concentration of power was in the Peloponnese, with Pylos ruling Messenia and Mycenae dominating the strongholds of the Argolid. While no Mycenaean centre has been located in Laconia, traces of an early palatial-style building are known to exist close by the Menelaion, a shrine dedicated to Menelaus and Helen some three kilometres east of Sparta. With the exception of Pylos and possibly Iolkos, these Mycenaean palace-strongholds were eventually fortified with strong walls of large boulders and hammer-dressed blocks of stone, which later Greeks thought had been put up by a race of giants – the one-eyed Cyclopes.

The prelude to this civilization was for seventy-five years the grave circle uncovered by Schliemann, until Greek archeologists restoring the Tomb of Clytemnestra in 1951 found a second group of shaft-graves outside the citadel walls of Mycenae. Grave Circle B, as it is called to distinguish it from the first one discovered, has been excavated with such meticulous attention to detail that we now have an idea of the rites involved in Mycenaean burials. Both circles were part of an extensive cemetery that reached to the foot of the citadel. Later on in the thirteenth century BC when the defences were enlarged and the Lion Gate was constructed, Grave Circle A still received so much veneration that it was separated off from the rest and incorporated within the Cyclopean walls. The double row of stones marking its circumference today date from this time.

Grave Circle A contained six deep burial shafts, cut vertically into the earth and the soft rock under it. The smallest measures three by three and a half metres; the largest four and a half by six and a half metres; and the deepest shaft reaches to four metres. Their floors were covered with a layer of pebbles, upon which bodies were placed in contracted or extended postures. Rubble-lined walls and wooden roofs protected the dead, earth being poured into the shaft to ground level, where stelai were set up. Although Schliemann recorded some confusion of bones and offerings, this would have been caused by the collapse of the roofs when their wooden beams had decayed, as the sanctity and awe in which the old kings buried here were held was enough to prevent spoliation. The bones found in the fill of the grave circle may be those of sacrificial victims, since Linear B inscriptions from Pylos mention the practice of human sacrifice to the gods. Archeological testimony of this gruesome custom is not entirely clear, for as George Mylonas has pointed out the supposed sacrificial pit of the royal tholos-tomb at Dendra could simply be filled with remnants of previous burials. Dendra, the ancient fortress of Midea, was the seat of a lesser prince to the south-east of Mycenae. Whether those buried in Grave Circle A were sufficiently exalted to be accompanied into the afterlife by sacrificed servants we cannot be sure, but a visitor to the National Museum in Athens is bound to be impressed with the richness of the funeral furnishings recovered from their graves. Over 400 items came from Grave IV alone. These include three gold masks, two gold crowns, eight gold headbands, one gold necklace, three gold armbands, two gold rings, two silver rings, seven gold vases, eleven silver vases, three alabaster vases, twenty-seven bronze swords, five bronze daggers, and the remains of several boar's-tusk helmets.

Equally remarkable are the carvings on the grave markers. Since it was impossible for a chariot to be handled effectively in the chase or on the battlefield by a single person, the three chariot scenes represented must be of races, perhaps held in honour of the dead. While the work of the sculptor looks less assured than that of the gemcutter, it does bear witness to the arrival in Europe of the chariot. As in the *Iliad*, the Mycenaeans appear to have used chariots as a means of transport rather than for fighting, not least because few parts of Greece south of Thessaly would have been suited to the massed chariot charge favoured by the Egyptians and the Hittites.

Hardly a tomb in Grave Circle B compares in wealth with the poorest in A. Of the twenty-four tombs in Grave Circle B, fourteen qualify as older shaft-graves, dating from around 1600 BC. The circle itself is located some 130 metres west of the Lion Gate and only ten metres west of the apex of the vault of Clytemnestra's tholos. Today there are just a few stones left of its circular wall; destruction was severe during the construction of this tholos tomb and the laying of a modern road to the citadel. The contrast between the grave furnishings of the two circles underlines the growing wealth of chariot-riding military elite installed at Mycenae. Because some of the late interments of Grave Circle B are contemporary with Grave Circle A, which is dated from 1600 to 1510 BC, it has been suggested by Marinatos that this dual use may indicate the existence of two branches in the royal family of Mycenae. In the *Iliad*, a tradition of alternating succession is preserved: Atreus was not succeeded by his son Agamemnon, but by his brother Thyestes, after whose death Agamemnon became king.

As in the case of Grave Circle A, most of those buried in Grave Circle B were warriors. An amethyst bead from Grave Gamma may show the bearded face of one of these powerful men, whose average height was well above that of Mycenaean commoners. Grave Gamma contained four men in extended postures. Two of the skeletons have been pushed aside to the walls, and a third, with almost no gifts at all, was placed in an east-west position along the width of the grave, beyond the feet of the others. The latter, thought to be a man of aabout twenty-eight, could have died as a result of surgery, for his fractured skull had three neat holes bored through it. This is the earliest known example of trepanation in Europe. The strange placing of the trepanned young man probably indicates his lowly status; as an unimportant member of the family, or a person who died before he had a chance to amass wealth and fame, he would not have been entitled to an elaborate funeral. The pushing aside of the two skeletons, however, had nothing to do with prestige, as the spoliation of graves, even by relatives, was apparently not considered an impious act. Vases from the earlier interments of Grave Gamma were found smashed outside the shaft, along with a great quantity of potsherds from other graves.

According to Mylonas, one of the excavators of Grave Circle B, the contrast between the scrupulous care taken over the deposition of the body and the arrangement of its equipment at the time of burial and the indifference shown to the skeletal remains and belongings once the flesh had decomposed, reflects a belief among the Mycenaeans that the spirit had departed for the nether world as soon as the body disappeared. Fear of the dead lasted only until decomposition, after which grave goods and bones were irrelevant to both the living and those who have gone before. Support of this belief exists in the Homeric conception of Hades, an abode of powerless shades no longer interested in their living descendants. The parallels between Mycenaean and Homeric burial customs are several – funeral feasts, grave equipment, the raising of mounds, stelai – but in one very crucial aspect they differ, namely the disposition of the dead: whereas the Mycenaeans generally used interment, the Homeric heroes preferred cremation, as did their traditional enemies the Trojans.

In Grave Circle B the tombs were occasionally used for the burial of one person, but usually a family group occupied the same grave. Very often, as in Grave Gamma, the bones of previous interments were brushed to the sides of the grave in order to make room for later ones. On these occasions grave furnishings were either thrown out, pushed into corners, or taken away by the living. Grave Lambda even appears to have been despoiled without a subsequent burial, its flagstone roof having collapsed before the shaft was filled with earth. The dead were sometimes lowered on an animal pelt which was left in the grave. After gifts were laid out next to the corpse, a funeral meal occurred, then the grave was closed and a stele erected. Exquisitely fashioned artifacts have been recovered from Grave Circle B, in particular from tombs holding a single burial like Grave Omikron. The woman interred here had a charming range of gifts, including amber beads, gold ornaments, pins with rock crystal heads, and a rock crystal duck-bowl. The realistic head of the duck, turned to look backwards, over the bowl, echoes Egyptian taste.

It used to be thought that the shaft-grave kings of Mycenae gained their personal wealth as mercenaries in Egypt. This now seems improbable, as even Crete in the sixteenth century BC was on the outer fringe of the Egyptian world. The contents of the two grave circles are better regarded as an index of mainland interest in the Aegean and beyond, since the Mycenaeans were beginning to turn to the sea and to the possibilities for trade and conquest its command was soon to offer them. The rugged nature of Greece always made it difficult for any one ruler to assert his authority over all of the mainland, but a powerful fleet gave an opportunity for riches overseas. Homer's catalogue of the ships sent to Troy leaves us in no doubt of the naval strength of Agamemnon, as Mycenae and Pylos provided the largest contingents for the expedition.

The origins of the two grave circles are likely to remain obscure, though some scholars feel that the shafts developed normally out of older cist-graves. The absence of any trace of a contemporary palace or town adds to the uncertainty. Quite possibly at this period warriors lived in Mycenae behind a wooden stockade on the citadel hill, whose steepness, combined with denudation and later occupation, ensures that archeology is of no avail. All that can be reasonably said concerns the advent of a new power in the Aegean. The Mycenaeans, with their war chariots and long swords, were about to step onto the international stage and replace the Minoans as the leading people of Europe. Their advance at Mycenae is documented as much in tomb architecture as anything else: 1500 BC to 1220 BC was to be the era of the magnificent tholos-tomb.

Well over a hundred tholoi have been excavated. Although they are spread across mainland Greece, there is a special concentration in Messenia, where the earliest known example is near modern Koryphasion. Only at Mycenae are the tholoi later than the shaft-graves; elsewhere, they appeared at the same time as chamber tombs. Whereas the rock-cut chamber tomb was used by people in general, the tholos-tomb, with its domed and stonelined chamber, was reserved for the burial of the king and the immediate members of his family. The circular underground tomb is of course more convenient than the cist-grave. It is easier to build, provided the underlying rock is not too hard, and easier to reuse than a deep shaft. A horizontal passage or dromos, open to the sky, led to a walled-up doorway; the chamber behind sometimes had pits or shallow shafts sunk into the floor and covered with slabs for extra protection. Signs of fire in many burial chambers are understood to be the results of fumigation and purification; often the fires were lighted on the floor without regard to previous burials, so that both grave goods and bones were blackened and disfigured.

A unique chamber tomb is Tomb Two at Dendra. On the floor of the grave were found a stone slaughtering block, a sacrificial hearth, two stone tables, and two pits cut into the rock. One of these depressions contained animal bones, the only skeletal remains in the whole tomb. The absence of human bones as well as the presence of comfortable furnishings identify the sepulchre as a cenotaph erected for the benefit of two persons who had perished away from home, the intention being to lure back by special rites the wandering spirits of these unburied men. On the edge of Hades, Odysseus performed similar rites to attract the shade of the blind seer Teiresias in book eleven of the *Odyssey*. He 'dug with his sharp sword a trench of a cubit's length and around it poured libations to all the dead, first with milk and honey together, then with sweet wine, and last of all with water.' Over all this was sprinkled 'white barley' before prayers were addressed 'to the helpless dead'. Then, having 'cut the throats of sheep over the trench so that the dark blood poured in', Odysseus 'sat on guard, sword in hand, and prevented any of the feckless ghosts from approaching the blood before Teiresias came.'

One of the two impulses behind the development of the tholos-tomb in Messenia came from Crete, the colony of Kastri on the island of Cythera acting as a staging post for Minoan influence to the Greek mainland. Specifically, it was the circular rock-built tomb common on the southern Messara plain of Crete since the third millennium BC. The second impulse was the local tumulus, which already had a long tradition in the south-western Peloponnese. Several tholoi in Messenia stand on

Schematic view of a Mycenaean tholos tomb.

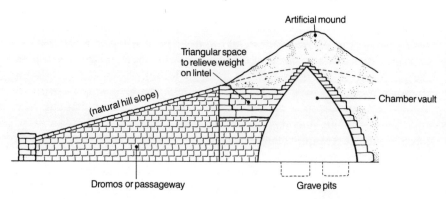

the ground, as in Crete, with a mound of earth raised over them. This method of construction had to be abandoned, the underground chamber becoming the norm, when it was realized that the weight of the mound was insufficient to counteract the outward thrust of the vault and to prevent collapse.

For Pausanias, the grand tour of ancient monuments had to take in at Orchomenus the Treasury of Minyas, 'one of the greatest wonders of Greece and of the world. It is built in stone, the shape is circular but the top does not stick up too sharply; they say the topmost stone is a keystone holding the entire structure in position.' Complaining about the tendency of his contemporaries 'to be wonderstruck by the exotic at the expense of sights at home', Pausanias regretted that 'distinguished historians have described minutely the Egyptian pyramids, and not made the slightest mention of Minyas' Treasury and the walls at Tiryns, though these are no less marvellous.' The tholos-tomb at Orchomenus, like 'the underground chambers of Atreus and his sons where they kept their wealth' in Mycenae, was termed a treasury because it was open. Except for a small tomb in the vicinity of the Pylos palace, all the tholoi so far discovered were plundered, an historical circumstance sadly restricting our knowledge of the associated burial customs. The Treasury of Minyas is now in a sorry state; the dromos was destroyed long before Schliemann reported in 1870 that the ceiling of the vault had caved in. How different it must have been in the Mycenaean period: Homer has Achilles reject the overtures of Agamemnon's ambassador, Odysseus, with the boast 'not for all the revenues of Orchomenus'.

The era of the tholos-tomb was that of the Mycenaean supremacy, when mainland activities reached outwards to Sicily and southern Italy, to the Cycladic islands, to Crete, to Rhodes, to Asia Minor, to Cyprus, and to northern Syria. In Hittite records for the fourteenth and thirteenth centuries BC there is reference to Ahhijawa, a powerful kingdom of the sea. Even if this is meant to be Rhodes, then a very strong Mycenaean principality, it is evidence of Hittite awareness of an enterprising civilization, newly in contact with that empire's own vassal states close to the Aegean seaboard.

At Mycenae the tholoi are nine in number. A.J.B. Wace, an excavator of the site for many years, divided them into three chronological groups: four primitive tombs built of rubble masonry, with unlined dromoi and entrances level with the top of the ground so as to avoid difficulties in setting door lintels in place; a second group of three tombs, whose vaults and extended passageways used dressed stone, and a relieving triangle above the door lintels prevented cracking; and the final group, which included the Treasury of Atreus and the Tomb of Clytemnestra.

Constructed about 1250 BC, the so-called Treasury of Atreus is the culmination of tholos-tomb development. It is excellently preserved, and has been one of the highlights of a visit to Mycenae for generations. The tremendously long dromos, measuring thirty-six metres, was cleared in 1878; its walls are lined with rectangular blocks of ashlar masonry, some of the larger stones being taken from an older building. At the entrance of the tomb itself the walls of this passageway reach ten metres in height. Though the façade of the grave is still uncracked, the remains of its decoration were removed during the nineteenth century. Fragments of carved half-columns are in the National Museum in Athens, and in the British Museum, which also houses carved slabs with bulls from the interior of the tholos. Once the doorway, some five and a half metres high by two and three-quarter metres wide at the base, was framed by half-columns of red and green carved stone in two storeys and closed by bronze double doors.

Mycenaean worship of a deity in the form of a column patently recalls Minoan reverence for the sacred post, but the ornate pillars here, like the one represented between the two lions on the relief above the Lion Gate, probably stand for the sanctity of the building rather than a divinity. The stomion, or door passage, is roofed with two giant lintels, the outer one weighing an estimated 120 tonnes. The relieving triangle above can now be readily distinguished from the dromos because of the removal of the decoration. The chamber comprises thirty-three courses of dressed ashlar blocks, rising in a corbelled vault nearly fourteen metres above its floor of solid rock. A small doorway, surmounted by a lintel and a relieving triangle, gives access to a rock-cut chamber on the north side of the tholos. Holes at irregular intervals on the interior of the vault may have held the nails of bronze rosettes and other decorative features. The outer side of the tholos was plastered with layers of clay in order to prevent the seepage of moisture into the joints, before a mound was raised. Wace found traces of a low retaining wall surrounding the base of the tumulus, which now is somewhat eroded.

The latest tholos at Mycenae, the Tomb of Clytemnestra, dates from 1220 BC. In spite of remaining undetected till the beginning of the nineteenth century, when the local Turkish pasha cleared its contents by breaking through the top of the vault, this tomb is poorly preserved. The collapse of the damaged vault through the action of rain water was only just stopped in 1951, the year the Greek Service for the Restoration and Preservation of Ancient Monuments made extensive repairs. The height of the restored vault is slightly under thirteen metres, and it seems not unlikely that the mound of this tomb, not far from the Lion Gate, was pointed out to Pausanias as 'the grave of Atreus'.

Recent investigation of tholoi at Peristeria in Messenia has disclosed three tombs within an oval enclosure wall, reminiscent of the precincts of the shaft-graves at Mycenae. Dating from around 1500 BC, they were excellently constructed with dressed stone, a mason's signs on the door-post of the largest one showing a double axe and a bough. To the south of this site, near the palace of Pylos, is the single unplundered tholos we possess. Its lucky escape from robbers was largely due to the total collapse of the structure within a few centuries of construction. Only the foundations of the vault are intact; they measure five and a half metres in diameter. The earliest burials were in pithoi, one of which is a Minoan import. The other pottery includes the so-called Palace Style jars, large storage vessels elegantly decorated with marine and plant designs. Although these jars originated at Knossos at the time of the Mycenaean occupation of the Palace of Minos, they were more popular on the Greek mainland, where their purpose could have been almost entirely funerary. The rest of the interments in the Pylos tomb took place in shallow pits, all of restricted dimensions except the last, which alone was adequate for a full-length burial. The final corpse was laid to rest with various cere-monial objects: a bronze dagger by his left side, an arrow shaft between his legs, a bronze mirror on his stomach, a terracotta figurine and a bronze awl with an ivory handle on his chest, a small bronze bowl at the head and an ointment jar by his right side.

The female figurine is a unique discovery, for nowhere else has this kind of votive offering been found as part of an adult burial. Derived from Crete, two small models of standing women prevalent in Mycenaean graves show one with wing-like arms outstretched in the manner of the Minoan mother goddess, the other with hands clasped below the waist. While the former are accepted as representatives of a divinity, whether unearthed from houses, shrines or graves, the latter have been called nurses, since they tend to be associated with infants' graves. The clasped hands of the Pylos figure must place the once popular theory of the divine nurse in jeopardy. Our problem in determining its religious significance is that, notwithstanding the lists of gods, goddesses, servants and offerings on the Linear B tablets, Mycenaean religion remains archeologically less apparent than Minoan. Not until the unexpected find by Mylonas and Lord William Taylour in 1968-9 of two sacred areas inside the citadel at Mycenae was there any certainty about a ritual building within a palace complex.

At Pylos a small chamber has been tentatively identified as a shrine. This palace also possessed a Minoan-style bathroom, which seems to have been available for general use. In the *Odyssey* it is related that Tele-machus, when inquiring about his father Odysseus from Nestor, was as a guest 'bathed and anointed with olive oil' by the king's daughter Po-lycaste, so that 'he appeared as one of the immortals'. The son of Odys-seus may have worshipped at the shrine or cult room too, as Pylos seems the palace under the strongest Cretan influence. The focus, however, of the Mycenaean palace was the circular hearth surrounded by four columns in the inner megaron, or throneroom. From the remains of a table with votive cups and a libation channel, cut into the floor of the throneroom, we may assume that Nestor performed religious ceremonies here. As wanax, the title for ruler in Linear B, the king of Pylos was not considered divine. Unlike Minoan rulers, Mycenaean royalty never acted as priest-kings, their subjects regarding them less as intermediaries with the gods than as leaders in peace and war on earth. Of course the regulation of the calendar, the oversight of festivals and observances, and the maintenance of sanctuaries were in the hands of the wanax, but the affairs of the religious realm devolved in effect onto a priestly class that appears to have been numerous and powerful. Its members included both men and women.

These keybearers – so the Linear B title of klawiphoros has been translated – would have ministered at the Cult Centre uncovered by Mylonas and Taylour in Mycenae, which comprises a number of buildings at the foot of the acropolis and just within the Cyclopean walls. The Cult Centre itself was destroyed shortly before 1200 BC. In 1950 at the nearby House of Tsountas, named after C. Tsountas who excavated the citadel from 1880 to 1902, Wace cleared a room with a stuccoed floor, a large hearth, and narrow platforms along two of its walls. A libation channel running to a sunken jar, rather like the arrangement in the throneroom at Pylos, leads to the belief that the room may have served as a shrine, though no idols were discovered there. It is possible that the House of Tsountas was part of the Cult Centre because Mylonas has recently uncovered a round altar and a room suitable for a high priest on its west side. The fact that Tsountas himself found in this area a painted limestone tablet of a war goddess only strengthens the case.

The damaged painting reveals a goddess almost hidden behind a figure-of-eight shield, attended by two female worshippers. Her domain could have been war in general or armour in particular; the large silver model of the figure-eight shield from Grave IV of Grave Circle A was probably a talisman relating to her cult. We are inevitably reminded of Athena who at Athens was identified with the tree, the bird, the snake, and, above all, the shield. The ferocity of the patron goddess of the Athenians is taken for granted by Homer: she is a female Ares, the god of war. In the *Iliad* we read that the day-long struggle between the Trojans and the Achaeans over Patroclus' corpse 'would not have displeased even warmonger Ares, or Athena, in their most belligerent mood. Such was the toil and agony that Zeus sent to man and horse alike.'

The two areas of the Cult Centre apparently contained separate cults. The chief one could be described as a small temple: it has an anteroom, with an outside storeroom attached; a cult room measuring approximately five by four metres, in the centre of which is a low rectangular platform, while at one end there is a series of narrow platforms; behind these platforms a window opens onto a small expanse of natural rock; next to three wooden columns, on one side of the cult room, a flight of six stairs gives access to a tiny storeroom. The excavators were amazed to find not only large clay statuettes in the cult room, but also sixteen others in the tiny store as well as three clay tables of offerings and six coiled snakes.

The snakes are significant in that here alone they are modelled without human figures; elsewhere in the Aegean, but especially on Crete, snakes normally tended to be associated with female divinities or priestesses. In Greek religion the snake belonged to the cults of Athena, Apollo and Dionysus, but down to our own times southern European peasants have kept non-poisonous snakes in their homes as household pets, a custom descending from worship of the household goddess. The serpent is an arcane symbol of earth and water: like a river winding its way, the serpent creeps silently along the ground; it dwells in the earth and issues forth like a spring or new shoot from its hole. In addition the serpent can

The Cult Centre at Mycenae. **A** 'The small temple'. 1. Anteroom. 2. Cult room with platforms. 3. Alcove with natural rock. 4. Position of mother-goddess statue. 5. Stairs. 6. Storeroom and statuettes. **B** 'Lesser sacred area'. 7. Anteroom. 8. Storeroom. 9. Room with hearth. 10. Shrine room. 11. Bath tub. 12. Hearth. 13. Bench.

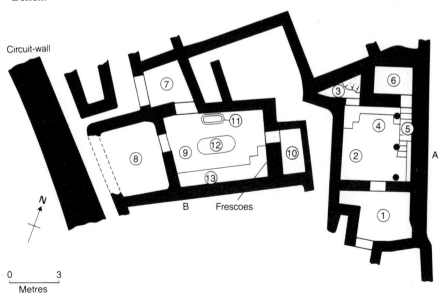

penetrate the tomb, and in the sloughing of its skin, it symbolizes the afterlife of the dead. Because of this the Greeks regarded the snake as a representative of both the dead and the gods, an Athenian law making the disposal of dead snakes a sacred duty. Taylour must be right then in proposing that 'the snakes were ... in some way associated with the unhewn, natural rock in the temple, as representing the underworld.'

The hollow statuette, sixty centimetres high, found standing on one of the narrow platforms, may be a Mycenaean version of the Great Mother, who for the Minoans was the mistress of mountains, vegetation, animals and the household. That the Indo-European cult of the sky god Zeus was gradually superimposed on an indigenous Aegean tradition in which an earth goddess was predominant can be observed from the development of Greek mythology, though for the Mycenaean period there is little definite information about relations between divinities. The statuette in question stood on the highest platform, hidden from immediate view by one of the columns; before her, a low, round table was ready for offerings. In Linear B the goddess was simply called 'Lady', Potnia.

Whereas Potnia is mentioned on many tablets, often as the protectress of a place, Zeus appears once in the Pylos archive, and several times at Knossos. In the Peloponnese, the most respected of the Mycenaean gods was not Zeus but his brother Poseidon, lord of earthquakes and water. Originally worshipped as a fertility god in the form of a horse, Poseidon became eventually the ruler of the waves, riding the deep in a chariot pulled by splendid golden seahorses. In the *Odyssey* the deity is the implacable foe of Odysseus, whom he pursues 'with relentless malice till the day he reaches Ithaca': the animosity of Poseidon was aroused by the blinding of his one-eyed son Polyphemus. When at Athena's instigation Telemachus arrived at Pylos, he encountered king Nestor on the shore with his followers sacrificing eighty-one 'jet-black bulls to Poseidon, the earthshaker, god of the sable locks'. Homer says that 'they had just tasted the victims' entrails and were burning some of the thighs in the god's benefit, as the trim ship approached them.' Confirmation of Poseidon's initial pre-eminence comes from a Pylos tablet: it lists the offerings due to four divinities; for Poseidon one gold cup and two women, for Zeus one gold bowl and one man, for Hera one gold bowl and one woman, for Hermes one gold cup and one man.

Hera, literally 'Lady', was the spouse of Zeus and the chief goddess of the Argolid, where a shield was awarded to the winner of the athletic contests held in her honour. During the Mycenaean age the strength of her local cult, as a manifestation of the mother goddess, was sufficient to cause the assimilation of the earth goddess as sister and wife of Zeus. It seems conceivable that later legends about her jealousy and quarrelsomeness recall the intense rivalry once existing between their two cults.

Although pre-Greek Hera was finally sublimated as the protectress of marriage, childbirth and the home, her 'harsh anger' is said to have led to disaster for gods, heroes and men, when she harried Zeus' other consorts and their children. Against the baby Heracles, whom Zeus begot on Alcmene, she sent two serpents, but the infant hero strangled them in his cradle, an event still celebrated on British gripe-water bottles today. Heracles means the one who won fame through Hera. Maybe the legendary twelve labours collected around an historical prince of Tiryns, who expiated a blood guilt at her behest, as six of them were accomplished in the Peloponnese. Though we lack direct evidence, the female statuette unearthed by Mylonas and Taylour could well be Potnia-Hera and the smaller figurine from the Pylos tholos the goddess in the chthonic aspect of her divinity.

Of the terracotta idols from the small temple, ten are female figures, seven male and two hermaphrodite. Slightly taller than the goddess we have called Potnia-Hera is a male deity; he swings in his right hand a hammer-axe, an obscure attribute unless it was connected with the construction of Cyclopean walls. Although the size of this statuette implies an important position in the Mycenaean pantheon, we are unable to determine the identity of the god. The hammer-axe had no connection with the iconography of Zeus, who as a weather god was remote from the concerns of men, and it cannot be readily attributed to the smith god Hephaestus in spite of a Linear B reference to his worship at Knossos, because the potter has made no attempt to show that the deity was lame. While the Greeks knew Hephaestus as the god of fire and especially the smithy fire, his cult being particularly prominent during the classical period at Athens and other industrialized cities, the Bronze Age character of the god was associated with volcanoes. It is thought that he originally came to mainland Greece via the volcanic island of Lemnos from Asia Minor. Greek myth blames his disability on having interfered in a quarrel between his parents, Zeus and Hera. So angry did Zeus become that he threw his son out of Olympus and let him fall heavily on Lemnos. As the concentration of so many deities in one small temple could have been accidental, perhaps as a precaution at a time when an enemy attack was expected, we need to hesitate over making assumptions of their relations with each other.

The lesser sacred area consists of four rooms: an anteroom; a storeroom; a central room with a hearth, an undecorated clay bath, a platform along one wall, and two damaged frescoes; and a small shrineroom. Both murals are Minoan in style, though the smallest goddess holding two handfuls of garnered corn in the scene with figures has been traced to Ugarit. Large quantities of Mycenaean pottery at the site of this Syrian port bear witness to its close trading ties with the Aegean. But demonstrably Minoan in the second fresco are the three horns of consecration and the row of beam-end capitals, painted alternately red and black. The sole idol from the shrineroom is a terracotta goddess with raised arms, nearly thirty centimetres high. Following the discovery of the pottery deities at Mycenae, similar figures have been excavated in the citadel at Tiryns and in a shrine at Phylakopi on the island of Melos. Other traces of Mycenaean temples exist at Eleusis in Attica and on the islands of Delos and Ceos, all places at a distance from princely strongholds. The building on Ceos possessed five rectangular rooms of different sizes. In the middle of the largest a stone platform was once the resting place of several terracotta deities, one of which could have been nearly lifesize. A fragment of a bronze figurine of a youth raising his hand in the Minoan fashion of worship suggests continuity of use at a sacred site. The Mycenaean structure was erected in the fifteenth century BC, repaired following earthquake damage two centuries later, and destroyed before 1100 BC. During the classical period a shrine to Dionysus stood there.

Two further tholoi deserve our attention because of the artifacts graverobbers overlooked in them. They are situated at Vapheio in Laconia and at Dendra in the Argolid. Explored by Tsountas in 1888, the Vapheio tholos was not cut into a hillside but constructed on top of a hill, and then covered by a mound. Besides bronze, stone, clay and silver vases, beads and carved gems, bronze knives and daggers, Tsountas was fortunate in locating two gold cups of exquisite Minoan craftsmanship. On these vessels, scenes connected with the bull games are portrayed in repoussé work. They narrate the ensnaring of a wild bull by means of a decoy, the tethering of one of his hind legs, and the drawing tight of a strong net: in the final event of the sequence the captured bull vents its ire on two male bull-leapers. The early collapse of the tomb may account for the preservation of these splendid drinking cups. The tholos at Dendra, the burial chamber of the kings of Midea, also suffered a cave-in of the vault. Scattered about in disorder on the floor were found the remains of at least three interments, but in two undisturbed pits lay the grave goods of a king and queen. The precious objects – gold cups, silver goblets, jewellery, bronze swords with gold-mounted hilts and ivory pommels – illustrate the riches deposited with the noble dead in Mycenaean tholos-tombs.

The palaces these wealthy rulers inhabited were fortified, with the very notable exception of Pylos. Their development into the palace-fortresses we recognize in the impressive ruins of today happened around 1300 BC, virtually at the close of the tholos age. In the next chapter we shall examine this stress on war, especially in the Argolid where the art of fortification reached a zenith; here we are concerned with the nature of the earlier citadels. At Tiryns, a narrow, oblong hillock almost one kilometre from the sea, the foundations and tiles of the circular building mentioned in Chapter One prove that an important settlement existed on what was to become the citadel prior to the arrival of the Mycenaeans. The initial defences of the newcomers have not survived, but in the evolution of the site three main phases are distinguished. The first palace on the very summit of the hill was surrounded by stone walls, a bastion in the south-east corner protecting its sole gateway. In the second phase the citadel was enlarged in three directions: to the north an open space was enclosed: to the south a number of buildings, probably for storage, were built within the extended wall; to the east the gateway was strengthened with the addition of a north-south passage containing two more doors. The layout of the final citadel, whose Cyclopean masonry has been the wonder of visitors from Pausanias onwards, was entirely dictated by military considerations, its chief feature, an elongated northern extension, offering shelter to people settled close by.

Only the ruling family and certain privileged members of the community lived permanently in Mycenaean citadels, the majority dwelling in villages within sight of the ramparts or at a greater distance away. Pylos would seem to have been exceptional in having an extensive settlement earlier than the construction of its palace. While population grew apace from 1400 BC, the density on mainland Greece never compared with that of Minoan Crete, save in Messenia. Indeed, the large houses in the shadow of the citadel walls of Mycenae could have been an adjunct

The citadel at Tiryns. 1. Lower Citadel. 2. Underground passage. 3. Ramp. 4. North-south passage. 5. Galleries. 6. Bastion and Postern Gate. 7. Propylons. 8. Altar in Inner Court. 9. Throne room.

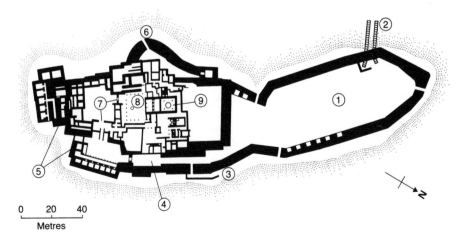

of the palace workshops rather than the residences of merchants, given the commercial activity of the wanax.

The throneroom remained the core of the Tiryns palace throughout the expansion of the citadel. It was approached in the third phase of development through two propylons. In the inner courtyard between these entrances was built a round altar, one and a half metres in diameter, surrounded by a rectangular pavement. The altar and the hearth in the throneroom were aligned on a north-south axis. The royal megaron had three sections: an outer porch supported by two columns and raised two steps above the courtyard: a vestibule with three doors opening onto the porch, one side door leading to inner apartments, including a bathroom, and the door giving access to the throneroom; the latter had bright paintings on the walls, a plastered pavement divided into coloured squares, and a vent in the ceiling to allow the escape of smoke. An older and smaller megaron to the rear is thought to have belonged to the queen and her ladies. Damage from the elements has obliterated the functions of the rooms arranged around these two principal units, though fragments of pithoi would make us suppose that some of them were the storerooms and kitchens which provided the substance for the feasts and entertainments dimly remembered by Homer. It is curious to note that ever since Schliemann's work on the site, scholars have pointed out similarities between Tiryns and descriptions of the palace of Odysseus in the *Odyssey*.

Before 1300 BC the town of Pylos was already populous. Set back from the sea to avoid surprise attack, the site enjoys from its low hill a sweeping view of the Navarino bay as well as the stark outline of Sphacteria, an island on which the Athenians achieved a rare land victory over the Spartans in 425 BC. Some time in the fourteenth century BC the town was burned and a dynasty installed itself in an unfortified palace on the hilltop. Legend says that the conqueror was Neleus of Iolkos, who was 'a son of Poseidon', a deity worshipped fervently in both Thessaly and Messenia. The Neleid palace, in turn fired like most Mycenaean sites about 1200 BC, was divided into three separate wings. The central building housed the state rooms and the king's quarters, its outer gateway having on one side the archives, on the other a guardroom with a tower. An inner paved court, open to the sky, conducted visitors to the fluted wooden columns of the entrance to the megaron. The rooms surrounding the throneroom were either stores or pantries, excavation bringing to light some 3,000 drinking cups and 6,000 vases. Adjacent to the guardroom were a smaller megaron and the bathroom Homer says that Odysseus' son used. Partly because this megaron had its own enclosed courtyard on the outside of the central complex, it is named the Queen's Hall, but in the west wing a larger room with four column bases may have better served the queen, especially if she supervised female slaves domiciled there. Quarrying this century has destroyed much of the west wing, possibly the hearth belonging to the megaron included, and left us with tantalizing fragments of wallpaintings. The three-columned vestibule of the large room had, for instance, above a dado a frieze of pink griffins as part of its decoration.

Although the majority of the east wing was given over to storerooms and workshops, it contained what could have been a shrine. This was a three by three and a half metre chamber, open to a stuccoed court in which was an altar of limestone covered with painted plaster. Linear B inscriptions unearthed nearby refer to chariots, leather and a horse goddess. The detached northern section of the east wing, a building with a narrow vestibule, served as the palace wine cellar, we gather from four sealings marked with the sign for wine. A tablet from the archives provides a list of offerings for an initiation ceremony, which was held away from the palace. Besides flour, barley, figs, olives, honey, an ox, sheep, goats and pigs, the king dedicated nearly 600 litres of wine. For Homer

Plan of the chief buildings of the Pylos palace. 1. Entrance to State Rooms. 2. Archive Room. 3. Guardroom with tower. 4. Inner Court. 5. Throne Room. 6. Stores and Pantries. 7. Queen's Hall. 8. Bathroom. 9. Enclosed courtyard. 10. West Wing. 11. Wine Cellar. 12. Shrine. 13. Altar.

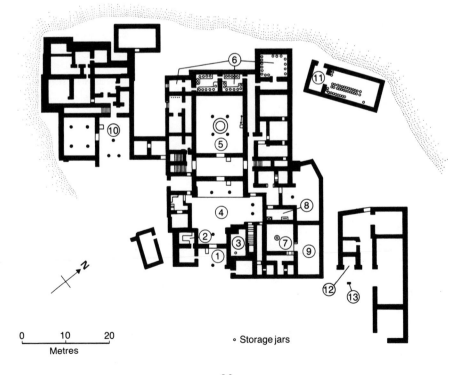

0   10   20
Metres

∘ Storage jars

93

too, the generosity of Pylos was renowned, guests 'ever finding their golden cups brimming full of wine'.

The ancestor of the Danaans, one of the names that Homer gives the Greeks, is linked by some scholars with the shaft-grave dynasty at Mycenae. According to legend, Danaos came from Egypt, challenged Gelanor for the throne, and was crowned as king of the Argolid. Pausanias tells us that the most glorious sight in the city of Argos was the sanctuary of Apollo Lykaios, 'the wolfish', which Danaos dedicated on his accession to the throne. The Argives could not decide between the descendant of their first king, Argos, and the would-be usurper, until they received a divine sign in the form of a wolf killing a bull by the city wall. This was taken to mean that Danaos should become king, because like the wolf he was an outsider attacking Gelanor. Whilst the Egyptian origins of Danaos have been advanced to explain the upsurge of activity in Mycenae, Greek tradition never suggests that he was a foreign prince, so there is no valid reason to regard Danaos as a Hyksos refugee who fled to the Aegean when the Egyptians drove the Hyksos invaders from the Delta about 1567 BC. The only outside influences on Grave Circles A and B are those of the Cyclades and Minoan Crete. The absence in the archeological record of any non-funerary construction prior to 1500 BC ensures that we are ignorant of the early citadel. Later levelling of the summit has also left little of the first palace, merely a filled-in room, broken foundations and fragments of wallpaintings, but the north winds blowing over the exposed site must have necessitated placing the entrance to the megaron in the south. The second palace built on the levelled and terraced upper slopes of the citadel had two stages of development, the last one following a devastating fire in the thirteenth century BC. The date of its final destruction by enemy action at the close of the Mycenaean period remains unsettled, Wace arguing that the sack occurred after 1200 BC.

The many similarities between the palaces at Pylos and Mycenae have encouraged the view that the builders of the former were influenced by those of the latter, if they did not belong to the same association of craftsmen. While the direction of influence may be deduced from the more elaborate and regular form of the Neleid building, it is possible that one innovation at least travelled back to the older palace at Mycenae, namely the introduction of a side door in the portico of the megaron so as to allow easier communication with the domestic quarters. The measurements of the megara of Pylos and Mycenae were almost the same, both had terracotta pipes above their great hearths in order to deal with the smoke and, unlike the Tiryns megaron, single doorways connected their porticoes and vestibules. The construction of the second palace at Mycenae coincides with the southward extension of the Cyclopean walls, which in the thirteenth century BC enclosed Grave Circle A next to the

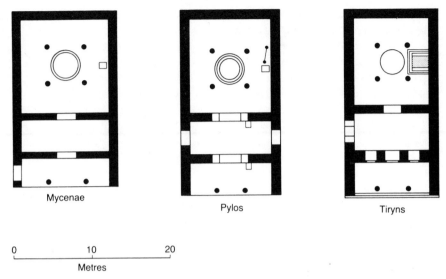

Mycenae

Pylos

Tiryns

0   10   20

Metres

Megara, throne rooms, compared.

Lion Gate. We can be sure of this, even though the exact date remains unfixed, because a section of the defences acted as a retaining wall for the terrace on which the megaron itself stood. The foundations of the megaron and a few other ceremonial buildings survive, but of the palace complex there is scarcely a trace, the only other section visible today being a possible east wing in what Wace named the House of Columns.

Ancient visitors to the king of Mycenae entered the citadel through the Lion Gate, passed the Granary, which may have functioned as a control centre for daily business like the archive rooms at Pylos, turned up a steep ramp just beyond Grave Circle A, and then progressed to the inner entrance of the palace. This consisted of an enclosed staircase. The first flight of twenty-two steps were stone, the second presumably wood. Having ascended the stairs, visitors had to cross a good-sized room before entering the large court in front of the megaron. The entrance to the staircase is an amazing vantage point for viewing of the Argive plain, spreading away as it does south-eastwards to the Aegean and south-westwards to the Arcadian hills. Dismounting from his chariot here, Agamemnon could have surveyed his realm on the day he is supposed to have returned from the Trojan War, just before he entered the palace and met his own death inside at the hands of his wife's lover, Aegisthus. In the *Odyssey* the leader of the Achaean host is slain at a banquet given in Aegisthus' stronghold, a storm having forced Agamemnon to make landfall outside his own territories. Later accounts shift the scene to the Argolid, and usually Argos, but there is every reason to suppose that the

95

assassination of a king at Mycenae was part of the unrest experienced by mainland Greece immediately after the fall of Troy.

Mylonas draws attention to a Homeric feature of the megaron at Mycenae. Both the inner throneroom and the vestibule had a border of gypsum slabs placed along their walls, an arrangement of imported Cretan stone which tallies with the description of the palace of Alcinous in book seven of the *Odyssey*. 'Inside the hall,' Odysseus observed, 'high chairs were ranged along the walls on either side ... and on them the Phaeacian chieftains sat and partook of generous quantities of food and wine.' Obviously the firmer border was intended to spare the rest of the stuccoed floor from unnecessary wear. Both Tsountas and Wace dug the House of Columns, but its close resemblance to the home of Odysseus on Ithaca was first remarked by Wace. A corridor from a recessed entrance joined a peristyle court, which may have once contained as many as ten wooden columns. Off the west side were four magazines, off the south a three-storeyed structure, the lowest level being another magazine, while the north and east side doors led to more formal rooms and a staircase to the upper floors. The megaron, situated on the northern side of the court, had a side door from its inner chamber opening onto the passage where the staircase was. Although the House of Columns appears to have been separated physically from the palace complex, the impressive central courtyard recommends its interpretation as an annex, perhaps the residence of members of the royal family. The rectangular tower in the Cyclopean wall next to this building would seem to have been built to cover a large drain rather than as a lookout post over the Argive plain. It is fanciful to imagine that the House of Columns was the abode of the lawagetas, 'the leader of the people', the war host, yet a beacon on the tower could have been a signal of impending military action, a call to arms for the warriors upon whom the authority of the wanax depended. Mycenaean rulers were obliged to rely on the support of a military aristocracy, whose leaders must have been kept loyal by the ties of kinship. From the Linear B tablets of Pylos there can be no question concerning the importance of the lawagetas and his followers.

Within the citadel of Mycenae the other excavated residences are clustered near Grave Circle A. Extensive damage hid the identity of their occupants until the uncovering of the Cult Centre in 1968-9, when it was surmised that they were intended as accommodation for priests in attendance at the shrines. The four houses here were constructed above a solid stone basement in rubble and timber, which was surfaced with painted plaster. Like Minoan buildings, they had flat roofs, the Mycenaeans remaining in ignorance of the tiled gables developed previously at Lerna and Tiryns. So thorough was the pillage of this section of the citadel that no more than the lower walls remain.

Previous page: View across the approach to the Grand Stairway on the left of the Palace at Phaestos. Notice the outline of the earlier palace which had been destroyed by earthquake about 1700 BC.

Right: Part of the final fortifications of Tiryns, whose massive walls still excited the admiration of Pausanias in the second century AD. At this site Mycenaean architecture reached its military apotheosis.

Below: The Palace of Minos at Knossos. Looking southwards from the Central Court, across the monumental horns of consecration towards Mount Juktas, on which Evans found in 1909 an extensive enclosure as well as a cult building with a plaster floor.

Above: The famous bull-leaping fresco which was unearthed at Knossos. It shows the various stages of the dangerous sport.

Below: One of the giant pithoi found in the Minoan palace of Mallia. The storage of agricultural produce was a chief concern of Bronze age rulers.

Above: The bee pendant discovered at Mallia. Exquisite craftsmanship was always associated with the Minoans, whose greatest exponent the Greeks remembered as Daedalus.

Right: One of the two frescoes from the West House on Thera. Here for the first time classical nudity has been applied to an ordinary man.

Above: The Phaestos Disc, about fifteen centimetres in diameter, its signs were evidently stamped on the clay when wet, thereby representing the first example of printing known in Europe.

Above: The smaller (about thirty centimetres high) of the famous pair of second-palatial faience statuettes found at Knossos. Argument still continues as to the figure's significance: is she a priestess or a goddess?

Below: The vault of the Treasury of Atreus at Myceneae. The interior is 14 metres high.

Above: Acragas, modern Agrigento in Sicily. Founded in 580 BC by the Greek colony of Gela to the east, Acragas grew prosperous on trade with North Africa and its citizens spent much wealth on a great temple terrace which was situated in the southern section of the city.

Below: Archaic painting of a long ship. Familiarity with the sea made the Mediterranean a Greek lake despite the efforts of the Phoenicians, Carthaginians and Etruscans.

Above: A view of the site of Miletus, the birthplace of philosophical speculation in the West. Its famous sons were Thales, Anaximander and Anaximenes.

Left: Funeral scene on a large Attic bowl, *c.* 750 BC. By the close of the Dark Age potters had reintroduced scenes with human figures and animals, albeit painted in silhouette.

Above: Relief of officials from the great ceremonial city of Persepolis, founded by Darius as the Persian capital. From here orders were dispatched to Egypt, Asia Minor and Syria, so as to prepare for expansion into Egypt.

Left: The elaborate plate-armour from the Mycenaean chamber tomb at Dendra, ancient Midea. Above is a boars' tusk helmet which was especially favoured by warriors in the Bronze Age.

Chapter Five

THE FALL OF THE MYCENAEANS

Mycenae was the home of warlike men. Even without the violence of their family and dynastic quarrels as remembered in Greek mythology, the archeological record speaks of an overriding concern with military dangers. The best energies of the population were directed to the building of the Cyclopean circuit walls, which in the thirteenth century BC attained a length of more than 3,000 metres. Like the other strongholds of the Argolid, the function of Mycenae was to deter foreign invaders, to resist the ambitions of rival kings, and to subdue the lowly inhabitants of the surrounding countryside.

At the apex of Mycenaean society stood the armoured warrior-lord. Although bronze plate armour did not remain fashionable throughout the Mycenaean period, the panoply from the Dendra chamber tomb so anticipates the equipment of the medieval knight that it invites comparison with feudalism. Dating from the fourteenth century BC, the main component was an elaborate cuirass, consisting of a front and rear plate, on which were hung a high neck guard and shoulder guards: three curved plates gave protection to the lower part of the torso. This incredible suit of body armour divulges the connection between political power and metal monopoly. While the rulers of Pylos for reasons we shall review later in this chapter felt safe enough to eschew fortifications, their archives plainly bring out a decisive palace influence over metallurgy. Linear B tablets record the levying and distribution of large amounts of imported bronze, most of which was used in the manufacture of arrowheads and spearheads. Against these sharp points, the Dendra warrior wore greaves on his legs, the earliest example of metal shin guards known in Europe.

Our understanding of Mycenaean society is not only restricted to the mature palatial epoch of the thirteenth century BC but even more to the kingdom of Pylos, though similarities between the palaces of Mycenae, Tiryns and Pylos led us to suppose that there was a common political and economic system at least in the Peloponnese. The insight we enjoy in Messenia derives from interpretation of the extensive archives which Blegen unearthed next to the entrance of the Neleid palace. These tablets depict a very different kind of society from the simple and largely unstructured world of the *Iliad* and the *Odyssey*. Despite disagreements among scholars over the meaning of several key Linear B terms, we can infer from the archives that a person's status was measured by amounts of grain. One tablet records the land held by the king and his principal followers: the size of each holding is calculated by the quantity of seed required for a sowing. The royal demesne is given as three times bigger than that of the lawagetas, the second personage in Pylos. The amount of seed corn the king needed was just short of 3,000 litres, enough to sow a very large area indeed. It may also be the case that this tablet refers only to crown land at one particular place.

The title of a Mycenaean king, wanax, is one of the two words Homer uses for a ruler. Basileus, the second, which occurs in Linear B inscriptions in the form of guasileus, had a less exalted meaning for the Mycenaeans, who employed the word generally as 'head' of a group. Although this use is still evident in Homer, basileus survived in classical times as the word for king, along with a military connotation. In Athenian legend, for example, the sons of Pandion, one of the earliest kings, are credited with a division of sovereignty. To Erechtheus went the basileia, and to his brother Butes, the hierosyne or priesthood. As war leader, even the re-inventor of the chariot, Erechtheus, was dominant until his death in battle, whereupon his sons contested for power. Perhaps the situation in Ithaca on the homecoming of Odysseus helps to explain the changes in kingship following the collapse of Mycenaean civilization. Telemachus, the hardpressed son of Odysseus, is merely one of the local basilees, or heads, no matter how often he tries to assert his position as master of the house. The suitors make no real effort to obey their host's wishes and they show restraint towards neither his womenfolk nor his belongings. Only the strong arm of Odysseus, who turns his powerful bow on these unruly peers, is able to recover the family prerogatives. While we should assume that the military abilities of the wanax were of the utmost importance, the palace organization would have ensured that royal authority rested on much more than personal valour. The disappearance of the wanax after the destruction of the palace-strongholds must have left political power in the hands of petty chieftains, whose influence varied according to the fighting strength of their supporters.

Besides the possession of considerable estates, the wanax owned workshops and storehouses, the adjective meaning royal being applied to such crafts as fulling, pottery and metalwork. His wealth can be seen in the gifts he dedicated regularly to gods and goddesses. Next to the wanax in social prestige came the lawagetas, who in the *Iliad* commanded the war host. Whether this later role was undertaken in the Mycenaean period by

The so-called 'Tripod Tablet' from Pylos. Its inscription provided dramatic support in 1953 for the decipherment of Linear B as an archaic form of Greek.

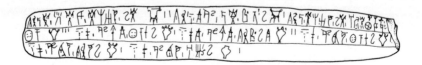

the lawagetas is not absolutely clear; some tablets imply an association with religion, but like other leading nobles he would have taken a keen interest in the service of the cults. Immediately surrounding the wanax and the lawagetas were the hequetai, the 'followers', who formed the royal retinue. These men either headed a military unit or acted as liaison officers between the palace and commanders in the field. As companions of the king, they represent the upper classes of Mycenaean society, the well-born group which dwelt in the palace precincts. From the Knossos tablets it is apparent that the hequetai wore an outer garment of special design, with white fringes, as a uniform. We are aware too that they were well supplied with slaves and chariots. Whereas the Mycenaean dynasts at Knossos maintained a force of about 200 chariots, the kings of Pylos seem to have managed with a rather smaller number. The heavily armoured and chariot-riding hequetai would have been in charge of the foot soldiers, who at Pylos were formed into eleven regiments.

In addition to the aristocracy centred on the palace there appears to have been a second, less influential, group living in the countryside, from whose ranks the wanax probably drew the officials responsible for the sixteen administrative districts into which Messenia was divided. These local landowners may be the telestas frequently mentioned in the Pylos archives; the tablet dealing with the estates of the wanax and the lawagetas informs us that three telestai together had lands of the same size as the royal demesne.

Each administrative district was under a governor, koreter, and his deputy, prokoreter. These officials seem to have had extra titles, including klawiphoros or 'keybearer'. The cult duties of keybearers are recorded on a number of tablets, where the person concerned can have been a woman, but it would be surprising if administrative appointments were held other than by men. Governors and deputy governors probably combined secular and religious offices, especially in districts containing famous cult centres, yet their prime duty was the enforcement of orders issued by the palace authorities. An illustration of this task is an instruction to collect bronze for 'spearheads'. The purpose of the levy, which included the collecting of old votive offerings from shrines, was to provide raw material for the armaments industry, a sign that Pylos preferred to improve its weaponry rather than to engage in an exhausting programme of defensive wall building. The main weapon of the Mycenaeans was the spear, whose straight-edged blade compared favourably with the length of a sword; besides the tremendous weight of its thrust, the giant spearhead could be employed at close quarters for a sideways slashing stroke. Its prestige is echoed in the *Iliad*, that celebration of heroes 'famous with the spear'. On the Trojan plain the fighting was always full of 'long, flesh-tearing spears', like the one Achilles drove through the neck of Hector.

Another term of note in Linear B is damos, which J.T. Hooker sensibly translates as 'community'. The demos in classical Greece was the ordinary people, but in Attica a deme could also mean a local administrative district. Given the continuity of Athenian traditions, we can accept that damos once referred to the inhabitants of a specific locality. It even appears that the damos possessed land, which was leased out to individual holders, a tenure arrangement somehow separate from the land owned by telestas, whose plots were called kotona kitimena, 'settled land'. The question of private ownership is difficult to resolve from the tablets we have at present, not least because the wanax may have been looked upon as the ultimate landlord as in feudalism. If this were so then the Pylos archives comprise a kind of Messenian Doomsday Book.

The tablets found in the Neleid palace are chiefly concerned with the nobility and landholding class on one hand, and with royal dependants and slaves on the other; the mass of the ordinary people do not feature at all. Several references occur to subtenants, small plotholders who are also called teojo dero or 'slaves of the god'. Whatever this title may have meant originally, Hooker is surely correct in regarding it as merely honorific by the time that the archives were formed. The real slave class seems to have been largely female and engaged in humble occupations on behalf of the palace authorities; they were corngrinders, bath attendants, flaxworkers and weavers. Their children lived with them, but no mention is made of their husbands. As Chadwick points out, this arrangement would have prevailed for the reason that after a slaving raid it was easier to slay the men and to take captive only the women and children. One tablet actually refers to groups of men as the sons of certain women, implying that they grew up enslaved. Though another says that five young men and a boy were the sons of rowers, we should not necessarily conclude that the 600 men who served as rowers in the fleet were themselves slaves. This naval contingent and a coastguard of some 800 soldiers defended the Messenian coast.

The origins of the female slaves listed at Pylos are intriguing. The majority were brought to mainland Greece from Asia Minor, but whether the palace of Pylos recruited these women through raids of its own or relied on slave markets run by Mycenaeans settled in the Aegean there is no way of knowing. Only at Knossos does a Linear B inscription bear witness to the purchase of slaves. Of the 750 female slaves belonging to the wanax at Pylos, 450 were located in and about the palace itself. The others lived on various crown lands, the greatest number at Leuktron, possibly an unidentified secondary capital of the fertile territories lying in the Pamisos valley. From a detailed analysis of Messenian place names in Linear B, it is thought that two provinces constituted the kingdom of Pylos: these were the western coastal strip where the palace stood and to the east the Messenian plain watered principally by the Pamisos river system. Between them stands a mountain range, known to the Mycenaeans as Aigolaia and the classical Greeks as Aigaleon.

In spite of the difficulties of interpretation, the Pylos archives show a complicated political and social structure. Scribes kept records of landholdings, craft activity, religious festivals and military operations. The interests of the wanax seem to have extended to almost every aspect of life. Tablets note the call-up of rowers and their assembly at a place named Pleuron, the movements of troops guarding frontier areas both inland and along the coastline, the arrangements for collecting and distributing raw materials and foodstuffs, the products made in the royal workshops, and the offerings awarded to the gods. What they fail to do is provide sufficient data on the size of the population, since the numbers of cultivators, shepherds, foresters and fishermen at work were never tallied. A cautious estimate puts the figure for the whole kingdom at 50,000 persons, which appears far too low for such a prosperous state. Although the suggestion of 178,000 may be slightly excessive, it is more in line with the population density sustained by the Minoans on Crete and therefore commands greater respect. Homer's 'sandy Pylos' could have been the home of 6,000–7,000 people.

If nothing else, the Pylos archives offer crucial negative evidence on the religious role of the wanax. There is no more support for the idea of a priest-king than there is for the palace to be looked upon as a divine residence. Unlike the Minoans, the Mycenaeans preferred to keep separate palaces and cult centres. The religious complex discovered by Mylonas and Taylour at Mycenae may be within the Cyclopean walls of the citadel, as is Grave Circle A, but its location is at a distance from the entrance to the palace.

One of the besetting problems for understanding Mycenaean belief has been the tendency to treat Mycenaean-Minoan religion as a unity. Even such a perceptive scholar as Jean-Pierre Vernant can still yoke together the Cretan legend of Minos' nine-yearly meetings with Zeus and the ordeal which Spartan ephors imposed on their two kings every nine years, when they searched the sky in order to read whether the rulers had committed any errors. Divine approval of a sovereign, however expressed in the elements, does not automatically imply a divine king. The ruler of Pylos, like his Bronze Age peers elsewhere, would have sought to maintain the best relations with the divinities his people revered by ensuring that the proper rites were regularly performed. Earthquakes, eclipses, comets, droughts and other unusual natural phenomena obviously caused alarm, and received the attention of seers, but whatever meanings were given to these startling events, there is nothing to indicate that they were held to be other than signs of divine disapproval. The king's actions would have had to be pleasing to the supernatural realm in the same way as the behaviour of his own subjects was expected to conform with established practice. The wanax was the chief of men, never the least of the gods.

Nor is there unequivocal testimony of a cult of the dead. The stone identified by Schliemann in the centre of Grave Circle A at Mycenae as an altar was in later Mycenaean times well below ground level. Mylonas' patient excavation of nearby Grave Circle B has shown that rites were performed on burial, as the piles of grave goods recovered from both enclosures would lead us to expect, but proof of the existence of a proper cult depends on evidence of continued rites in honour of the dead. Whilst the construction of mighty tholos-tombs argues for their use as miniature dwelling-places of the noble dead rather than as temporary shelters for the journey to the afterlife, their re-use for burials and their subsequent despoliation effectively denies us first-hand knowledge.

Though monumental tombs would seem to have been a purely My-cenaean development, the funerary traditions of the Minoans being more modest, archeologists can find nothing akin to the ancestral cults practised in contemporary China, whose warlike sovereigns had very similar interests to the wanaktes. The Bronze Age Shang nobility there lived in fortified towns, controlled trade and industry, rode to battle in chariots, and built elaborate royal tombs. As a closely knit kinship group, they traced their descent through their chief member, the king, from the supreme god, Shang Ti, the founder-ancestor of their people and the ruler of the natural world. Shang Ti was thought of as ruling on high, and his realm extended beyond the world of their deceased ancestors to include control of the sun, moon, stars, rain, wind and thunder. When a king died, he was said to have gone up to heaven to join his great ancestor, bequeathing to his son the role of chief worshipper as priest-king in the ancestral cult. Upon the goodwill of Shang Ti and the deceased forbears everything hung: they received the appropriate sacrifices for the seasons and major events, such as birth, marriage and death, besides providing guidance and help when governmental decisions arose. Hence, political power was linked in Shang China (c. 1650–1027 BC) with spiritual power, and the ruler as Son of Heaven, by his harmonious relationship with the spiritual realm, ensured the welfare of the state.

Our greater knowledge of ancient Chinese religion derives from the innumerable oracular inscriptions left by the Shang, who recorded both the questions they asked the ancestral spirits and the answers they received. In contrast, the Linear B tablets are preoccupied with the function of the palace in running the economy and in maintaining law and order. The tablets relating to sacrifices at Pylos inform us of the generous provision made by the king for cult purposes, but there is not the over-riding concern felt by the Shang for divine guidance. In the inscriptions we encounter no requests, no thanks; the names of gods and goddesses are mentioned only when they are beneficiaries of the palace storerooms: the wanax appears to have been as detached from divinities as he was from the world of the dead, for he was never the chief functionary of an ancestral cult based on the tholos-tomb. The inconvenience of incorporating Grave Circle A within the extended Cyclopean walls at Mycenae during the late thirteenth century BC is insufficient to prove that it was required there for purposes of worship. Indeed, the entrance through the double row of stones then placed along its circumference faces towards the Lion Gate and away from the Cult Centre.

It is hard to imagine a situation in which a clear distinction can be drawn between a Minoan and a Mycenaean religious artifact from a site on mainland Greece. Further discoveries of Linear B inscriptions may help, provided they go beyond palace book-keeping and outline some of the attributes of Mycenaean deities. At the moment we cannot take the double axes in gold foil, or the other symbols of Minoan religion found in Grave Circle A, as direct imports of the cult of the Cretan mother goddess. Since these objects were found among so many other ornaments, the Mycenaeans may not have connected them with cult at all.

Our uncertainties are perhaps best focused on the Great Goddess Ring, which we discussed at length in Chapter Three. Hooker has drawn notice to its crowded design, and wondered about the engraver's need to establish that the whole picture was a cult scene by inserting religious symbols – the double axe, the sacred tree, and the row of animal heads. He believes that the ring was a Mycenaean attempt to display a typical facet of the Minoan religion, then about 1500 BC becoming known on the Greek mainland. His case rests essentially on the small figure with the figure-of-eight shield, whom we regarded as a descending god. Given that no descending figure is portrayed with a shield in Minoan art and that a similarly armed diety is the Mycenaean war goddess, Hooker concludes that the figure with the figure-of-eight shield should be seen as a mainland divinity superimposed upon a quasi-Minoan cult scene. Even though this aspect of the composition appears unusual, the rest is so Minoan in temper that the epiphany of the Great Mother with her poppies remains quite undisturbed as the subject. All that we are able to say is that there is a possibility that the ring was manufactured at Mycenae and not imported from Crete, but beyond this lies pure speculation. The extent of the assimilation between Mycenaean and Minoan religions is notoriously difficult to determine.

The cult of the mother goddess, which had dominated religious life throughout the Aegean since the advent of agriculture, found expression in Linear B in the title of Potnia, 'Lady'. At Pylos one goddess is addressed as athana potnia, Lady Athena; potnia is associated with bronze in the Pylos archives, with sheep on the tablets from Knossos. Besides the income shepherds and smiths would have provided for her shrines and attendants, the goddess probably acted as protectress of their occupations. South of Knossos, a cave at Arkalokhori was used as a workshop by bronzesmiths as well as a sanctuary.

In classical Athens the city goddess Athena shared with Hephaestus the allegiance of metalworkers, an overlap in function presumably of Mycenaean origin. Both deities were always closely connected with armour and weapons by the Greeks, so that in the principal myth of Athena's birth the head of Zeus was split open with an axe swung by Hephaestus, and the goddess leapt out, fully armed and uttering her war cry. Less combative in Knossos, the mother goddess also appears as dapurito potnia, Lady of the Labyrinth. A tablet from Thebes speaks of Potnia's 'house', or shrine, and reveals the widespread continuation of worship given, under different guises, to the Great Mother, but it was in Hera, the wife of 'Father Zeus', that the Aegean earth goddess attained her apotheosis. In later versions of Greek legend, she is credited with saving Zeus from Kronos, who swallowed his sons because he feared that he would be overcome by one of them; she becomes too the mother of Ares, Hephaestus, Eileithyia and Hebe. The last two goddesses were rather extensions of Hera's own powers, Eileithyia in connection with childbirth and Hebe, the cupbearer of the gods, with domesticity. While Eileithyia was often a title given by the Greeks to Hera herself, the goddess of birth and nursing does occur separately on a tablet from Knossos, near which she inherited a cave previously sacred to a pair of Minoan goddesses.

Although we cannot say which deities were thought to patronize commercial activities as opposed to the processes of manufacture, Linear B tablets leave us in little doubt over the dominant role played by the wanax in trade. There is neither reference to merchants nor to their business. Palace archives of West Asia prove that traders were looked upon as a valuable source of revenue, whereas the Pylos archives merely record the economic arrangements initiated by the palace authorities themselves. Even the apparent lack of some form of currency would not have been enough to prevent the widespread barter of goods, unless there was political pressure against independent trade on any scale. The picture we get from the Linear B inscriptions is of a centralized government, dependent on a network of roads connecting with distant areas whose agricultural produce was essential to its survival. In good years there would have been a surplus of corn and oil in Messenia for export; the commodities were exchanged abroad for raw materials in short supply as well as luxury items. Then state trading probably took place, the wanax dispatching a couple of ships laden with articles under the care of his officials and 'followers'. The boat wrecked off Cape Gelidonya in southern Turkey during the thirteenth century BC could have been engaged in such a transaction. The home port of the sailing vessel remains undetermined, but its cargo was precious bronze, copper and tin ingots; on board too were the toolkit of a metalworker and a set of trading weights. We should remember that metals formed the largest Aegean import right down to the classical period of Greece.

If we discount the existence of a merchant class in Mycenaean society, then there is a need to reconsider the ownership of several of the substantial houses outside the Cyclopean walls at Mycenae. Four of these buildings lie together next to the modern road leading to the citadel: they are named the West House, the House of Sphinxes, the House of the Oil Merchant, and the House of Shields. Best preserved, because of the massive retaining wall built to hold up its artificial terrace, is the House of the Oil Merchant. It comprised a two-level building, divided by a long internal corridor giving access to storerooms, in one of which pithoi were used to store large quantities of olive oil. Excavations between 1958 and 1961 of the immediately adjacent West House have brought to light both a low, mud-brick fireplace suitable for heating massive cauldrons, and nineteen Linear B tablets listing the herbal ingredients of perfumed oil. The inevitable conclusion is that the buildings here were engaged in the production of perfume as an adjunct of the palace workshops. Their location beyond the protection of the walls indicates the confidence once general at the site.

From po-ro-wi-to-jo, the month of sailing – our April – the Mycenaeans put out on the Aegean waters, the stormy winter weather having safely passed. They rowed and sailed the seas as widely as the Minoans had done, but unlike their Cretan predecessors they also founded numerous colonies. There cannot be much doubt from pottery finds that the Cycladic islands became virtually part of Mycenaean Greece during the thirteenth century BC. Crete, we have noted, had already fallen under the sway of a Mycenaean dynasty based on Knossos. Recent excavations at modern Khania, in the north-west of the island, confirm a long period of Mycenaean settlement there, apparently uninterrupted by the sack of Knossos some time before 1370 BC. On Rhodes too, the identification of some eighty chamber tombs indicates a permanently established Mycenaean population. It seems, indeed, that Rhodes was second only to Mycenae in power in the Aegean. Apart from its strategic position on the trade route to Cyprus and northern Syria, the island enjoyed easy access to south-western Asia Minor, whence it may have taken slaves for resale to the Mycenaean principalities of mainland Greece. The great island of Cyprus was certainly settled by Mycenaeans in the early twelfth century BC, if not before. The scale of commercial activity in the eastern Mediterranean from 1300 BC onwards must have involved the more or less permanent presence of Mycenaeans on the Cypriot coast.

Relations between Cyprus and the Aegean during the Bronze Age are far from transparent. In particular, there is the unresolved question of the Cypro-Minoan script, as Evans labelled the linear writing first found on a fragment of a baked clay tablet at Enkomi and dated to 1500 BC. Very few documents survive in the earliest form of this script, thus obscuring a possible Cretan parentage, and when after 1400 BC it was in general use, the cushion-like tablets favoured lean more towards West Asian scribal traditions. If the Minoan origin of Cypro-Minoan is accepted, then two methods of transfer for Linear A might be considered. One is its arrival in Cyprus through the direct trading activities of Cycladic or Minoan vessels. The alternative suggestion is that the Cypriots borrowed the script from Aegean traders residing in northern Syria, especially Ugarit. The late settlement of Cyprus by the Mycenaeans effectively rules out Greek as the tongue recorded, though Cypro–Minoan remained in use in the twelfth century BC when the ruling classes at Enkomi and elsewhere along the southern seaboard were certainly Mycenaeans. The only explanation for this oddity must be the employment of local scribes.

Cyprus was claimed by the Hittites to be part of their empire from about 1400 to 1200 BC. According to their records, Shuppilulima II successfully fought a sea battle in 1190 BC against Alashiya, or Cyprus, which he followed up with a land campaign and the exacting of tribute in the form of silver, copper, women and children. Periodic raids on wavering vassals comprised the standard policy of the Hittite kings, who were primarily interested in maintaining a regular flow of tribute as well as secure frontiers. How close their control of tributary peoples was, it is now hard to reckon, except that known contacts between Cypriot kings and Egyptian pharaohs during the Hittite overlordship lead to the conclusion that the concern of the conquerors was mainly economic. Copper ingots recovered from Hattusha, the Hittite capital, support this view.

The influx of Mycenaean pottery, therefore, probably means no more initially than the replacement of Minoan by Mycenaean traders in Cyprus after 1400 BC. Some of these wares are of tremendous importance for our understanding of religion. A large two–handled vase from an early fourteenth century BC tomb at Enkomi provides us with one of the first representations of a Greek mythological scene. It illustrates the authority of Zeus who, dressed in long robes, holds the scales of destiny. Later grave goods from the same site reveal a mixture of styles, as local craftsmen blended motifs from both West Asia and the Aegean. The peaceful conditions which encouraged these artistic developments came to an end prior to the intervention of Shuppilulima II. The balance of power achieved in the eastern Mediterranean between the Egyptian and the Hittite empires following the battle of Kadesh in 1285 BC was rudely shattered by the movements of restless groups, whom the Egyptians called the Peoples of the Sea. At Kadesh on the River Orontes, in north-eastern Syria, the Hittites under king Muwatalli had forced the Egyptians under Ramesses II to a draw, no matter what pharaonic propaganda was to claim later, and gained the ascendancy in that region. But this stability was breaking down even before Ugarit was overwhelmed in the first quarter of the twelfth century BC. A letter from the king of Ugarit to the king, or a king, of Alashiya sounds a note of anxiety and despair. It announces that seven enemy ships had attacked the Syrian coast, burning and looting cities, at a time when the army of Ugarit was on service with Hittite troops and the navy was off the land of Lukka, probably Lycia. Although the king admits that a faulty disposition of his forces had allowed a small enemy squadron to discomfort him, he closes the letter with an urgent plea for any information Alashiya may possess about enemy movements at sea.

The Sea Peoples, according to Egyptian records, came 'from the midst of the sea' and were 'all at once on the move, scattered in war'. Their two attacks on Egypt ended in crushing defeats. About 1218 BC pharaoh Merenptah destroyed in a six-hour battle a Libyan army supported by the Shardana, Lukka, Teresh, Shekelesh and Ekwesh, peoples from Asia Minor and possibly the Aegean. On rather weak grounds the Ekwesh have been called Mycenaeans, but rejection of this equation should not exclude the possibility that either adventurers or refugees, escaping from the disorders on the Greek mainland, crossed to Anatolia where they joined forces with other groups before moving on to Cyprus, Syria, Palestine and Egypt.

The second attack of the northerners, without the Libyans, was defeated in 1182 BC by Ramesses III in a land battle on the edge of the Sinai desert and a naval engagement on a branch of the Delta. The colossal stone reliefs at Medinet Habu show Ramesses smiting 'the chiefs of all the countries' before the god Amon. Many of the defeated Sea Peoples sported a stiff headdress of feathers, reminiscent of the plumped hieroglyph stamped on the Phaestos Disc, carried round shields, and wore short kilts like Mycenaean warriors. After this second defeat some of the attackers stayed as prisoners in Egypt, while others settled more peacefully in Palestine - the Tjeker on the coast around modern Haifa, part of the Danuna in the Jordan valley, where they may have become the Israelite tribe of Dan, and the Peleset in the cities of Ashkalon, Ashdod and Gaza. The Peleset, the biblical Philistines, cannot be regarded as Mycenaeans on the strength of the Aegean-style pottery they made. The only direct evidence for Mycenaean settlers among the Sea

Peoples comes from a cemetery near Ashdod and comprises five rock-cut chambers with dromoi.

The Medinet Habu inscription ascribes all the widespread destruction in the eastern Mediterranean in the later thirteenth and early twelfth centuries BC to the depredations of the Sea Peoples. 'No one stood against them, from Hattusha, Kode, Karchemish, Arzawa and Alashiya', except the Egyptians. That they perceived their attackers in 1182 BC as a great migration of peoples from north to south is evident in the relief of the land battle: fighting takes place around oxcarts carrying women and children. Elsewhere the activities of the Peoples of the Sea are less easy to identify, notwithstanding the list of victims given in the inscription. Egyptian bombast should not be permitted to inflate the role played by roving bands of migrants, set in motion by political breakdown in Asia Minor and the Aegean. It seems incredible that Ramesses can claim credit for routing singlehanded an enemy capable of subduing the Hittite empire and its vassal states. On the contrary, the actual sequence of events could well have been the reverse, the collapse of Hittite power through a combination of internal difficulties and external weakness providing the opportunity for a sharp revival of piracy and pillage. The Lukka, for instance, had already been a source of trouble for more than a century. They would have welcomed the crippling pestilence which struck the Hittites at this period, just as tributary states may have seized the chance to revolt. If this were the situation, the 1190 BC campaign of Shuppilulima II in Cyprus may represent a final desperate attempt to restore Hittite authority. Hattusha was destroyed in a great fire shortly afterwards and with its destruction the Hittite empire came to an end.

On Cyprus the devastation at the coastal cities of Kition and Enkomi was followed, after a partial abandonment, by reconstruction. The old mud-brick city wall of Kition, built on its foundation a century earlier around 1300 BC, was replaced by a Cyclopean wall of dressed stone. Both cities flourished down to 1050 BC when an earthquake levelled their buildings and overturned Kition's defences. Although Kition was rebuilt, the inhabitants of Enkomi quit the site and founded Salamis, a new city around a natural harbour. Some time in the twelfth century BC, Mycenaeans are thought to have assumed control of these two cities, taking advantage of the weakened condition of the Cypriot population. Those who left mainland Greece or the Aegean would have been members of the upper classes, the lords and their immediate followers. Outright domination was not entailed, as local practices in architecture, religion and record keeping continued undisturbed, but intermarriage did not submerge the Mycenaean heritage either. Several tombs at Salamis, dating from the eighth to the seventh centuries BC, had the dead man's chariot, complete with its slaughtered horses, buried in the dromos, a Mycenaean custom known from a tomb at Marathon in Attica. A Cypriot contribution to mainland Greece, we shall see in the next chapter, may have been expertise in iron working, brought from the island at the beginning of the Dark Age.

In Asia Minor there were Mycenaean settlements at Iasus and Miletus, both of which had strong fortifications. The Minoan foundation of Miletus had come within the Mycenaean sphere of influence after the invasion of Crete about 1450 BC, and its considerable size indicates that in trade with Anatolian peoples only Rhodes was a serious rival. However, the key emporium of West Asia was Ugarit, which probably housed a Mycenaean enclave. Despite the fact that in Syria Mycenaean pottery is usually associated with Cypriot ware, it would be wrong to conclude that all commercial activity was in Cypriot hands. The presence of Semitic loanwords in Linear B tends to support direct links between the Ugarits and the Mycenaeans. Four words borrowed from Ugaritic are 'ki-to' – tunic, 'ku-mi-no' – cummin, 'ku-ru-so' – gold, and 'sa-sa-ma' – sesame.

Greek tradition says the heroes who settled in Cyprus – such as Teukros the founder of Salamis – arrived there 'after the end of the Trojan war'. Two dates are currently advanced for the destruction of Homeric Troy: 1270 BC and 1220 BC. While archeological testimony suggests the second date, which is close to that of the sack of Mycenae, Pylos and Tiryns, we must be careful not to link events in the Troad or mainland Greece with the Sea Peoples. Nor should the armada under the command of Agamemnon be automatically accepted as the cause of Troy's downfall. There is little outside Homer to prove that a protracted siege of Troy, or another north-west Anatolian city, was successfully mounted by a confederation of Mycenaean principalities. It is questionable whether the Mycenaeans had the capability of a large overseas expedition during the troubled times of the late thirteenth century BC. A destruction of Troy (actually Troy VIIa) did take place, but we are uncertain of Mycenaean participation. Troy had enjoyed several centuries of prosperity and was in consequence a prime target in the last confused years of Hittite decline. The Trojans themselves may have been drawn into the fighting connected with the great rebellion led by the powerful kingdom of Arzawa against the Hittite king Tudhaliyas IV shortly after 1250 BC.

Schliemann's excavation of the site of Troy between 1870 and 1890 uncovered seven 'cities' piled one on top of the other to a depth of nearly sixteen metres. Subsequent exploration has identified nine settlement levels, the earliest dating from before 2500 BC and the latest from the Roman period. Homer's Troy, Schliemann believed, was Troy II, a squarish, strongly fortified citadel of modest dimensions, measuring scarcely eighty metres across. As its carefully constructed fortifications would have given refuge to few people, a town with an outer wall was also assumed to have once existed, but nothing of it has ever been found. Countering criticism in his *Trojan Antiquities*, Schliemann wrote: 'If people are disappointed in their expectations and consider that Troy was too small for the great deeds of the *Iliad*, and that Homer exaggerated everything with a poet's freedom, they must, on the other hand, find great satisfaction in the certainty now established that the Homeric poems are based on facts.' Troy VIIa, now favoured as the Homeric foundation, extended over more than twice the area of Troy II, and had five gateways let into its strong defences, plus a tower built on the east side. Though this huge structure, still nine metres high on excavation, is temptingly labelled the 'great tower of Ilios' mentioned in book six of the *Iliad*, we need to take such identifications with a pinch of salt. After all, the identification of Troy itself rests on negative grounds. No inscription has been discovered at the site which might reveal its ancient name; nonetheless, if Troy was a real place then this is the only likely site in north-western Asia Minor. At the very least, we have to admit that Greek epic tradition preserved memories concerning the ruin of an important eastern city at the close of the Bronze Age.

Whatever the truth about Troy's fall, Homer seems to have correctly recalled the melancholy of mainland Greece in the later part of the thirteenth century BC. The *Odyssey* tells of ill luck besetting many of the heroes who survived the Trojan war: Agamemnon slain on his return home, Odysseus compelled to wander the seas, and other leaders either shipwrecked or forced to seek their fortune abroad. The crews of the seven ships that attacked Ugarit could have easily included Mycenaean exiles. Their surprise assault reflects the dislocation of the times, a process which sudden acts of violence did little to mend. The causes of breakdown on the Greek mainland are by no means agreed, but there is no longer any consensus placing the blame on an invasion from the Balkans. The growth of defences during the thirteenth century BC was generated by internal warfare rather than an external threat.

At Mycenae three destructions punctuate the history of the site after 1300 BC. The first was confined to the area outside the citadel, the second affected both the citadel and its surrounding town, and the last ravaged only the citadel itself. Following the second destruction by a devastating fire, the inhabitants thoroughly renovated the site. The final stage of palace development was reached and, no less significant, the west wall of the citadel was demolished so that a considerable area could be added to the south and west. From the south side of the newly constructed Lion Gate a Cyclopean wall was erected which, after enclosing Grave Circle A, ran south-east towards a ravine before swinging northwards to rejoin the older defences south of the palace hill. The Lion Gate today remains an imposing entrance, its four huge monoliths of sawn and hammer-dressed conglomerate still acting as serviceable door jambs, threshold and lintel. The double wooden doors have gone, but pivot holes are visible at either end of the threshold and the lintel. On vertical beams positioned in these holes the doors once pivoted, being made secure when closed by a cross-beam which fitted in sockets cut into the jambs. The depressions on the threshold are a drain as well as the wear and tear of chariot and wagon wheels. In front of the relieving triangle above the lintel stone is the impressive relief from which the gateway derives its title. We are fortunate that in 1801 Lord Elgin was advised it was not 'portable': the block with 'two colossal lions in bas-relief over the "Gate Way" was too gigantic, and too distant from the sea to give any hopes of being able to obtain so renowned a monument of the Fabulous ages.' The sculpture consists of two lions, standing on each side of a column, their forefeet planted on the column plinth and their heads probably turned towards anyone approaching the gate. The heads were apparently made of different material and are now missing. It has been proposed that bronze casts were used, like the 'gold and silver dogs, which Hephaestus had made with cunning skill, to keep guard at the palace of king Alcinous'. Book seven of the *Odyssey* specifically states that the splendour of this prince's dwelling so 'filled with misgivings' the heart of wandering Odysseus that 'he hesitated before setting foot on the bronze threshold'.

The Lion Gate was defended by a long stretch of wall on the east side and on the west by a rectangular bastion fifteen by seven metres in width. Between them lay a narrow passageway, which served to reduce the numbers of an attacking force and to concentrate the fire of the defenders. Attackers would have been unable to use their shields to deflect missiles from both left and right at the same time, a severe military disadvantage which caused the adoption of an identical arrangement in the north-south passage at Tiryns. The postern gate, another late addition to the defences of Mycenae, was set back in the northern Cyclopean wall and furnished with a small bastion too. Ordinary sally-posts pierced the final extension of the defences in the north-eastern corner of the citadel; they consist of tiny corbelled corridors, akin to the galleries of Tiryns. The southern one gave access to an observation platform overlooking the ravine, along which enemy soldiers might have tried to creep, while another in the north facilitated sorties against an enemy assaulting the postern gate or the subterranean cistern.

The subterranean cistern, the most amazing example of engineering at Mycenae, explains the last realignment of the walls. As the problem of the water supply was serious even without a siege, witness the numerous cisterns for catching rain on the rocky citadel hill, it is hardly surprising that the rulers of Mycenae determined to eliminate this fundamental shortcoming. They drove stairs through the living rock down to a cistern,

111

which collected the waters of a spring below and outside the walls. The location of this reservoir was probably a closely kept secret, not least because an enemy could have broken through the corbelled roof of the underground stairway just beyond the defences, before it began a steep descent. The cistern, some five metres deep, received water through a terracotta pipe, but the thick watertight plaster also covering the bottom section of the stairs meant that in winter a higher water level could be accommodated. So daunting does the Cyclopean stair appear that modern visitors usually take a deep breath on descending into its gloom.

Destruction was visited upon Tiryns at least three times during the thirteenth century BC, though as at Mycenae reoccupation of some sort occurred after 1200 BC. At its greatest extent, the citadel entirely covered the small hill on which it stood, fortifications tracing the irregular outline of the contours. 'The walls', Pausanias noted in awe, 'are made of un-wrought stones, each stone so large that a pair of mules could not move the smallest of them.' They range in thickness from four and a half to seventeen metres, their total height probably reaching ten metres when the mud-brick battlements originally built on top are taken into account. The northern extension of the walls to form the so-called Lower Citadel may have been occasioned by two considerations: the need to offer sanc-tuary to the surrounding population from increasing internecine strife and the absence of springs on the hill itself. For excavation has revealed at the north-west corner of the Lower Citadel two subterranean passages stretching more than twenty metres outside the walls, presumably to a reliable source of water. These stonelined tunnels measure one and a half by three and a half metres in height, and have steps cut into the solid rock where the incline is quite steep. A guardroom seems to have covered the two entrances, or at all events disguised their purpose to strangers. The other remarkable piece of late Mycenaean engineering at the site also involves concealed passageways, not underground, but within the Cyclo-pean walls themselves. They are the galleries on the southern and south-eastern sides of the citadel. Averaging just over one and a half metres in width, their side walls rose vertically for nearly two metres before leaning inwards as a V-shaped corbel vault.

Defensive measures at Tiryns centred on the security of the main entrance on the eastern side of the citadel. Access was gained initially by climbing a ramp, which exposed an enemy force to attack on its unpro-tected right flank from defenders on top of the wall. Even if entrance was gained through the unbarred opening at the head of the ramp, enemy soldiers would have been stranded in a narrow section of the north-south passage, with two doors still barred between themselves and the outer courtyards of the palace. The north-west passage was in effect a further refinement of the bastion developed next to the Lion Gate at Mycenae.

To protect the postern, at the base of a long flight of stairs to the west of the palace, the Tirynthians constructed a massive semicircular bastion, which archers could man in order to give covering fire to parties leaving or entering the citadel by this route. On the acropolis at Athens the remains of a similar projection, a great square tower, were found in 1936 beneath the bastion supporting the temple of Athene Nike, 'wingless victory'. The protection this goddess of citadels afforded the acropolis was such that no destruction took place during the Mycenaean period, a singular achievement for the rather minor principality based there. The resulting historical continuity must account for the strength of her cult in Athens, since she assumed ownership of the acropolis when it ceased to be the dwellingplace of rulers.

The enormous bronze statue of Athena Promachos, 'the champion', which stood behind the classical Propylaea and whose speartip and helmet crest Pausanias tells us could be seen by ships at sea, was a war trophy presented to the Athenians by the allies after the victory over the Persians at Marathon. Erected in 456 BC the statue was the work of the famous sculptor Phidias: it appears to have survived in Constantinople until 1203, when it was broken up by drunken rioters, whom a chronicler caustically remarked were unable to bear even a symbol of courage and wisdom.

Of course the acropolis of Athens was easy to defend, especially when its summit was surrounded by Cyclopean walls. The tower already mentioned guarded the western entrance, while a bastion like the one belonging to the postern gate at Mycenae was built for the entrance through the northern wall. Though the Bronze Age relics of the acropolis are meagre in comparison with those of Mycenae and Tiryns, they exhibit typically Mycenaean characteristics. The preoccupation with the water supply is obvious in the eight flights of stairs, made of wood and stone, which were constructed in a fissure to the west of the northern entrance. This chasm, some thirty-five metres deep, collected water from nearby springs and was entirely free from enemy interference. Perhaps the advantage it gave to the defenders helped to ensure that they became victims of neither assault nor treachery.

Except for Pylos, our knowledge of the remaining Mycenaean palatial settlements is fragmentary and incomplete. Iolkos and Thebes are buried under modern towns; Orchomenus and Gla are still only partially explored: but all of them suffered destruction, Iolkos being the last to fall in the early or middle twelfth century BC.

Virtually no trace of fortifications has come to light at Pylos, which was destroyed and abandoned around 1200 BC. Its ruling house, the Neleids, chose to rely on an efficient army and navy rather than defensive works, the Linear B tablets giving us full details of the elaborate early warning system of 'watchers' deployed along the frontiers. Lookouts, it is estimated, were posted every two hundred metres on the coast, clearly regarded as the kingdom's most vulnerable border. The heaviest military concentrations are also recorded close to the Navarino bay, where an enemy landing would have directly threatened Pylos. Whether a seaborne attack brought about Pylos' downfall we cannot tell, but there is no reason to believe that such an occurrence, if it happened, was part of the ravages of the Sea Peoples, because even the combative Lukka lacked a fleet capable of facing that of Pylos. The archeological evidence points more to warfare between Mycenaean states, combined with internal collapse. Tradition says that the defeated Neleids took refuge in Attica.

Hostile relations between Mycenaean rulers must account for the concentration on military architecture in the Argolid during the thirteenth century BC. To argue that Tiryns simply guarded the coast on behalf of Mycenae is to overlook the immense efforts required to raise these citadels to a level of mutual impregnability. The adoption of the bastion at both sites does not constitute cooperation as much as competition in a late Bronze Age arms race. War had become more bitter, more organized: arms and armour no longer reflected the glories of noble combat – the days of decorated blades and plate armour had gone. Swords were shorter and stouter, as were spears, and a rounded shield with hand grips replaced the old neck-slung body shield. On the so-called Warrior Vase, found by Schliemann at Mycenae and dated to about 1200 BC, a line of identically equipped soldiers is depicted attending a funeral. They carry spears and

Conjectural defences of the Mycenaean acropolis at Athens. 1. Great Tower and Postern Gate. 2. Main Entrance.

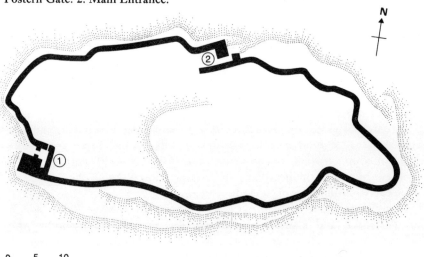

114

rounded shields, are dressed in stiff leather, certainly non-metallic jerkins, kilts and greaves, and wear plumed helmets. Although Schliemann rightly drew attention to the close parallel in equipment of the Homeric heroes, he ignored the plain and unheroic manner in which the painter worked. The warriors are deliberately portrayed as ordinary troops; they move in formation as part of a well-drilled force, their light armour allowing a greater mobility than ever before. Their co-ordinated charges would have superseded the single combats of the chariot-riding aristocracy admired by Homer. Tactics, not noble display, had become the norm.

Yet the *Iliad* does recall in the personal rivalries of the Greek leaders something of the political conditions of Mycenaean times. Nothing the epic narrates would make Agamemnon ruler of a centralized empire, nor even overlord of the Argolid, for it is his personal prowess as well as his forces that raises him to the rank of greatest king. Book two is quite explicit on the subject. In the hundred ships Agamemnon led were troops from Mycenae, Corinth, Cleonae, Sicyon, Hyperesie, Gonoessa, Pellene, Aegion and Helice. When he drew up his contingent on the plain of Troy, 'he was a proud man ... armed in gleaming bronze, the greatest captain of all, in virtue of his rank and as commander of the largest number of men'. Likewise, the other powerful princes are listed with their forces: Menelaus the husband of Helen, 'cunning' Odysseus from Ithaca, Nestor 'with ninety vessels', and Diomedes fellow ruler of the Argolid. In the eighty ships of Diomedes, son of furious Dydeus, the legendary victor of the Theban Games, sailed men from Argos, Tiryns, Hermione, Asine, Troezen, Eionae, Epidauros, Aegina and Mases. The placing of 'Tiryns of the Great Walls' in the realm of Diomedes means that Agamemnon exercised no political authority over him and that as far as Homer was concerned, Mycenae and Tiryns were situated in completely separated and independent kingdoms.

War alone cannot be blamed for the fall of the Mycenaeans, though the increasing emphasis on military activity would have exacerbated any decline. The archeological record indicates that the late thirteenth and early twelfth centuries BC were a period of acute political instability, repeated destructions of major sites, and movements of peoples. There is no evidence of a universal invasion, despite the possibility of a Cyclopean wall being built across the Isthmus, and in some areas, such as Attica, the Cyclades and the Dodecanese, we are unable to discover signs of disruption altogether. The conclusion forced upon us, until archeology provides alternative information, is of a breakdown of the civilization itself under a combination of pressures. The traditional view that the arrival of the Dorians coincides with the end of the Mycenaeans we shall discuss in the next chapter, where population changes will be placed in the context of the general pattern of migration during the Dark Age.

Suffice it to say here that the story of the return of the Heraclids, the sons of Heracles, was in all probability a myth justifying the domination of the Peloponnese by the later Dorian states, and notably Sparta.

What then were the causes of Mycenaean collapse? Perhaps the fate of Knossos after 1450 BC offers a clue. There a usurping Mycenaean dynasty brought disaster either through insurrection of the peasantry or armed intervention by rival princes, or both. The overconcentration of power at Knossos, after the destruction of the other Minoan palaces, was patently unworkable, having stretched to breaking point the means of production and communication. The Linear B tablets from Knossos belong to a highly centralized military state, which relied on an efficient bureaucracy to exploit the wealth of the countryside. Without agricultural surpluses the palace could not exist, no matter how aggressive its soldiery might be, and therefore any drop in productivity was very serious. Too much shepherding in Crete, too much corn growing in Messenia; an overspecialized economy, too dependent on a central administration: these were the likely factors weakening the Mycenaeans at the close of the turbulent thirteenth century BC.

The destruction of Mycenaean civilization meant the firing of the palaces, save at Athens; with them went the ruling classes as well as the scribes and craftsmen. Literacy was lost in the Aegean for nearly half a millennium, inevitably as the sole function of writing on the evidence of the presently available Linear B texts was palace record-keeping. When the Greeks recovered literacy not later than 750 BC, at the close of the Dark Age, the writing system was totally different. Not only was it based on an alphabetical form from which our own is still derived, but more its users were individuals rather than members of a bureaucracy. Initially, they scratched details of ownership or personal comments on pottery, often in verse: this surge of graffiti, so dear to the archeologist, suggests that in Mycenaean times very few people could read and fewer still could write. The palace, inhabited by a warrior-king and his privileged followers, had vanished from the Aegean scene, thus freeing the Greeks from the absolute monarchal rule common in the rest of the ancient world.

That the palace departed so completely after the twelfth century BC should not surprise us when the differences in population density between the Aegean and West Asia are appreciated. Apart from Crete, and further east Cyprus, Mycenaean civilization was scarcely urban, its settlements being little more than villages clustered around palace-strongholds. And because there were no cities of any size, the immediate consequence of breakdown was a reversion to subsistence agriculture and the formation of small inward-looking communities. Only in Attica did the Mycenaean inheritance transform itself into a new cultural phase, which immigrants were soon to carry to the south-western coast of Asia Minor.

PART THREE

THE DARK AGE

Chapter Six

THE COMING OF IRON

The Dark Age was as impenetrable to the ancient Greeks as it remained to us before the advent of modern archeological technique. The 400 years succeeding the final disintegration of the Mycenaean world around 1100 BC were not viewed as a gulf between two eras of civilization for the precise reason that Greek historians lacked any inkling of this spectacular collapse. Thucydides mentions disturbances immediately after the Trojan war, stating that within sixty years the Boeotians came down from Thessaly to settle in Boeotia, and within eighty years the Dorians together with the Heraclids gained control of the Peloponnese; but, other than these two events at the outset of the Dark Age, he gives no impression of the swift cultural decline which occurred in most areas of mainland Greece. Though he admits a lengthy period elapsed before peaceful conditions prevailed, his narrative tends to assume a gradual process of improvement down to classical times, accompanied by the spread of colonies to Asia Minor, North Africa, Italy and Sicily. The *Iliad* and the *Odyssey*, composed in Ionia during the eighth century BC and three centuries before Thucydides wrote, confine themselves to the heroic deeds of Mycenaean princes: they ignore actions unconnected with the Trojan war and its aftermath. Hesiod, on the other hand, does have a view of the Dark Age as a falling off from earliest times but his awareness of deterioration is based on nostalgia, a sense of loss he personally felt towards the close of the eighth century BC. While he may have echoed traditions concerning the fall of Mycenaean citadels in the powerful condemnation he made of 'harsh-voiced and sullen-faced' men who took delight in destroying towns, the tenor of the complaint was very applicable to the poet's lifetime. The Lelantine war of about 700 BC between Chalcis and Eretria, the main cities on the island of Euboea, comprised the first recorded large-scale conflict of the post-Mycenaean period. 'On this occasion,' Thucydides ruefully comments, 'the rest of the Greeks joined in with one side or the other.'

Modern archeology reveals the extent of the impoverishment in material culture during the Dark Age. It provides a picture of general decay in the eleventh and tenth centuries BC – with the exception of Attica, which seems to have afforded a refuge for people fleeing from other Mycenaean kingdoms on the Greek mainland – and then picks out the physical details relating to the slow re-emergence of the Aegean from 900 BC as a centre of ancient civilization. The recovery of this outline, however incomplete it still is for certain areas, must be regarded as an invaluable contribution to the history of Europe's origins, not least because without it we would have no chart for a gulf of time in which the distinctive social, political and economic developments of the Archaic Age were inaugurated. The future lay not in states run by palace bureaucracies but in a new kind of society which was to award responsibilities and privileges to a large section of its members, who were expected to live according to written laws.

Because of the virtual isolation of the Aegean until just before 900 BC we are unable to take advantage of archives maintained by powers in West Asia and Egypt. The absence of Greek affairs in these records has compelled scholars to reassess tales about the movements of peoples after the Trojan war in the light of archeological evidence. Of the several explanations which have been proposed for the turmoil at the end of Mycenaean civilization, two place the blame on population movement. Our problem is that the widespread evidence for warlike activities, such as destroyed citadels and abandoned settlements, gives no indication as to the identity or geographical origin of the aggressors. The ruins do not tell us whether those who wrought the havoc came from within or outside Greece. The details of the chief destructions are as follows: Pylos was burned and abandoned just after 1200 BC; at Mycenae there were three fires, one before 1200 BC, a second near the time of Pylos' destruction, and a third between 1150 and 1120 BC; Tiryns also suffered three disasters but it is unknown exactly when the palace was destroyed by fire, though after 1150 BC the site ceased to be of any importance; Thebes was burned before 1200 BC, then reoccupied; Orchomenus and Gla were destroyed at uncertain dates; and Iolkos was overwhelmed after 1120 BC. No detectable destruction, however, occurred at Athens. Here we have an impressive catalogue of violence, yet no clear pattern for a general invasion. Equally startling is the testimony for the reduction in settlement sites, which suggests that the population by the end of the twelfth century BC had dwindled to about ten per cent of what it had been one hundred years earlier. Even in Attica, despite an influx of refugees, the number of settlements was halved.

How do we account for the Dark Age? What brought down the Mycenaean palaces at the height of their prosperity? In the last chapter we hinted at a breakdown of the civilization itself and we shall return to this notion once the various theories have been considered. Four command attention. The first envisages an armed invasion from outside the Mycenaean world, followed by the invader's settlement of the conquered lands. For this there is no archeological proof, though N.G.L. Hammond has tried to show that grave goods in burials dating from after the last destruction at Mycenae have connections with finds in southern Albania. He cites finger rings with spiralling ends, ornaments known from both cist-graves and tumuli there. Yet these few artifacts, and others from

119

burials in Elis, on the north-western coast of the Peloponnese, hardly alter the residual Mycenaean characteristics of the surviving culture.

The weight of the evidence from buildings and graves indicates that the few inhabitants of mainland Greece at the beginning of the Dark Age were descendants of those who had lived there for centuries. Three major changes affecting daily life did take place – the replacement of bronze by iron as the useful metal, the adoption of cremation for the disposal of the dead, and the burial of corpses singly in cist-graves – but they happened with neither suddenness nor uniformity. The use of the cist-grave cannot be attributed to invaders from the north, because this form of tomb, as we saw in Chapter One, had a long history also in the Cyclades, and even on mainland Greece it never quite went out of favour during the Mycenaean period. Where cist-graves first appear in great numbers, on the island of Salamis and in the Keramikos cemetery to the north-west of the acropolis in Athens, there are no signs of armed intrusion at all. The only conclusion to be drawn is the revival of an old burial custom at a time when people were disinclined to invest in the labour needed to construct a family chamber tomb. Evidently the same feeling of transitoriness and insecurity brought about the importation of the new rite of cremation; its ready acceptance by Athens and Lefkandi, another town with connections oversea on Euboea, points to Asia Minor as the source of the idea.

In a similar manner the metallurgical field was transformed through the coming of iron. Knowledge of its working was conveyed to Attica by Cypriots, or returning Mycenaeans, who had learned about the more advanced processes involved as a result of Hittite weakness. Prior to the fall of the Hittite empire some time in the early twelfth century BC and the flight of its survivors to newly founded states in northern Syria, expertise in ironworking was a secret belonging to the smiths of Kizzuwatna, a province which encompassed the ore-bearing Tarsus mountains. A letter sent in the thirteenth century BC from the Hittite king Hattusilis III to a contemporary ruler, probably the Assyrian monarch, shows how close was state supervision of the industry, since Hattusilis could write of production difficulties and low stocks of smelted iron delaying the delivery of the items requested. In Greece, deposits of iron allowed the continuation of metallurgy in the early Dark Age, when supplies of copper but especially tin ceased to flow from Cyprus. It is thought that the establishment of a bronze foundry at Lefkandi in the late tenth century BC signals resumption of trade with that island.

For those who connect the destructions with the Dorians, the theory of an armed conquest is most attractive. Both Herodotus and Thucydides refer to Doris, a narrow mountainous tract situated between Phocis and Locris in central Greece, quite beyond the Mycenaean cultural sphere, as the homeland of the Dorian people. At this point it would seem advisable to look at Greek traditions about population movements on the mainland. Accounts are contained in widely scattered sources, but it was Thucydides who perceived the cause of such upheavals, when he wrote:

> Where the soil was most fertile there were the most frequent changes of population, for example in Thessaly, in Boeotia, in most of the Peloponnese except Arcadia ... For in these rich areas it was easier for men to secure greater strength than their neighbours: this led to disunity, which often toppled these states, and to the unwanted attention of foreign invaders.

The initial movement around 1160 BC, if 1220 BC is reckoned to be the date of Troy's fall, is said to have been the descent of the Thessalians from the hills of Epirus onto the plain which they named. Thucydides notes that 'the modern Boeotians were driven out of Arne by the Thessalians and settled in what is now Boeotia, but was before the kingdom of Kadmos. Some Boeotians had already settled there and taken part in the Trojan War.'

The inability of the Mycenaeans to resist this second push could have been the sacking of Thebes by a coalition of southern Mycenaean principalities before 1200 BC, a conflict celebrated in Aeschylus' play *Seven against Thebes*. The clearing of Boeotia would have left the way open for an attack further south on the Peloponnese, which the Dorians are supposed to have spearheaded about 1120 BC. A southward thrust by a vigorous enemy could have threatened Mycenaean strongholds already undermined by internecine warfare, but the dates for the chief destructions do not readily suit this scenario. Even pushing back the end of the Trojan war to 1270 BC – for which there is no real justification – does not solve the range of dates the violence covers. A protracted assault by the Dorians, or any other northern people, would surely have left us with some archeological trace too.

The traditional reason given for the Dorian invasion of the Peloponnese was the return of the Heraclids, whose allies the Dorians were. These descendants of Heracles had originally been driven out by Eurystheus, who feared that the hero's sons, and in particular Hyllos, would remove him from the throne of Mycenae. According to Diodorus Siculus:

> The young Heraclids and their followers saw that they were no match for Eurystheus in combat, and determined to escape ... Travelling from city to city they beseeched sanctuary but none dared receive them except the Athenians, who, out of a sense of justice, allowed them to settle ... Having achieved manhood and become proud of their illustrious descent, the sons of Heracles posed a threat to Eurystheus, who took the field against them

with a large force. But the Heraclids had aid from the Athenians and made Iolaus, a nephew of Heracles, their leader, and under his command and that of Theseus and Hyllos, they routed Eurystheus in a pitched battle. The majority of Eurystheus' army fell and the king himself, his chariot wrecked when he tried to flee, was slain by Hyllos, Heracles' son. All of the sons of Eurystheus also died in the battle. After this success ... the Heraclids ... invaded the Peloponnese with Hyllos as war leader ... [Against them marched] Atreus, the new king of Mycenae. When the opposing armies met at the Isthmus, Hyllos issued a challenge: he offered to face in single combat any of the enemy who would fight him, on the understanding that if Hyllos overcame his opponent the Heraclids should receive the kingdom of Eurystheus, but if Hyllos were beaten, then the Heraclids would quit the Peloponnese for fifty years. Echemos, king of the Tegeans, accepted the challenge, slew Hyllos, and compelled the Heraclids to withdraw ... When fifty years had passed, they successfully returned.

A later source than Diodorus Siculus tells us that after their return the Heraclids set up three altars to Zeus, sacrificed on them, and cast lots for the territories of the Peloponnese: Cresphontes won Messenia, Temenus Argos, and the sons of Aristodemus Laconia, thus establishing the dual kingship of Sparta.

Perhaps this connection with the Spartan constitution is the telling indictment against the Dorians as destroyers of Mycenaean civilization. Of all the differences between the Dorians of the historical period and the other Greek tribes the most obvious was a selfconsciousness over their lineage. The Spartan kings regarded themselves as the direct descendants of Heracles. The commander of the Greek force which held the pass at Thermopylae against the Persians in 480 BC, the Spartan king Leonidas, is provided by Herodotus with a faultless pedigree. The historian says that 'Leonidas traced his descent directly back to Heracles, through his father Anaxandrides, his grandfather Leon, Anaxander, Eurycrates, Polydorus, Acamenes, Teleches, Archelaus, Agesilaus, Doryssus, Labotas, Echestratus, Agis, Eurysthenes, Aristodemus, Aristomachus, Cleodaeus, and so to Hyllos, who was Heracles' son.' Such a king-list is properly regarded as an example of state propaganda which sought to legitimize Sparta's hegemony in the Peloponnese, as well as its leadership of the Greek resistance to Xerxes, king of Persia. Since the Spartans had to admit that their forebears lacked any connection with the Trojan War, they obtained genealogical contact with the great heroes of the past via the semi-divine Heracles, a device accounting for the inconsistencies apparent in the ramifications of the king-list. A motive for this deception could have been guilt on the part of the Dorians that their ancestors sometime in the Dark Age had seized power in the Peloponnese by force.

It is interesting to note that Plato preserves an account of the Dorian invasion, albeit in late Mycenaean times, as a power struggle between two generations, even two sections of society. The returning exiles are those who were ousted by younger men: their leader was a certain Dorieus, after whom they were called.

Having agreed with V.R.d'A. Desborough that the probability of the Dorians having been responsible for the disasters at the end of the thirteenth century BC and the further decline of the twelfth century BC is exceedingly small, there still is the possibility of a mass incursion by outsiders who afterwards withdrew. This second theory at least has less dependence on archeological data. The sack of Troy VIIa, Homeric Ilios, is an indisputable fact, but the destruction level discloses nothing of its perpetrators. Yet there are convincing arguments against a population movement which simply passed through mainland Greece. A seaborne attack, an offshoot of the activities of the Sea Peoples, seems unlikely as the refuges the stricken Mycenaeans fled to lay in the path of any invader. In the west people moved into Achaea, on the north-western seaboard of the Peloponnese, and onto the island of Cephallenia, close by Ithaca; in the east new inhabitants appeared on the islands of Chios and Euboea as well as in Attica. In addition, the totally ruined site of Pylos possessed one of the most powerful navies afloat. The alternative of an overland raid is more feasible and might explain the Isthmus wall, if it actually was a defensive work.

Against this kind of invasion we may object that it is odd for invaders to decide not to remain in such a depopulated land. We might wonder too at the power of those who managed to capture the mighty citadels of Mycenae and Tiryns, whose massive fortifications, storage facilities, and secure water supply would have made a prolonged siege inevitable. Although there is nothing to disprove a great incursion, a series of increasingly effective attacks by hillsmen on the Mycenaeans seems more promising, especially when the latter were locked into bitter internal squabbles. 'It was many years before the army returned from Troy,' writes Thucydides, 'and this alone encouraged many changes. There were conflicts in almost all the cities, and those who were expelled founded cities of their own.'

This civil discord brings us to the third theory, namely that the Mycenaean rulers were deposed through an uprising of their subjects. Though enticing to the moden mind, revolutions of oppressed peasantry are not easy to square with the archeological information now available. Again we have to reckon with the defences of the citadels in the Argolid, though Mycenae could have been denied water once the attackers had located the reservoir beyond the walls, broken through the roof of its single subterranean approach, and filled the cistern with rocks. Whilst a popular rising on its own cannot take the credit for the widespread destruction, which affected major and minor settlements alike, rural unrest would have played some part in the Mycenaean collapse, but rather as a concomitant of the breakdown in civilization. The fourth theory, of some natural disaster, has the merit of creating the conditions in which violence would have occurred; it also explains the drastic reduction in agricultural prosperity in many areas of mainland Greece. What it fails to take into account is the survival of remnants of Mycenaean society, reduced as to quality it is true, in Attica and the Cyclades. There is, moreover, firm climatic data to support neither drought nor flood, the only known alteration being a slight drop in the annual mean temperature during a prolonged period of moister and cooler weather. We would look then in vain to nature for the outbreak of devastating famine and plague.

Possibly the shortcoming of each of the preceding hypotheses is a reliance on one event. Ancient civilization was dependent on numerous factors for its maintenance – such as agriculture, metallurgy, craft specialization, trade, communications, population, settlements, literacy, religious and social beliefs – and these needed to remain in harmony with the environment. Colin Renfrew has expertly delineated their interaction in the gradual emergence of civilization in the Aegean during the third millennium BC, and so it might well be argued that the Mycenaean collapse represents a dislocation of this finely balanced system. To suggest that the Mycenaeans disappeared because of a breakdown of civilization does not beg the question. All that is intended is a more comprehensive approach to an otherwise mysterious sequence of events. The signs of violence and insecurity are plain enough, their causes are not. Although we are obliged to offer another scenario for which no clear archeological proof exists, it is hoped that readers will be encouraged to pursue the matter themselves.

The thirteenth century BC witnessed Mycenaean power and impotency. Thucydides has no hesitation in blaming external and internal wars for the discontent, 'the state of ferment ... [which gave] no opportunity for peaceful development'. Mycenaean thrones suffered usurpations galore when ambitious but unfavoured nobles bid for supreme authority. As palaces changed hands the loyalties of the influential telestas would have come under increasing strain, so much so that these provincial landowners may have banded together against rapacious upstarts. The Pylos archives do not feature these conflicts, possibly because Messenia was away from the main centre of turmoil in the Argolid, but the enforced collection of surplus bronze we noted there might also be construed as a measure to concentrate weaponry in the palace storerooms, since an unarmed population would pose less threat to the royal forces. The palace at Pylos, though unfortified, had been founded after all by princely opportunists who had come from Thessaly. Further conflict was generated by feuds between the various royal houses, the early attack on Thebes setting a climate of mutual mistrust.

The fortifications at Tiryns, the apotheosis of Mycenaean architecture, must have taken many years to complete, from which we may deduce they were not put up against a sudden and unexpected foe. The growing militarism, a sort of late parallel to the experience of Mycenaean Crete, was expensive, time consuming and perilous. Enforced labour and military service as auxiliaries would have reduced peasant manpower on the land and decreased agricultural productivity, while raids and sacks disrupted trade and industry. Added to this, the presence of barbarian mercenaries and adventurers from Greek hill tribes may have aggravated an already volatile situation. From archives in West Asia and Egypt we are aware of the extensive use made by Bronze Age rulers of mercenary contingents, a practice fraught with danger in times of uncertainty, as many states found to their cost on the onslaught of the Sea Peoples. Our assumption of mercenaries in Greece rests primarily on finds of weapons of Balkan and central European origin, types soon copied by Mycenaean armourers; for in Linear B, no word has so far been interpreted to mean 'hired soldier'.

Pylos itself, as an internal Troy, may have been destroyed through an overland attack by Mycenaean and mercenary troops from other Peloponnese states. We cannot be sure, but about the economic crisis following the destructions there is no doubt. Depopulation, abandoned settlements, uncultivated fields, empty workshops; these are telltale signs of catastrophe. Could it have been that increased violence was the *coup de grâce* for a system at the limits of its resources? Were there in the overspecialized palace economies sufficient reserves to sustain for long such a high level of military activity? Did Mycenaean civilization just fall apart?

The second series of population movements remembered by the Greeks involved migration overseas, though usually preceded by changes of habitation on the mainland. The devastation of so many Mycenaean sites naturally precipitated movements of people. The survivors tended to disperse into more widely scattered settlements, except for Achaea, Attica and the area round Iolkos in Thessaly, where refugees congregated in large numbers. Mountainous Achaea seems to have been used by Mycenaeans from the Argolid; they founded a number of towns and reoccupied the damaged coastal fortress of Teichos Dymaion. This stronghold, however, suffered a further attack about the time of the last destruction at Mycenae, after which the refugees abandoned Achaea for Attica. Herodotus says that these people were the Ionians, who later established themselves in twelve cities on the coast of Asia Minor: no more than this number of colonies was founded because 'they were divided into twelve states when they lived in the Peloponnese, just as the Achaeans, who drove them out, are nowadays'.

Though an Ionian tradition claims that under king Cordus, a scion of the Neleid dynasty of Pylos, the Athenians kept their homeland safe at this time by repulsing a Dorian attack, the greatest pressure on Attica would have come from the Boeotians, or whoever else moved into the vacuum created through the elimination of Theban power. Clear evidence of Mycenaean continuity is the cemetery of Perati in eastern Attica. Most of its graves are chamber tombs; inhumation remains the general rule, and grave goods comprise not only objects with purely Mycenaean antecedents but imports from places overseas with which the Mycenaeans had long been trading. Pottery from Crete and the Cyclades, glass from Egypt, metalwork from Syria, and amber from the Baltic show that those buried in Perati belonged to no enclave of refugees. According to Thucydides, the poverty of the Attic soil discouraged invaders and gave to Athens the stability which acted as a magnet to the most wealthy refugees. 'These took up residence in Athens: they became citizens, and soon made the city more populous than it had been before, with the result that later Attica became too small for her inhabitants and emigrants were sent off to Ionia.' This movement across the Aegean started soon after 1050 BC, but it was not the first of the eastward migrations of the Dark Age.

In Thessaly similar circumstances had already forced Aeolian Greeks to leave Iolkos for the island of Lesbos and the adjacent Anatolian coast. The migration may have begun as early as 1120 BC and it continued until about 1000 BC. These emigrants, and especially the Ionians, were to be in the Archaic Age responsible for the intellectual enlargement of the Greek world. Four of the Seven Sages hailed from the eastern Aegean, including the founder of physical science, Thales. With Anaximander and Anaximenes, fellow citizens of Miletus, he initiated a detached and systematic approach to natural phenomena, thereby beginning the process through which reason was freed from the shackles of superstition. Of course, the overall length of time it took to settle the seaboard of Asia Minor is incalculable, but Greek settlements stayed there right down to the expulsion by the Turks in 1923.

When the revival of literacy permits the identification of dialect groupings a pattern emerges which authenticates population movements. Three parallel dialect bands then spread across the Aegean. In the north, Aeolic was spoken in Thessaly, Boeotia, Lesbos, and on the coast of northwestern Asia Minor; at the centre Ionic existed in Attica, Euboea, most of the Cyclades, Chios, Samos, and on the central portion of the western coast of Asia Minor; to the south Doric was present an Aeotolia, Acar-

126

nania, Phocis, Locris, the Peloponnese (except Arcadia), the southernmost Cyclades, Crete, Rhodes and on the coast of south-western Asia Minor. An exception occurs in the tongue of the Arcadians, whose dialect had affinities with the Greek spoken in Cyprus.

Some scholars still hold that the distribution of Doric speech is consistent with the tradition of a Dorian invasion sweeping down from Doris, through the Peloponnese, where it isolated hilly Arcadia, and on to the islands. Thera and Melos are supposed to have been conquered from Laconia around 1120 BC. But the sudden arrival of backward hillsmen, burning and destroying a civilization with which they had had little contact, fails to explain how the Dorians managed to communicate with other Greeks. Distinct though the dialects were in their development, the differences were never great enough to render speech between them unintelligible, not even in the case of Arcadian, which represents a survival of a dialect common during the Mycenaean settlement of Cyprus in the twelfth century BC. Tradition recounts that Agapenor, leader of the Arcadians in the Trojan War, was the founder of Paphos, a city on the south-western coast of Cyprus. Excavation of the site has turned up an inscription in the Arcadian dialect: it is the oldest known example of Greek on the island.

If Doric was not a primitive tongue from the fastness of Doris whence did it derive? The answer is amazingly simple: from the Mycenaean world. For, with John Chadwick and others, we prefer to regard the Dorians as the lower classes of much of the Mycenaean Peloponnese. The breakdown of civilization, accompanied by the flight of the Ionic-speaking nobility and its immediate followers to Attica, and then abroad, left Doric speakers as the chief element in the population. Subsequently, the Dorians may have inaugurated their own migrations to Crete and Rhodes, where the grip of Mycenaean princes was probably less strong than in the Cyclades. Above all we should not allow the pattern of dialects to obscure the essential unity of the ancient Greeks. As A.M. Snodgrass has well remarked, 'the growth of the great Doric/Ionic antithesis seems to be to a considerable degree the result of the political climate of Greece after the Persian Wars.'

The general outline of deterioration and recovery in material culture vouchsafed by archeology for the Dark Age is not easy to present because of conspicuous regional variations. A nearby uniform retreat to unimaginative forms, as if the adoption of iron had ushered in a bleak utilitarian phase, is only gradually transformed into a new cultural phase, the Geometric. This name, derived from a style of pottery whose decoration was at first assisted by compasses, has been given to the last 200 years of the period, 900 to 700 BC. Its origins are to be discovered in the 'protogeometric' pottery of late eleventh century Attica, where sub-Mycenaean styles may have been amalgamated with Cypriot techniques such as the use of the multiple brush: the complete transition to less spherical shapes and painted designs is documented by vases from the Keramikos cemetery in Athens.

The material progress achieved by the Athenians was not immediately emulated elsewhere on the mainland of Greece, for Corinth and Thebes were slower off the mark, while Argos and Sparta lagged even farther behind. Population grew considerably in geometric times, the number of identified settlements doubling those known for the eleventh century BC, yet the densities of the Bronze Age were still not regained. Nevertheless, these small towns and villages were the genesis of the cities which later so bravely resisted the massed ranks of the Persian invaders. It seems that contacts oversea were almost completely severed for the first half of the tenth century BC, after which the Euboeans and the Athenians took to the seas. By 800 BC, the Euboeans had established at Al Mina, near the mouth of the River Orontes in northern Syria, a trading station, the first permanent settlement on the Levantine coast since the thirteenth century BC. It never formed a colony in the understood sense of the term: no land was owned, nor were its deities entirely Greek. Rather Al Mina (its ancient name is unknown) functioned as an entrepôt for the materials and products the Greeks needed at home, presumably metals, ivory and luxury goods.

Aegean mariners sailing eastwards would have had the advantage of friendly ports of call in Cyprus as well as renewed access to its mineral wealth. The Cypriot Greeks shared the great island with oriental people – the first Phoenician colonists arriving in the mid-ninth century BC – so they were in a good position to direct their Aegean cousins to the civilizations of West Asia. On the Anatolian mainland too there were Mycenaean settlers at Tarsus from the twelfth century BC; in this city, they flourished until the Assyrian king Sennacherib wiped out its inhabitants during the Cilician revolt of 696 BC. Unquestionably the momentous gain for the Greeks in the eastern exchange was the alphabet, taken from the Phoenicians.

As the chief innovations of the Dark Age sprang from the soil of Attica we shall turn our attention to the Athenians, before looking at developments in the rest of the Aegean. Geometric pottery, which in Athens had evolved from the 'protometric' style not later than 900 BC, is characterized by the exact matching of a vase's decoration to its shape. Moving away from the circles and semicircles of 'protometric' ornament, artists painted in prominent places zigzags, meanders, battlements and lozenges. Sometimes these linear designs run right round a pot in a horizontal band, otherwise they are contained in an isolated rectangle positioned on the necks of larger vessels or on the sides of drinking cups and small containers. The shift away from circular ornament continued throughout the geometric period, until a point was reached when the whole surface of a piece of pottery was covered in abstract motifs.

A final decorative feature was the addition of figured scenes, painted in silhouette. This profound artistic reawakening in the late ninth and early eighth centuries BC initially served funerary purposes; burial urns show rows of mourners, funeral games, favourite horses, even the deceased on their biers. Eventually, the events depicted took on legendary implications. Although we need to be careful in identifying episodes from the *Iliad* and the *Odyssey*, as well as mythological subjects, the Greeks were definitely becoming more aware of their heroic past, through the collection of epic narratives and the revival of local cults, often centred on Bronze Age tombs.

From the eighth century BC, Agamemnon received offerings at Mycenae and Menelaus near Sparta, while in Attica the cult of Iphigenia, the daughter whom Agamemnon had to sacrifice in order to gain a fair wind to Troy, combined with the goddess Artemis, the virgin huntress. At Brauron, on the eastern coast of Attica, a cave near Artemis' sanctuary was held to be Iphigenia's tomb or cenotaph. Legend recounts how the goddess snatched Agamemnon's daughter from an altar at Aulis, where the expeditionary fleet was stranded, and left a hind in her stead. Iphigenia may have been Artemis' priestess, since she was charged with the sacrifice to the goddess of all strangers caught in the country of the Tauri, a Scythian tribe. Even in classical times the vestiges of human sacrifice could be found in the worship of Artemis, as blood was drawn from a slight cut on the throat of a male victim by female devotees. Here the descent of her agricultural cult from the Bronze Age is testified by a Mycenaean settlement on a hillock close to Brauron.

Geometric ware was soon copied in the Argolid, Boeotia and Corinth, but non-Athenian potters were not so proficient in using the faster wheel necessary for its pure profile. Not until 800 BC did the Corinthians develop a style of their own and challenge Athens' position at the chief exporter of fine pottery. The diffusion of Attic, and later Corinthian, designs throughout the Aegean underlines the steady improvement in communications. Oriental influences were very marked after 750 BC at Athens, where an expansion of representational art occurred, inspired by metalwork and ivory carvings brought from the Levant. So accomplished are the small ivory statuettes of naked girls recovered from the Dipylon cemetery that they excel the Astarte figurines they imitate. The Canaanite goddess Astarte, from whom even the Hebrews had to be deterred from giving reverence by the prophet Jeremiah, stands behind Aphrodite, the Greek goddess of love. Aphrodite's most important shrines were in Cyprus at Amathos and Paphos: a great temple was constructed in honour

Restored clay model of a temple, dating from the late eighth century BC. It was probably a votice offering for Hera, whose sanctuary stood on the promontory of Perachora north of Corinth.

of Astarte at the latter site by the Phoenician king Ethbaal, who ruled both of the maritime cities of Sidon and Tyre between 887 and 856 BC. Like Astarte, who is sometimes shown equipped with helmet, battleaxe and spear, Aphrodite possessed a darker side, being titled androphonos – 'man killer', tymborychos – 'gravedigger', epitymbidia – 'she upon the tombs', and, above all, pasiphaessa – 'the far shining queen of the underworld'.

Competition with Hera, the indigenous Aegean mother goddess and wife of Zeus, obliged Aphrodite to specialize as a love goddess, becoming in time the mother of Eros (with whom, originally, she had nothing to do). Her sanctuary on the acropolis at Corinth maintained the oriental custom of sacral prostitution down to Roman times, as did her shrines in Cyprus. When on Mount Eyrx, in western Sicily, the Romans rededicated the Carthaginian temple of Astarte to Venus in 241 BC, they also retained the services of its prostitutes. The westerly penetration of Aphrodite's cult was a symptom of Greek responsiveness to West Asian ideas, not least among the Athenians who knew her as 'pandemus' – goddess of the whole people. In this title of praise was enshrined the notion of her authority over affection and all the impulses that underpin social life, besides sexual love.

The reopening of trade relations in the eastern Mediterranean possibly explains the recurrence of bronze artifacts on the mainland of Greece at the close of the tenth century BC. Techniques of working iron at first gave the metal little advantage over bronze, though its novelty and accessibility must have ensured that smiths persevered with its use. Bronze seems to have acquired a ritual role during the period iron was being mastered; the expensive votive offerings made in the eighth century BC at the newly thriving sanctuaries of Delphi in central Greece, Olympia in Elis, and Delos in the Cyclades tend to be cast in bronze. An almost complete cauldron with solid legs riveted to the bowl, from Olympia, is a sign of the surplus wealth now available for displays of piety. Still, the growing demand for iron weapons and cutting implements also stimulated exploration oversea, the Euboeans establishing before 750 BC the first trading post in the western Mediterranean on Ischia, a tiny island near the entrance to the Bay of Naples. The settlement of Pithecusae, built on a steep headland between two good anchorages, was easily defensible and excellently sited for the Etruscan metal trade. The settlers from Chalcis and Eretria turned it into another Al Mina prior to the departure of the Chalcidians to the Italian mainland about 725 BC. Their foundation of Cumae, which had a safe beach rather than a sheltered harbour, resulted from a quarrel with the Eretrians, a commercial rivalry which flared into the Lelantine war at the end of the Dark Age. Although the Athenians did not voyage to such distant shores, they made the Aegean their own and in the process discouraged the troublesome activities of pirates. It became possible to live closer to the seashore, though precautions were still taken against surprise attacks from envious neighbours. Life became less uncertain and trade increased. 'The Athenians', Thucydides tells us, 'were the first to give up the habit of carrying arms and to adopt a way of living that was more relaxed and more luxurious.'

This prosperity was connected with a political revolution only dimly recalled by Greek historians: the synoecism of Attica. While some kind of unity may have existed in the Mycenaean period, based on the citadel of the Athenian acropolis, the turbulent conditions at the outset of the Dark Age would have rendered any such arrangement hollow. Furthermore, Mycenaean rulers were entrenched warrior lords who dominated subjects living at a markedly inferior level: they enjoyed luxuries only partially shared by local magnets and not at all by the mass of the peasantry. Quite different in character was the unification of the inhabitants of Attica during the ninth century BC, when it was agreed that Athens should act as the capital of a single city-state, a polis.

The polis was a typical Iron Age development, though at this early period in the Aegean solely an Athenian innovation. In contrast with the Bronze Age, metallurgy became both more widespread and more local-ized, metal tools were cheaper and easier to obtain, and a larger propor-tion of the population used them. The division of labour and of labour skills steadily expanded in industry, agriculture and trade, so that a varied economy could be sustained over a considerable territory. In Attica the disruption of farming on the fall of the Mycenaeans seems to have been not quite as serious as elsewhere. Cemeteries show that there was con-tinuity in at least twenty-five per cent of the countryside, without which arboriculture is impossible. In many other parts of central Greece, on the other hand, as well as the Peloponnese, depopulation had let olives and vines revert to their wild states. A relatively secure economic base un-derlay the political unification of the Athenians. For Thucydides the change was a question of unifying the laws. He writes:

> When Theseus became king he was as clever as he was powerful. In his reorganization of the country one of the chief things he did was to abolish the separate councils and governments of the towns and to concentrate them all in the present city of Athens, thus forming a single deliberative assembly and a single government. Individuals could look after their own property just as before, but Theseus compelled them to have one centre for their political affairs, namely Athens, of which they were all citizens.

Discounting the obligatory nod to Theseus, a fundamental realignment of loyalties is described in this passage as an historical fact. The accept-ance of Athens as the political, and in consequence religious, centre of Attica created a state in which no formal distinction can be said to have existed between city and countryside. Essentially an anti-monarchal in-stitution, the polis was often at first in the hands of a king, as Athens was, though the city and its satellite villages were really controlled by a landed nobility. In the Archaic Age this ruling aristocracy was to attain an increasingly privileged position, socially and economically; as a result, those citizens who were unable to find land to cultivate or employment in urban areas migrated to colonies oversea. Quite possibly the size of Attica provided an outlet which other city-states had to find abroad, for the Athenians sponsored few colonies, and tended to seek their fortunes as individuals in other states' foundations. The second safety valve was to be mercantile trade. Membership of the citizen body depended upon the constitution of each city-state, but in every case the polis was regarded as identical with the totality of its citizens. They formed in due course a ruling class, even in democracies such as fifth-century Athens, for there were always submerged groups in existence: not simply women, but dependent servants, slaves, foreign residents and allies.

An influence on the evolution of the polis could have been Phoenicia, which consisted of a number of mutually independent cities, each with its own deity, monarchy, assembly and surrounding territory. But this stimulus would have merely confirmed a trend already encouraged by the geography of the Aegean, with its division into many separate plains, peninsulas and islands. The same devotion to a city cult, nonetheless, was a crucial factor in ensuring lasting unity in the Greek city-state, and this religious centralization must have taken a great deal of effort to achieve, given the multiplicity of local beliefs inherited from the Bronze Age. Here again, the Athenians pointed the way forward. No longer were buildings at Athens grouped around a royal palace on the fortified acropolis; they spread instead, Thucydides writes, from its southern flank, the acropolis itself being reserved for Athena's sanctuary. As yet fortifications were unbuilt around the city, so that fields began where houses stopped and a sense of the Attic countryside was ever present. The agora, the 'gathering-place', was readily accessible to town and country people alike, and its use for the exchange of produce as well as a forum for political discussion explains our perception of it as a market place.

Rudimentary though Dark Age Athens was, the new arrangements it devised formed the embryo of the classical polis, the best organization for civilized life according to Aristotle. Writing in the middle of the fourth century BC, the twilight of Greek liberty, Aristotle was convinced 'that man is by nature a political animal' and that the free association of the villages of a hinterland with a larger settlement as a city-state was a 'natural phenomenon'. Characteristically, the philosopher was unconcerned about a minimum size, a position which comfortably accommodated the several hundred Greek city-states then flourishing.

We also need to be cautious over settlement size. Athens remained small, as did Corinth, where in the eighth century BC there is reason to believe synoecism happened too. Smyrna, which was the first city to have been defended by a city wall, was built shortly after 850 BC and had a population of fewer than 3,000. Situated at the sheltered head of a long gulf on the Anatolian coast behind the island of Chios, Smyrna was protected by a series of effective fortifications. The unusually early defences here, as at Iasus farther south, may be explained by the hostility of the indigenous inhabitants. Herodotus records a bloody start for Miletus, a settlement reoccupied by the Ionians. He says:

> the newcomers brought no women with them, but married Carian girls, whose parents they had killed. Because these women were forced into wedlock after the murder of their fathers, husbands and sons, they bound themselves by oath, as well as their female descendants, never to sit at table with their husbands or to call them by name.

An additional cause of friction on the Anatolian coast, Herodotus adds, was rivalry between the Greek colonists themselves, and he offers as proof the story that certain Ionians from neighbouring Colophon seized Smyrna from the Aeolians. Having been expelled from their own city and taken in as refugees, the Ionians assumed control of the city while the inhabitants were celebrating a festival to Dionysus outside the walls. Although other Aeolians came quickly to their aid, the defences were strong enough to compel a compromise, whereby the Ionians kept Smyrna but handed over all movable property to its inhabitants, who were enfranchised in the remaining eleven Aeolic city-states on the mainland of Asia Minor. Weakness in siegecraft, combined with a short campaigning season, largely accounts for the perennial indecisiveness of inter-Greek wars and the survival of so many city-states.

The alternative political organization to the city-state was the ethnos, or tribal confederation. It departed from Aristotle's ideal in the loss of autarkia – 'self-sufficiency', as low population density precluded the growth of cities and their associated industries. Yet between the extremes of the ethnos of the Locrians in central Greece and the polis of the Athenians there were many intermediate stages of development. A famous one is Boeotia. The twelve city-states of this area, which was only slightly larger than Attica, steadily refused to acknowledge the position of the largest of their number, Thebes, and did not cooperate in an effective league under its leadership till the late fifth century BC. On the whole, poleis emerged during the Archaic Age in parts of mainland Greece where the Mycenaeans had previously dwelt, on the Aegean islands, and in colonies overseas. Ethne were always located on the borders of resurgent Greek civilization.

Continuity from the Bronze Age is evident on the island of Euboea, whose favoured position away from Aegean storms encouraged its inhabitants to become the pre-eminent traders. In about 1200 BC Lefkandi received a considerable influx of refugees, but unlike Athens cremation was immediately adopted as the standard rite. Bones were deposited with pottery and personal belongings in cist-graves, then in simple rock-cut shafts closed by slabs. At the turn of the eleventh century BC, Lefkandi was abandoned; it was slowly reoccupied and stayed inhabited down to about 700 BC, when in the Lelantine War a good harbour was found to be no compensation for an exposed site. Although Lefkandi furnishes archeological proof of the earliest examples of eastern Mediterranean imports as well as locally manufactured bronze tripods, neighbouring Chalcis to the west was to become the chief city on the island and renowned for its metalwork. Chalcis, 'bronze city', could have tapped Euboean sources of copper and iron at the start of the Dark Age, though a shortfall in minerals soon drove abroad the Chalcidians and their commercial rivals the Eretrians, whose own city to the east of Lefkandi was established around 770 BC. While these two peoples seem to have initially collaborated in overseas ventures, both in the Levant and Italy, there is a tradition of separate Eretrian enterprise in the Adriatic. In 733 BC the Corinthians evicted Eretrians from Corcyra, modern Corfu, which must have acted as a staging post for westward voyages. The settlers are said to have founded an alternative colony at Methone on the shores of the northern Aegean coastline – henceforth, the area for Eretrian colonization.

One theory for Lefkandi's fall and Eretria's rise in the eighth century BC argues that the former was once the port of Chalcis, which stood next to the awkward currents of the straits between Euboea and the mainland. The majority of its inhabitants are presumed to have moved to Eretria and disputed with the Chalcidians the fertile Lelantine plain situated between the two cities. The scale of the conflict was long recalled, but not the outcome, which leads to the conclusion of an exhausting draw. Certainly the Euboeans after this war forfeited their commanding lead as international traders.

Over at least three northern islands in the Cyclades the Eretrians may have exercised some dominion. Ceos, Teos and Andros have yielded representative pottery, and the fortified site of Zagora on Andros seems to have been a safe anchorage for eastward-bound shipping. This influence did not continue into the Archaic Age, when the islanders were strong enough to join the colonization movement on their own account. The relative isolation of the Cyclades, plus Ionian settlement, doubtless contributed to the slower transition from Mycenaean culture. But even on the sacred island of Delos, a narrow granite oblong some five kilometres in length near the centre of the archipelago, there is evidence of a break in settlement in the eleventh century BC. Temporary desertion of this infertile island should not be taken to imply any abandonment of cult practices there during the Dark Age, notwithstanding the replacement at some unknown time of the Aegean mother goddess by Apollo. The Greeks maintained her worship in the subsidiary cult of Artemis, the twin sister of the god.

To the south of the Cyclades the island of Crete commenced the isolation that left it on the periphery of Greek affairs. The Cretans were not unresponsive to outside influences, as the numerous Attic vases and the presence of oriental craftsmen testify, but the contrast with Minoan times is startling. Except for law-codes, music, and archers, the island was to export little. Crete, from the eighth century BC, turned into something of a cultural backwater, absorbed by its own inter-state rivalries and wars. Population movements were intense at the beginning of the Dark Age, a wave of Mycenaeans arriving shortly after 1200 BC and another wave of people with Minoan cultural traits leaving for Cyprus around 1100 BC. More settled conditions ensued in the tenth century BC, when the inhabitants of the mountain-top town of Karphi felt sufficiently confident to move down onto the Lasithi plain. Thereafter population increased steadily and new settlements were planted, but the cities usually lay close to Bronze Age sites.

Other than Corinth, the same pattern of a very slow revival can be apprehended in the Peloponnese, where widespread disruption marked the closing years of Mycenaean rule. For Laconia the archeological evidence is fragmentary and a complete picture difficult to piece together. Tradition ascribes two crucial events to the Spartan Dark Age: the unique institution of a double kingship and the reforms of Lycurgus, both of which should be understood in terms of religious belief. For a people who revered the Dioscuri, the twin sons of Zeus, the birth of identical sons to king Aristodemus was bound to be regarded as a divine favour, so that the two boys were invested jointly on their father's death. The long tradition of this constitutional arrangement must be partly responsible for Sparta's unusual retention of the monarchy as a political force, since Herodotus describes the duties of the kings as religious and military. They held 'two priesthoods, of Zeus Lacedaemon and of Zeus Uranius, and the power of declaring war on whom they please. In consequence, no Spartan can oppose their decision without being outlawed.'

Eunomia - 'good order' - the orderliness resulting from Lycurgus' reshaping of the Spartans way of life, is said by Thucydides to have begun around 804 BC, though the historian does not mention the reformer by name. The Spartans had no uncertainties about Lycurgus, however. They believed that he gained his wisdom from the oracle at Delphi, where the priestess acknowledged his own divinity, and by the fifth century BC he was worshipped in Sparta as a god. Until Lycurgus' revision, Herodotus states, 'the Spartans had the worst laws of practically all the Greeks, holding aloof from one another and from foreigners.' While recording the view that the new system may owe something to Crete, he has no hesitation in saying that 'the Spartans changed their laws for the better'. Typically, the first action of Lycurgus was to build a sanctuary to Zeus and Athena on the lowlying acropolis which served the cluster of five villages comprising Sparta.

Down until the third century BC the Spartans were exceedingly proud of their unwalled city, which never lost its rural air. Their ability to cope without defences was a direct result of Lycurgus, whose system dedicated every Spartan male from the age of seven to a punishing regime of military training and discipline which produced the finest army in Greece. The power that this military concentration gave to the Spartans on land unnerved their fiercest foes and allowed them to subjugate their near 'neighbours' - the perioeci.

The perioeci, unlike the helots who toiled for their Spartan masters in the countryside, retained local rights and the freedom of occupational choice, though they were obliged to fight in Sparta's wars and accept any decisions that Sparta might make for them. Helots, on the other hand, could not be sold by their masters, as they were ultimately the property of the state. They were cowed by brutal means, but remained the abiding fear of the Spartans, not least after the annexation of Messenia in about 720 BC. It is uncertain whether the helots were in origin ex-citizens, enslaved prisoners or non-Dorian folk. The practice of holding down servile populations, dependent inhabitants in the rural community, seems to have been widespread, but the repression exercised in Laconia and Messenia was recognized as exceptional by the ancient Greeks themselves. Aristotle thought that it was inevitable, given the Spartan preoccupation with military prowess. In *The Politics* he notes the heavy price paid:

> The Spartans are stable enough in the field but are less effective once they have gained a victory. They do not appreciate leisure and never engage in any kind of pursuit higher than war... Those like the Spartans who specialize in one and ignore the other in their education to turn men into machines. . . .

Reflecting on Sparta's miserable failure in Greek politics after the defeat of Athens in 404 BC, Aristotle sagely commented that an exclusively military training was no preparation for peace and, in the last resort, was itself a cause of defeat.

Sparta's chief rival in the Peloponnese, Argos, had made more progress materially by the close of the Dark Age. The high tide of Argive fortunes was to be the decisive defeat of the Spartans at Hysiae in 669 BC, after which Argos and her Arcadian allies gained control of Olympia with its important festival, and Sparta threw itself into a programme of even more intensive military training. Plentiful finds of iron near Argos give the impression of early prosperity and population growth, so much so that the city must have become the centre of the Argolid before 800 BC. The wealth of its leading families can be judged by the contents of a warrior's grave there. It contained a bronze helmet and plate-corslet, gold rings and a field kitchen; the last comprised two ample cooking pots, a cup, a bowl, two iron firedogs, two axes and twelve spits.

Farther north in Corinth there is some evidence of continuity from Mycenaean times in spite of changes in the locations of settlement-sites. Thucydides reports that these first settlers were Aeolians, whom the Dorians later subdued. What made the area attractive was its fine, pale clay, which the Corinthians exploited to rival Attic pottery. After 800 BC their ware was used quite beyond the Isthmus communities. Examples have been unearthed as far east as Smyrna in Asia Minor, as far west as Syracuse in Sicily, and as far north as Dodona in Epirus. Although Corinth seems to have pioneered improvements in shipbuilding, the popularity of its products ensured that they were carried by ships belonging to other Greek city-states as well. But Corinthian ships did expel the Eretrians from Corfu on their way to Sicily, where they founded Syracuse in 734 or 733 BC, eventually to become the richest of the Greek cities in the western Mediterranean. Hardship at home apparently prompted this expedition because it is recorded that many small farmers were among its members. City-states like Corinth and Chalcis possessed insufficient agricultural land to feed their growing populations prior to the end of the Dark Age. Pheidon of Corinth, a legendary lawgiver, acknowledged the problem when he laid down that the number of houses and the number of citizens should be kept equal.

Better times for the Corinthians may be dated to abolition of the hereditary kingship and the unification of the laws in the early eighth century BC. Thereafter the new polis was able to wrest territory from Megara, including the promontory of Perachora and its sheltered harbour, stand up to Argive pressure, relieve economic distress through the planting of two strong colonies oversea, and develop maritime trade.

The colonies of the Greeks who had migrated to Asia Minor in the early part of the Dark Age strongly suggested further settlement oversea. The resumption of trade in the Aegean reunited the Greek-speaking world and brought news back to the mainland of the flourishing condition of these city-states. Land hunger had been more than appeased, for with the notable exception of Phocaea, each city enjoyed easy access to rich soil and lush pasturage. Because of the infertile headland on which the Phocaeans lived, they were very active in seafaring, and dispatched ships to the Black Sea and the western Mediterranean. Before 700 BC a Phocaean outpost was built in the Troad at Lampsacus, guarding the eastern entrance to the Hellespont, and in the Archaic Age the trade route to Spain was dotted with similar settlements, the most important being Massilia, modern Marseilles. The spirit of the Phocaeans was to catch the besieging Persians by surprise in 544 or 540 BC, when most of the citizens preferred emigration to submission, and sailed away to southern Italy, where they founded Elea. Their robust independence, a marked character trait in the ancient Greeks, had already impressed Arganthonius, king of Tartessus in Spain. Finding that he could not persuade the Phocaeans to leave Ionia and settle in his own dominions, and learning of their danger from the Persians, Arganthonius helped to finance the construction of strong city walls. 'He must have given generously,' Herodotus says, 'for the wall at Phocaea is of great extent, and built of large stone blocks well fitted together.'

The early fortification of colonies on the Anatolian seaboard, as we noticed at Smyrna, was a consequence of local resistance to the new arrivals, but archeology does not substantiate poor relations between Greek and non-Greek everywhere. In Caria there was generally peaceful co-existence with the well-organized hill tribes of the interior: in Ionia an abundance of agricultural land in the lower valleys of the Meander and Cayster rivers helped to reduce friction, at least until the Lydian kings halted expansion inland; and the reports of cities intriguing with indigenous kingdoms as well as the occurrence of non-Greek names amongst the settlers show that close contact existed between the various peoples. Evidence for the conversion of the conquered into an under-privileged rural workforce is inconclusive, although we know this happened initially at Syracuse in Sicily and on the southern coast of the Black Sea at Heraclea Pontica, where Megarian and Boeotian colonists reduced the native Mariandyni to serfdom in 560 BC, but agreed not to sell them outside the territory of the city-state.

The ample resources of the Anatolian colonies met Aristotle's criterion of autarkia, encouraged them to pursue independent policies, and fostered a society capable of reflecting profoundly on the wisdom of West Asia and Egypt. Miletus became in due course the birthplace of Greek philosophy. Its first luminary, Thales, 'a Phoenician by remote descent' according to Herodotus, demonstrated the ascendancy of the intellect by successfully predicting a solar eclipse on 28 May 585 BC. The sudden darkening of the sky that day caused the Lydians and the Medes to break off the battle of Halys River and conclude a peace.

It used to be held that the Ionians in the Dark Age belonged to a confederation, and were under the rule not only of kings in each of their twelve cities but also of a supreme ruler of all Ionia. Scholars thought that the sanctuary of Panionium, on the northern slopes of Mount Mycale, was the site of a common festival and of a delegate conference in time of crisis. Recent excavation points to a later date for the inauguration of the shrine, from which we may deduce that cooperation between the inhabitants of the mainland cities and those on the islands of Chios and Samos arose through growing threats from inland powers. The first definite Ionian union was formed at the Panionium sanctuary in 499 BC by nine cities revolting against Persian suzerainty. The delegates formulated common policy, appointed a joint command, and issued an Ionian coinage. Assistance sent to the rebels by the Eretrians and by the Athenians, who regarded themselves as dwellers in 'the eldest land of Ionia', angered the Persian king Darius I and precipitated the Persian invasion of Europe. Those twenty-five ships were an insult not to be borne by an empire stretching from Asia Minor to modern Pakistan.

The action of the Eretrians and the Athenians was not irresponsible, nor was it looked upon by all the mainland Greeks as extraordinary. The Aegean and the vast expanses of the Mediterranean had been transformed by Greek nautical skills into a friendly lake, along whose shores stood cities which partook of a common culture. Even in the Dark Age there were incipient signs of Greek self-awareness, as communities sought the advice of national oracles at Delphi as well as Delos and adopted cults of the heroic Bronze Age dead. About 750 BC, for instance, the inhabitants of Eleusis in Attica enclosed within a wall several graves identified with the heroes celebrated in Aeschylus' *Seven against Thebes*. Whilst they mistakenly chose to honour pre-Mycenaean burials, the worship they accorded the dead served two distinct purposes: the local cult anchored their claim to the land they occupied and it emphasized their own descent from the mythological heroes of the past.

In the Homeric poems, above all else, the Greeks were reminded of the splendours of their ancestors during the Trojan war. All knew of and took delight in Agamemnon's largesse, Achilles' audacity, Odysseus' artfulness, Nestor's eloquence and Diomedes' chivalry. Perhaps this appreciation of a glorious past enabled the Greeks in the Archaic Age to respond creatively to the stimulus of direct contact with the older civilizations of West Asia and Egypt. For the two centuries down to the clash with the Persians witnessed a truly remarkable cultural renaissance in the Aegean world, and the crystallization of a European standpoint.

PART FOUR

ARCHAIC GREECE

Chapter Seven

THE RISE OF THE
CITY-STATE

Two developments which dominate the Archaic Age are the progress of the polis and the enlargement of the Greek world. They were intimately connected as more than ever before the Greeks made the sea their own element, but the scale of the historical change they cover between 700 and 500 BC necessitates separate treatment for each. In particular, the diffusion of colonies along the coast of the Aegean, Mediterranean and Black Seas brought about not only a significant expansion of the European cultural area but produced an intellectual revolution from which we have derived many of our present-day attitudes.

Renewed contact with West Asian civilizations was both the cause and the means of this growth of the mind. It has already been noted in the Dark Age how far Greece withdrew into itself after the fall of the Mycenaeans. That external assistance was required for the recovery of literacy merely illustrates the extent of the cultural retreat involved, though the uses to which the Greeks put the Phoenician alphabet were very different from those of palace archivists. From the start the inscriptions possess a personal ring, being largely the comments individuals scratched on pottery. A cup from a grave of a Chalcidian trader at Ischia, dated some time after 720 BC, bears this poetic message: 'I am Nestor's cup. Whoever drinks will be struck at once with desire for fair-crowned Aphrodite.' Its discovery in the Al Mina of the western Mediterranean serves to remind us of the decisive influence West Asia and Egypt had on Archaic Greece.

At the close of this period, too, the gathering cloud of Persian power on the eastern horizon forced the Greeks to assert their own individuality. The Persians appeared on the coast of Asia Minor about 540 BC, crossed to Europe in order to campaign in Thrace in 516 BC, and invaded the Greek mainland twice, in 490 and 480–79 BC. Despite the pessimistic pronouncements of the Delphic oracle, the Greeks threw back the Persian host, and at the same time the colonists in Sicily routed the forces of Carthage. The Persian wars were correctly looked upon as the coming of age of the Greeks: they marked in effect the termination of the original phase of European civilization.

The translation of polis as city-state is not really apposite, for only those who owned land qualified for citizenship. Because poleis depended on agricultural wealth it was general practice to restrict the ownership of land to full citizens. During the Archaic Age there occurred a switch to arable farming, with barley and wheat reducing the area of pasturage, and in Attica olive groves and vineyards became pre-eminent. As late as 403 BC, after the long and fruitless struggle with Sparta, seventy-five per cent of the citizens of Athens still remained smallholders. This is an impressive figure when it is recalled that Athens was the largest of all poleis with nearly 30,000 citizens. The question of the alienability of landholdings is unresolved, though Hesiod said that in Boeotia the purchase of fields was not uncommon. Pressures were certainly building up in the countryside, rural debt being one of the main targets of Solon's reforms in Athens in 594 BC, but the extent to which the well placed were able to consolidate property is uncertain. The attempt by Pheidon of Corinth to balance the number of dwellings and the number of citizens in his state seems to have been repeated before 700 BC at Thebes by Philolaus, another Corinthian lawgiver. According to Aristotle, the purpose of Philolaus' enactment on inheritance was the maintenance of a fixed number of estates.

Although rural slavery existed, there is no evidence for the wholesale replacement of freeholders by chattel-slaves on farms, if we exclude for the moment the oppressed helots belonging to the Spartans, and this is in striking contrast to the growing importance of unfree labour in industry by the close of the Archaic Period. The tendency in the countryside of Attica, about which we are best informed, was towards the impoverishment of the small farmer and his conversion into a peasant, who owed a proportion of his produce to a noble family. The surpluses so obtained were invested in the manufacture of luxury goods at home or their import from abroad. Prejudice against trades and crafts must partly explain the numbers of foreigners and slaves recruited to these newer activities: half the potters and vase painters in Athens had non-Greek names and rich foreigners were a recognized feature of its society. A metic, or resident alien, was distinguished from other non-Athenians in having been sponsored by a citizen, registered in a deme, and made liable for taxation. Speaking of the distaste exhibited towards handicrafts by most Greeks, Herodotus wonders,

whether they got their ideas about trade, like so much else, from Egypt. The sentiment is common enough. I have observed that Thracians, Scythians, Persians, Lydians, indeed almost all foreigners, reckon craftsmen and their descendants as lower in the social scale than those who are unconnected with manual work. Only the latter, and especially those who are trained for war, do they count as nobles. All the Greeks have taken up this attitude, and above all the Spartans: the feeling against handicrafts is least strong amongst the Corinthians.

But even busy Corinth had to import industrial skills. Hired labour was available on farms in the form of the thetes, poor countrymen, who may have equalled as much as half the Attic population. The lowest class of free men in a polis, the thetes were too poor to afford the equipment necessary to join the armoured citizen infantry and therefore they went to battle as support troops: either javelin throwers or bowmen. Solon admitted them only to the assembly, the ecclesia, but their service as sailors and marines in the fifth-century Athenian navy eventually led to the dropping of limitations on enfranchisement.

Archaic society remained essentially aristocratic. Though the social structure was becoming more complex and flexible as wealthy families moved upwards and sought a share in government, the issue of popular sovereignty did not arise until after the Persian wars, and even then it was largely confined to those poleis which were in the forefront of economic development. The ambivalence felt over the political aspirations of the lower classes is apparent in the word demos, from which we have obtained democracy: demos could refer to all of the people, or just the common people. Nevertheless, there were social and economic forces working strongly against the aristocratic order, with the result that political revolution did take place in many city-states during the seventh century BC. Sometimes change was accomplished peacefully through the introduction of a law-code or a constitution; but on occasions a shift in the balance of power meant violence between kings and aristocrats, or between the aristocrats themselves. The advent of tyrants, especially in the poleis concentrated around the Isthmus, the narrow bridge of land joining the Peloponnese to the rest of the Greek mainland, was a response to the increasing instability which accompanied this breakdown of aristocratic rule. Tyranny itself gave way in the fifth century BC to two forms of government: oligarchy and democracy.

From the outset of the Archaic Age we encounter a preoccupation with the past. Powerful aristocratic families constructed genealogies stretching back to the heroic figures of Greek legend, doubtless to justify their political leadership. They vied with each other in the pursuit of fame, believing that by so doing they emulated the exploits of the *Iliad*. This competition among equals had a crucial influence on the polis since it encouraged the notion that the state belonged to every citizen. The nobles in fact established a correspondence between martial skills and the right to participate in public affairs, a tenet of Greek political theory that was never again questioned. Initially, the battlefield was the exclusive domain of the horseriding aristocrats, the hippeis. Because metal was scarce and horses expensive to feed, the pattern of warfare seems to have comprised a series of cavalry raids and skirmishes, the outcome of any struggle depending on duels fought by dismounted warrior-nobles. Improvements

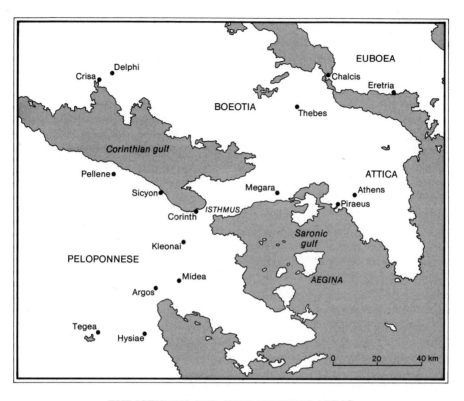

THE ISTHMUS AND SURROUNDING AREAS

in armour, notably the corslet, greaves, helmet and shield, quite soon added another combatant, the hoplite, or armoured infantryman, who asked for admission to the select band noted above by Herodotus.

Hoplite equipment cost a great deal and in consequence the development of the phalanx, the close-packed body of infantry in which hoplites deployed, cannot be regarded as the democratization of Greek armies. Only the professional Spartans received state aid for armour, a fact which ensured in most poleis that poor citizens were obliged to fight as light-armed auxiliaries on land. Yet the phalanx obviously gave an enlarged military role to those with more substantial means, and in time allowed them to exercise a similar one politically. In his *Politics*, Aristotle plainly underlines this when he states that the earliest constitutions, immediately after the disappearance of kings, were narrowly based; whereas, once the military strength of a city-state came to rely on the hoplite army, the basis of the constitution was necessarily widened. The Athenian hoplites are known to have been zeugitai, small farmers and craftsmen; under Solon's constitution the zeugitai enjoyed full citizen rights, except that

145

they were admitted to minor magistracies only. By the end of the Archaic Period, however, they could also be elected as strategoi, the board of ten generals who had operational command of Athens' forces for one day each in turn. At the battle of Marathon in 490 BC the successful offensive against the Persian invaders was initiated by a noble, Miltiades, to whom four other strategoi had awarded their days of command.

The efficiency of the phalanx rested on standardized weapons and regular training. It would appear that its possibilities were first perceived by the half-legendary Pheidon of Argos who, Aristotle says, exceeded the traditional bounds of royal power in order to become a tyrant. The patent superiority of the phalanx over the much looser formation used by aristocratic fighters was probably demonstrated at Hysiae, where a Spartan expeditionary force was overwhelmed by the Argives in 669 BC. Scenes of fighting between men in hoplite armour are depicted on vases from Corinth and Athens before this date. The chief item was the great round shield, the hoplon, from which the hoplite took his name. About three feet in diameter, the slightly curved hoplon was made of wood, reinforced with bronze, and held by means of an armband running across the inside as well as a handle on the rim. While we are uncertain as to whether the phalanx was a Greek invention or an adaptation of West Asian tactics, the custom of referring to the hoplon as the Argive shield does lend support to the proposition that Pheidon owed his unchallenged authority to military innovation. No army was capable of stopping him from breaking the Olympic truce, which forbade the presence of armed men within the precincts of Olympia during the Games. His sacrilegious intervention was dictated by diplomatic considerations, for domination of this national event was intended as a signal to the Greeks that Argos had taken over the hegemony of the Peloponnese from Sparta. Under the influence of Pheidon events were expanded from running and wrestling to include races for chariots and single horses, though the foot race always remained the principal contest. The race in armour was only instituted in 520 BC.

In addition to a shield, the hoplite was protected by a bronze helmet, corslet and greaves. The most popular helmet, the Corinthian, covered the whole head from the collar bone upwards, enclosed the cheeks and overhung the nose. An incredible feat of metalwork, each helmet was beaten from a single sheet of bronze. Possibly the single drawback of the Corinthian helmet, the temporary deafness it imposed on a wearer, explains the existence of other types, like the Chalcidian, which left the ears unobstructed.

Equally valuable in the thick of hand-to-hand fighting must have been the bronze corslet, a chest protector comprising a beaten breastplate and backplate, firmly secured at the sides. Its prototype was the plate corslet we have already noticed in the rich warrior's grave at Argos, but beyond this find origins are hard to trace. As the collapse of metallurgy in the Dark Age rules out an evolution from Mycenaean armour and the hot climate of West Asia and Egypt predisposed soldiers there to favour light scale-armour, leather, or simply linen, the only source outside of Greece for plate is Europe, from which the idea of strong body armour might conceivably have come. Herodotus leaves us in no uncertainty about the advantage it gave to the Greeks at Plataea in 479 BC. Once the Persians were engaged at close quarters the superiority of the phalanx told. 'In courage and strength,' the historian writes, 'they were as good as the Greeks, but they were deficient in armour, untrained, and greatly inferior in skill.'

For the Spartans, who bore the brunt of the Persian attack in the battle of Plataea, remaining in formation constituted a matter of duty. So imbued was their thinking with the phalanx that losing one's shield became the same as losing one's honour. The interdependence of the hoplites, their overriding need to fight as a unit if they were to win, had encouraged the view of the good citizen as a man who stood his ground in the line and sank his destiny in cooperating with his fellows.

A phalanx was never less than four ranks deep, so that an engagement between two tended to be a slow process of attrition and required a steady nerve – no mean test for the part-time citizen soldier. The weaponry for such close combat was the spear and sword. Vase paintings show hoplites with two or more spears, but it is unlikely that in battle a hoplite would have bothered to carry more than a single thrusting spear, besides a short sword as a reserve weapon. The importance of the spear, as in former times, is celebrated in a term often applied to captives; namely, doruxenoi, or spear-guests. For Aeschylus, who fought against the Persians at Marathon and Salamis, the struggle for Greek independence was symbolized as a contest between the spear and the bow. It is not surprising that iron spearheads made short work of an enemy wearing leather jerkins and linen tunics, since at Olympia archeologists have discovered votive bronze helmets and corslets punctured with holes.

The political power the newly introduced phalanx conferred on Argos was employed by the tyrant Pheidon to further his own territorial ambitions, which he vindicated by reference to the Mycenaean period. One of his closest allies, the town Sicyon on the Corinthian gulf, was said in the *Iliad* to be subject to Agamemnon. Cleisthenes, a later tyrant of Sicyon, made strenuous efforts to distance his city-state from Argos by downgrading this historical link. He tried to eclipse the local cult of Adrastos, a legendary Argive king who was buried in the city's agora. After receiving a dusty answer about exhuming the hero's remains from the oracle at Delphi, Cleisthenes brought from Thebes the bones of Melanippos, who was Adrastos' bitterest enemy, having slain his brother and his son-in-law in the conflict recorded in Aeschylus' *Seven against Thebes*. Revenge on Delphi for its unhelpfulness was one of the motives that prompted the tyrant to enter the First Sacred War, fought some time between 595 and 586 BC. The use of hallowed bones in inter-state rivalry was not unusual, the Spartans gaining the upper hand over the Tegeans of Arcadia about 550 BC after the Delphic oracle had instructed them to acquire the bones of Agamemnon's son, Orestes, which they located in an iron-smith's yard in Tegean territory. The influence of events at Olympia and Delphi on Archaic Greece, not unlike the media today, compelled tyrants like Pheidon and Cleisthenes to assert their positions. But the attempt Pheidon made to bring Corinth under his control caused his own death about 657 BC.

Pheidon was credited with the establishment of standard weights and measures in the Peloponnese, also the earliest coinage. Although Herodotus tells us that the Lydians first struck coins, the honour among the Greeks belongs to the island of Aegina, which issued silver denominations from the middle of the sixth century BC. Pheidon is supposed to have dedicated to Hera iron spits, the medium of exchange made obsolete by coinage, and such offerings have been dug from tombs as well as the temple of the goddess situated between Argos and Mycenae. Whatever the truth, Pheidon set the Argives on a collision course with the Spartans. During the Second Messenian war, which took place between 650 and 620 BC, the Argive navy was able to ferry troops to Messenia unopposed. Support for the Messenians, who were encouraged to revolt by Spartan weakness after the defeat at Hysiae, formed part of a broader strategy intended by Argos to confine Sparta to the Eurotas valley. At this time the island of Cythera, lying off the southernmost extremity of Laconia, was firmly in Argive hands, the Spartans having turned their backs on the sea. This singular lack of interest in ships stemmed directly from the Lycurgan reforms, since they had placed overwhelming emphasis on the army. The bitter struggle between Argos and Sparta for supremacy in the Peloponnese, and as a consequence leadership of the Greeks in opposition to Persia, can be looked upon as the perfection of the Spartan military machine, which only in 546 BC was ready to finally settle accounts with the Argives at the battle of Thyreae. Concentration on mastery of the battlefield is clearly expressed in the saying of the Spartan statesman Chilon, one of the Seven Sages: prior to the Argive defeat he used to say that Cythera would be better sunk beneath the waves.

Still, the course of events down to Sparta's emergence in 546 BC as the most powerful state in the Greek world was by no means smooth. The Messenian rebels fought with all the desperation of the cruelly oppressed. Daring to engage in pitched battles, they worsted Spartan units; and, even in the last years of the revolt when they were deserted by their allies, they sent out bands of guerrillas to waste Laconia and the recaptured parts of Messenia. During the critical moments at the beginning of the war, the poet-general Tyrtaeus rallied the Spartans with stirring songs, which idealized the phalanx and exhorted its members to put aside any concern for personal safety. Advancing together, step by step, shield pressing against shield, spears at the ready, the hoplites symbolized the Spartan way of life. There could be no question of retreat, an attitude to death that was to be unintelligible in 480 BC to the Persian king at Thermopylae. What cemented this ideal to Spartan tactics was the victory achieved at the so-called 'battle of the trench', the turning point of the Second Messenian War. It would seem that it was here that the Spartans first adopted with success the new infantry formation developed by the Argives. The remainder of the campaign was a series of ambushes and counterattacks until the last rebel stronghold of Eira fell in 620 BC.

Before considering the rise of the Spartan confederacy, which came into being following the suppression of the Messenians, alliance with the Arcadians, and the defeat of the Argives, it is necessary to describe the effect prolonged conflict had on the Spartan constitution. A political crisis after the First Messenian War had resulted in the foundation of Taras, modern Taranto in the instep of Italy. To this colony, whose excellent natural harbour backed onto extensive cornlands, the Spartans exiled the partheniai, illegitimate children born at home while the army was away on active service in Messenia. One tradition asserts that the oath the soldiers swore early in the war not to cease fighting until they were victorious, prompted the Spartan women to complain that they lacked the means to replace those who fell in battle. Hence they persuaded their husbands to allow them to bear children by men too young to serve with the army, but on the return of peace the offspring of these unions were disowned.

Though it is unlikely that the expedition to Taras arose for such a simple cause, quite apparent are the strains a hard-fought series of campaigns placed on Spartan society, not unlike the unrest at home that Thucydides says was fermented by the duration of the Trojan War. Another effect was that the apella, the assembly, did not represent the full citizen body and its relations with the council of elders, the gerousia, were acrimonious. Consisting of twenty-eight citizens over the age of sixty elected for life, plus the two kings, the gerousia not unnaturally remained very conservative in approach. In order to strengthen its authority during the war the gerousia claimed the power to make law and to determine state policy as long as unanimity prevailed, issues being referred to the apella only when there was more than a single proposal. The practice became permanent, thereby reinforcing the military hierarchy, but a check on the power of the co-equal kings also evolved in the ephorate. Five ephors, aged over thirty and elected annually by the apella, were charged with the administration of justice as well as the supervision of the dual monarchy.

It was soon customary at the beginning of each year for the kings to swear that they would rule in accordance with the laws of the state, and the ephors to swear on behalf of the state to preserve the position of the kings provided they kept their word. A popular safety valve, the ephorate gave a workable flexibility to the otherwise rigid Spartan constitution. The ephors spoke for the citizen body, men over thirty years of age, attended meetings of the gerousia, travelled with the kings on campaign, and declared war each year on the helots.

The doubling of the number of helots through the conquest of Messenia obliged Sparta to be continually on a war footing. Anxiety drove the ephors to sanction the actions of the notorious krypteia, the secret police responsible for the annual cull of helots. Recruited from young Spartans, this force was said to have been dispatched to kill secretly any of the rural slaves thought to be dangerous. There has been some argument about the origins of this bloody custom, which may have been a survival of early warrior initiation rites. Equipped with daggers and food, the assassins are supposed to have holed up during the day, then struck down unwary helots on the road at night; alternatively, they slew in broad daylight the strongest they encountered working in the fields. Although Aristotle ascribes the institution to Lycurgus, other commentators indicate a fifth-century date for its introduction. In 424 BC we know some 2,000 helots were done away, or the equivalent of a quarter of the Spartan citizenry. Five thousand Spartans had marched to the decisive battle of Plataea in 479 BC, brilliant infantrymen but the majority of the citizens in their prime of life, between thirty and fifty-five years of age. Unhealthy or deformed boys were always exposed at birth on the orders of the state; as a result of this policy and the tendency of women to marry late, the perennial shortage of men intensified Spartan fears, encouraged savage repression of the helots, and after the defeat of the Athenians contributed to the downfall of the Spartans in the early fourth century BC. Spartan women, unlike Athenian, enjoyed considerable economic freedom and their ability to become heiresses contributed to the enlargement of estates and, in consequence, the reduction of the number of Spartan citizens living off their landholdings, or kleroi.

Victory at Thyraea in 546 BC allowed the Spartans to intervene in the internal affairs of other Greek states, which they readily did where tyrants held power. Their opposition to autocratic government was an attempt to preserve the oligarchic status quo as well as an assertion of the value of traditional ways. The decision to eschew the new silver currency, with

150

an inevitable drop in imports, reflects the Spartan preference for plain living and is in striking contrast to the commercial activities of the chief states which experienced tyrannies: Corinth, Sicyon, Athens and Samos. A byproduct of colonial expansion was an enormous increase in seaborne trade, the main routes of which met at the Isthmus.

So intense were the activities of traders from both east and west here that some time before his death in 585 BC the second Corinthian tyrant Periander built the diolkos, a paved shipway between the Gulf of Corinth and the Saronic Gulf. Vessels were hauled on a vehicle – the grooves in which its wheels ran still being visible in the later version of the diolkos. It was to be expected that Periander should have done his utmost to facilitate commerce, since tyranny first appeared in Corinth about 657 BC through the inability of the Bacchiad aristocracy to handle effectively the new wealth derived from porterage, shipbuilding, manufacturing and trade. Despite their prosperity the Corinthians seem to have been under Argive pressure until the death of Pheidon, against whom Cypselus, the founder of the tyranny, may have organized resistance. Cypselus' *coup d'état* appears to have been regarded as a liberation, for long after the passing of the tyrants his rule was remembered for its mildness. His survival without a bodyguard underlines the general acquiescence, including that of the hoplite army, many of whose members would have acquired their status by means of trade. Like his defeated rival Pheidon of Argos, Cypselus secured his own position by incorporating the hoplites into the structure of the state. He also appears to have embellished the city cult: a new temple built for Apollo was the first building on mainland Greece to possess a tiled roof since the destruction of the House of Tiles at Lerna prior to 2100 BC.

To Herodotus Cypselus was a monster, whose usurpation of power negated the principle of self-government enshrined in the polis. The settled hatred of the historian for tyranny is not surprising, when we recall the pro-Persian sentiments of most of the dictators. Because Persia favoured tyrants as governors of the Greek cities in Asia Minor, it was easy for tyrants elsewhere to side with the Persians and bask in the warmth of their growing success. A notable collaborator was Polycrates, who seized power on the island of Samos about 535 BC. Yet his willingness to lend the Persians a part of his strong navy in 525 BC, in the attack on Egypt, failed to save his own skin when Oroetes, the Persian governor of Sardis, decided that the tyrant ought to be checked. Lured by promises of financial support for his schemes to dominate the Aegean, Polycrates was foolish enough to attend Oroetes' court, where he was killed in 523 or 522 BC.

The tale of Polycrates' ring particularly fascinated Herodotus because he thought it summed up the attitude of the gods to an arrogance that made the tyrant's power the talk of Ionia and the rest of Greece. All his campaigns ended in victory, his every venture in success. He possessed a fleet of one hundred and fifty-oared galleys and a force of 1,000 archers. His plundering raids were widespread and callous, as he said that his friends would always be pleased he returned to them what he had taken.

According to the story, Polycrates was warned by one of his allies that the continuous good fortune he enjoyed would provoke the anger of the gods, and he was advised to divest himself of the thing he valued most. Therefore, in a ceremony at sea Polycrates cast overboard his magnificent signet ring, an emerald set in gold. But it happened a week afterwards that a big fish presented to the tyrant by one of his subjects was discovered to contain the same ring. When he reported this to his ally, he was told that anyone whose luck held even to the extent of recovering what he deliberately threw away must be destined to die a miserable death. In 524 BC, Polycrates beat off an expedition of Spartans and Corinthians who sought to intervene on behalf of exiled Samians, and flushed with this achievement he could not resist walking in to the trap at Sardis, despite all the warnings of his family and courtiers.

Behind the tale of the ring stands a body of religious ideas and cult practices which relate to sacrifice. Evidently the ritual Polycrates performed on one of his warships proved unacceptable to the gods and called into question the legitimacy of his rule. The importance of public sacrifice in the duties of a tyrant is clear in the case of Isodamos, who briefly shared power with Cleisthenes in Sicyon. These two men displaced Myron, their feckless elder brother, in about 595 BC and ruled together until it was obvious that Isodamos' pollution by fratricide prevented him from making sacrifices. Cleisthenes persuaded Isodamos to seek purification outside Sicyon, then kept him exiled in Corinth so that he alone could exercise the tyranny. Since Cleisthenes is supposed to have encouraged Isodamos' murder of Myron, the episode has all the appearance of a carefully laid plot. Aristotle says that Cleisthenes was admired for his warlike character, however: no matter his rather poor military showing against the Argives, he continued the policy of the tyranny in 'treating the Sicyonians with moderation and adhering to the laws'. It also seems that Cleisthenes' secondary revolution within the tyranny received impetus from tribal antagonisms, on which he capitalized by renaming his own non-Dorian tribe as 'rulers'. What is interesting about the details of the dynastic squabble is the implication that an inability to sacrifice to the gods debarred a person from holding power.

A ring is rumoured to have played a crucial role in the fortunes of Gyges, the first person the Greeks called a tyrant. In 685 BC Gyges, a member of the Lydian royal bodyguard, murdered king Kandaules, married his wife and usurped the throne. He swiftly embarked on a programme of territorial expansion which ended in Lydia becoming the dominant power in Asia Minor. At the same time he had to deal with the Cimmerian invaders who, some time after 695 BC, had routed the Phrygians, destroying the kingdom of the legendary Midas. The wealth and power of Gyges was unequalled in Greek experience: it was typical of a tyrannos (possibly a Lydian word). The legend of Gyges' rise to absolute authority is simpler. As a shepherd in the service of the Lydian king, he stumbled one day on a cave in which he found a bronze horse, within which was a naked corpse wearing only a ring. Taking the ring, Gyges was amazed to perceive the magical quality of its stone, for he was rendered invisible whenever he turned it towards himself. With this advantage, he managed to make himself ruler. Possibly in both the stories of Polycrates and Gyges we have a reference to the seal, from the Bronze Age onwards a symbol of ownership, personal power, and identity. In the stone, doubtless engraved, the magic resided.

Although tyranny was a term of abuse by the time of Polycrates' rule, the policies of individual tyrants were often brilliantly successful; for as champions of the demos, in the Archaic Period essentially the hoplites, they curbed aristocratic privilege and eased the lot of ordinary citizens. Demands for the redistribution of land and the cancellation of debts form the background of their seizure of power, even in Athens, where Solon had already tried to establish justice. This wise lawgiver could not contain the social and economic conflicts that gave Peisistratus his chance to bid for domination. As Solon lamented: 'A city's ruin comes from great men, and the people in their folly fall into the slavery of a monarch.' Submission to tyrants lasted for three generations at Corinth, 657 to 583 BC, and for a century at Sicyon, 655 to 555 BC.

Like Cypselus, the first tyrant of Corinth, Orthagoras seems to have initially earned the obedience of the Sicyonians through his defence of threatened territory. Commanding a force of border guards, he kept at bay the Pellenes, with whom Sicyon had been for many years at war, and stopped the Argives from exploiting a boundary dispute with Kleonai. Aristotle adds as reasons for Orthagoras' elevation the respect he showed for the laws, his moderation in dealing with his subjects, and the demos. While Orthagoras may have eliminated rivals by execution or banishment, the Sicyonian aristocracy as a whole accepted the dynasty he founded, the citizen body itself concurring with a system of government that gave the state peace, prosperity, and justice.

Renowned for its bronzework, Sicyon was caught up in the trade boom of the late seventh century BC and the descendants of Orthagoras displayed this wealth through the lavish gifts they made to the sanctuaries of Olympia and Delphi. There was no sign of the antagonism between the Delphic Oracle and the Sicyonian tyranny which marred Cleisthenes' reign, about 595 to 564 BC; quite the contrary, the rise of Orchagoras to power was foretold by the priestess. The story goes that the oracle informed a Sicyonian embassy that whoever on returning home first heard that a son had been born to him, that son was to be the first of the tyrants who would scourge the Sicyonians for 100 years. With the embassy went a cook named Andreas, whom the noble envoys naturally overlooked, though his son was indeed Orthagoras. The sympathy the oracle at Delphi showed towards Pheidon of Argos, Cypselus of Corinth, Orthagoras of Sicyon, and Cylon, who with the aid of troops lent by his father-in-law, the tyrant of Megara, nearly secured Athens about 625 BC, tells us that Apollo was willing to back the new order around the Isthmus. Sparta, left out in the cold, needed a respite after the Second Messenian War to regroup its energies and to prepare for the showdown with Argos. Nonetheless, it was from the Delphic oracle that the Spartans learned how to isolate the Argives, as the advice concerning the bones of Orestes was intended to persuade these relentless soldiers from a foreign policy of annexation to one of alliance. The pact agreed with the Tegeans formed the cornerstone of the Peloponnesian league they built up after 550 BC. The league was the first large-scale military coalition in European history.

Involvement in the First Sacred War came to the Sicyonians through the ambitions of Cleisthenes, to whom Delphi had proffered unhelpful responses in his propaganda campaign against Argos. Nettled by the name leuster – 'stonethrower' – Cleisthenes was delighted to send a fleet to attack Crisa, the Phocian city which controlled the port of Itea on the Corinthian gulf and thereby monopolized visitors to the oracle. Harassment of these pilgrims was the ostensible reason for the joint expedition of Thessalians, Athenians and Sicyonians, but Cleisthenes had his eye on two things, personal influence at Delphi and the commercial benefits of destroying Itea. On the fall of Crisa in 591 BC, he received a third of the war spoils, which were used to enlarge a festival at Sicyon, called the Pythia. In due course his star rose at Delphi too, where he competed with success during festivals and built a treasury for the Sicyonians to store the offerings they dedicated to Apollo.

Divine approbation in the guise of favourable oracles remained important for tyrants, especially when their opponents in exile managed to affect the utterances themselves. Thus Peisistratus, the Athenian tyrant, was forced to turn his attention to Apollo's shrine on the island of Delos between 540 and 530 BC, because his enemies were too well entrenched at Delphi. Having secured the neighbouring island of Naxos as an ally by supporting there the tyrant Lygdamis, Peisistratus exhumed the dead whose graves were in sight of the precinct, reburying them elsewhere on

Delos, and then in the purified sanctuary he rebuilt the temple in Attic limestone. Though the task was also undertaken to enhance the claim of Athens to be leader of the Ionians, the awe in which Archaic Greeks held their gods was profound. Even the Persians, when in 490 BC they sailed through the Cyclades on their way to attack Eretria and Athens, dared not pass Delos without sacrificing to Apollo and Artemis and burned upon the altar there an immense amount of frankincense. After their departure, Herodotus notes, occurred the only earth tremor ever known on the sacred isle; he says, 'The shock was a divine sign to warn men of the troubles that were to come.' Polycrates of course sought approval from Delos in his own flamboyant way. He captured the adjoining island of Rheneia and by a chain attached it to Delos as an offering to Apollo.

Equally demonstrative were the preparations for the marriage of Cleisthenes' daughter Agariste to Megacles, a member of the Alcmeonidae, a noble Athenian family prominent in politics. His father, Alcmeon, had led the Athenian contingent in the First Sacred War. After winning the chariot race at the Olympic games, Cleisthenes publicly announced his intention of marrying his daughter to the best suitor in Greece. Those who deemed themselves worthy enough to be his son-in-law were invited to spend a year in Sicyon and undergo rigorous athletic and intellectual scrutiny. Herodotus tells us how Cleisthenes 'had a race-track and a wrestling ring specially built for the purpose', and how he 'spoke with the suitors sometimes individually, sometimes all together, in order to test the character, abilities, education and manners of each.' The Athenian Hippocleides, who was the preferred candidate because he was distantly related to the family of Cypselus of Corinth, ruined his chances on the final day at a great banquet, when the worse for wine, he completed a dance on a table, standing on his head and beating time with his legs in the air. Cleisthenes was not amused, for 'the most important test of all was behaviour at the dinner-table', and he betrothed Agariste to Megacles instead.

Little more can be gleaned from the histories about the final years of the tyranny at Sicyon, which ceased on the Spartan expulsion of Cleisthenes' successor, Aischines, in 555 BC. The Spartans appear to have intervened to forestall an internal revolution, which they feared would lead to a pro-Argive government. The Sicyonians had lost the initiative in the war their tyrants waged against the Argives, as separate reports of plague and famine attest, so a peace movement could have alerted Sparta to the danger of Aischines' imminent fall. Like all dictators, his survival depended on success. The great reign of Cleisthenes may have exhausted Sicyon, just as earlier at Corinth the energetic foreign policy of Periander prepared for his successor's demise.

Our problem with Periander, who ruled from about 625 to 585 BC, is

the conflicting judgements the ancient Greeks delivered about his government. On one hand, he was blamed for violent measures not only against
his own family – the death of his wife, the dispossession of his father-
in-law, and the quarrels with his sons – but more against outstanding
Corinthians, many of whom he cut down, Aristotle tells us, like the tallest
stalks in a field: on the other, tradition places the tyrant among the Seven
Sages, along with Chilon of Sparta, Solon of Athens and Pittacus of
Mytilene. Comparison with Pittacus is instructive for unlike Periander,
this tyrant was content to accept from the Mytilenaeans a period of power
limited to ten years, which duly elapsed without incident about 580 BC.
As aware as Solon of the shortcomings of aristocratic politics, Pittacus
introduced legislation against the extravagance of the rich, in particular
the crimes they committed during drunken revels, but he did not attempt
any Solonian reform of the constitution. With Periander the motive for
curbing the powerful was based on self-interest, the preservation of his
own position; it was one of the ways he controlled Corinth, the others
being chiefly a prohibition on assembly and a network of spies. Aristotle
credits Periander with an entire battery of repressive regulations and
notes that the methods of the Persian kings offered many parallels. Periander's ambitions as a ruler were fired by the strong colonial system he
inherited, the colonies overseas that assisted Corinthian trading activities
and were kept friendly by regular visits from the navies the tyrant maintained.

A policy of closer supervision may have derived from his father Cypselus, the first Corinthian tyrant, since three of Periander's brothers went
out as founder-rulers of new colonies. At Ambracia, a settlement on the
Bay of Actium, we know that a Cypselid tyranny endured for three
generations, contesting control of the rich coastlands with the Acarnani-
ans and Amphilochians. Periander's own sons were installed at Potidaea,
founded in Chalcidice about 600 BC for trade with Macedonia, and at
Corcyra, the strategic Corinthian colony in the Adriatic Sea. Renewed
hostility towards the mother-city could explain Periander's wish for more
direct influence in Corcyra; in 664 BC the Corcyreans and the Corinthians
had fought the first naval battle ever recorded between Greek fleets.
When his son was killed in a revolt there, Periander invaded the island,
crushed the rebels, and made his nephew tyrant. As further punishment,
he took 300 boys, the sons of leading citizens of Corcyra, and sent them
to Sardis with the intention of having them castrated. Fortunately for
the youths, however, they did not enter the Lydian court as eunuchs,
because on the way they were rescued by the Samians, who returned
them home.

Such a present for Alyattes, the king of Lydia, should be regarded as
an aspect of Periander's foreign policy, for the tyrant was sufficiently

powerful within the Greek world to exchange envoys with kings beyond its limits. Of all the archaic states, Corinth under Periander came closest to establishing a colonial empire. His fleets, operating from both the Corinthian and Saronic Gulfs, preserved a tight relationship with the colonies, as can be seen from the suppression of the Corcyreans, but no amount of naval manoeuvres was capable of halting the tide of political independence. Neither in Corinth itself could tyranny last for more than two years after Periander's death. How the Corinthians moved onto con-stitutional government in 583 BC is obscure, though at least one ancient author saw the hand of Sparta in the oligarchy they adopted. Even if a popular rising alone did not pull down Periander's nephew, the price of tyranny was plain to the people: the continual denial of freedom, the haunting fear of informers, and the lack of any influence on state policy. The famous caution of Solon springs to mind: 'It's easy to put up an autocrat, but not to put one down.'

The situation in Athens is almost an epitome of the aristocratic weak-ness. After their early recovery in the Dark Age, and the political unifi-cation of Attica as a single polics, the Athenians should have been set on a course of development second to none on the Greek mainland. But under the Eupatrids, the 'well-born', the state languished and economic stagnation was normal, for the aristocrats spent their best energies in internecine strife. So bitter were their feuds that they encompassed both the living and the dead; the graves of the Alcmaeonids were opened and their contents dumped outside Attica, while living members of Megacles' family sought safety in exile too. This attack was justified as a cleansing of the state for the blood the Alcmaeonids had shed in thwarting Cylon's seizure of the acropolis, in about 625 BC. However genuine the worries about pollution – some of the conspirators had been killed within the sacred precincts – the motives of the persecuting aristocrats were frankly partisan. 'Afterwards,' Aristotle remarks, 'for a long time conflicts took place between the nobles and the people.'

The publication of Draco's law-code in 621 or 620 BC needs to be seen in the context of the growing civil disorder. Although details are lost and a reputation for severity invests the lawgiver's name, an enlightened distinction was apparently drawn between manslaughter and murder. Revenge no longer rested entirely on the shoulders of the deceased's relatives, as Draco made justice the property of every citizen, a right and a duty for the first time publicly spelt out in Athens. We cannot be sure that Draco also established a constitution based on the franchise of hop-lites, as Aristotle believed, but he certainly intended his harsh laws to tame aristocratic excess. That a written law-code was agreed represents a decisive break with the past. As Confucius, the great defender of tradi-tional ways in China, astutely reminded progressive rulers, the setting down of laws was a dangerous practice for the nobility. He noted that the code of punishments inscribed on a tripod by the king of Chin in 513 BC would be learned and respected by the ordinary people above all else. In Archaic Greece, literacy swiftly took on a public purpose; it allowed the polis to disclose to its citizens the machinery of government as well as the code of law. Magistrates could never again evoke tradition in order to declare that their opinions were correct.

By 594 BC the Athenians realized that another lawgiver was urgently required and they turned to Solon, a moderate aristocrat engaged in overseas trade. He appreciated that the rapacity of the rich lay at the heart of the economic crisis, exacerbated by the use of coinage, and that political difficulties centred on the unfulfilled aspirations of the hoplites, who unlike the poorest farmers had benefited from expanding trade and commerce. Appointed as mediator, Solon cancelled debts, bought citizens out of slavery and prohibited all future loans on the security of the person. The abolition of enslavement for debt guaranteed the personal freedom of the humblest citizen; it crystallized, too, the concept of fundamental, inalienable civil rights without which citizenship would be rendered valueless. Solon himself considered this measure his most significant reform, which for the future development of European democracy it undoubtedly was. Nevertheless, he refused to extend the seisachtheia, 'the shaking off of burdens', to any redistribution of the land owned by the nobility. A free peasantry was Solon's ideal, and indeed throughout the period Athens was a polis, smallholders comprised the majority of its citizen-body. Those citizens whom Solon had redeemed from bondage, both at home and abroad, probably found employment in the growing commercial sector of the economy; they took their place in a social hierarchy based not on birth, but on wealth, a major change of principle.

Eligible for the highest offices of state were the pentakosiomedimnoi or 500-bushel men. Through one of these one-year posts, the archonship, they could gain entry to the peerage, the Council of the Areopagus, whose life members oversaw the direction of state affairs. Named after Ares' hill, a craggy knoll north-west of the acropolis, the council originally advised the king in his capacity as war leader, priest and judge, but with the decline and disappearance of the monarchy the aristocratic councillors were left virtually in charge of the government. The next two classes, the hippeis, or knights, and the zeugitai, or yokemen, were eligible for minor offices and the new council of 400, the boule, which Solon set up. As the minimum income qualification for either was not high, most citizens in these middle classes would have served as hoplites. At first the hippeis, as lesser nobles, may have had precedence over the zeugitai, though the latter were able to stand for election as archons from 456 BC. The lowest class, the thetes, citizens with less than 200 measures of produce a year, were restricted to the assembly, the ecclesia.

The opening of politics to men of substance marked the end of the nobility's stranglehold on government, although not its dominance. The new non-aristocratic pentakosiomedimnoi took the first steps along the path to the democratic system of government which flourished in Athens after the Persian Wars. Yet for Solon the new boule was intended as a counterweight to the ecclesia; along with the Council of the Areopagus, he saw it as one of the two anchors securing the ship of state, so that it would 'pitch less in the surf and make the people less turbulent'. Its middle-class members had the role of preparing legislation to be voted upon by the general assembly of citizens.

The calming effect they were supposed to have exercised over debate seems singly absent in the passing of the earliest decree known to us, the ill-fated granting of a bodyguard to Peisistratus in 561 or 560 BC. The would-be tyrant appeared in the agora, claiming that he had been wounded by his rivals: Herodotus says the wounds were self inflicted. Aided by the bodyguard he was voted, his clubbearers, Peisistratus then seized the acropolis and power, though he was careful not to disturb Solon's constitutional arrangements. No suspicious Periander, the first Athenian tyrant conciliated the upper classes, recognized the social ambitions of the hoplites, and protected the poorest citizens, to whom he may have given land confiscated from exiled political opponents. Like the reformer, Peisistratus came to popular attention through military success against Megara; whereas Solon encouraged the Athenians to fight for Salamis, Peisistratus actually captured the port of Nisaea nearby and secured the Athenian claim to the island.

Appropriately, the statesman responsible for the final overthrow of tyranny in Athens also developed the democratic potential of Solon's constitution. Cleisthenes, the son of Megacles and Agariste, daughter of Cleisthenes of Sicyon, persuaded the prophetess at Delphi, in return for the services of the Alcmeonids in the rebuilding of the temple, to recommend to all Spartans consulting the oracle the freeing of the Athenians. Taking advantage of the confusion following the Spartan intervention of 510 BC, Cleisthenes enlisted the support of the citizen-body to weaken further the power of all noble families except his own. He achieved this by undermining the geographic basis of tribal loyalties. Within three main divisions, the city, the country, and the coast, demes or wards were grouped in tens to form trittys. One trittys was selected from each area and the resulting three combined into a new tribe. In all, ten new tribes replaced the four previously in existence, and each one elected fifty members of the boule, now the council of five hundred. While the old tribes continued as religious organizations, political consciousness focused upon the deme, trittys and new tribe as the means of governing the polis. The boule itself functioned as the engine of democracy, for without its assistance the ecclesia could never have exercised its sovereignty effectively.

The reason the councillors were unable to dominate Athens in the fifth century BC was due to annual elections and the limitation of membership to two terms. The packing of the Council of the Areopagus with supporters of the tyranny had sullied its name, though during the crisis with Persia a temporary revival of its influence in state affairs took place. After 461 BC, the council was reduced to a minor, if venerated, part of the judicial system, the court for cases of violent crime and arson. At the close of the Archaic Period, in 500 BC, the constitution Solon framed had become democratic, much to the dismay of the Spartans who were uneasy about the demos even when led and guided by aristocrats.

The device Cleisthenes is reputed to have introduced to deal with unconstitutional ambition was ostracism, the banishment of any citizen for a decade. If the assembly agreed to hold the annual ostracism, which it could forgo, then the citizen against whom most votes were cast went into exile without loss of property. Scathing about its later abuse, Aristotle comments that the Athenians attached 'such immense importance to the principle of equality above all else that they ostracized and sent abroad for fixed periods anyone whose power was thought to be excessive, whether this power was due to wealth or popularity or any other influence in the state.'

Against Peisistratus ostracism would have been a handy weapon, for this determined descendant of the Neleids of Pylos cleverly exploited the discontent which broke out after Solon retired abroad. The reformer seems to have left in order to avoid the clamour for amendment. His constitutional arrangements may have disappointed the hoplites, just as his reluctance to interfere with land tenure upset the thetes; and whilst the encouragement to settle he gave to foreign traders and craftsmen in the form of citizenship did much to stimulate commerce and industry, the rise of a money economy hardly assisted the small farmers and even threatened the apparently secure position of the nobles. A humanely revised law-code benefited all, especially in its provision of a right of appeal to the assembly, but laws inscribed on wooden slabs proved insufficient to bind together Athenian society.

The continued social unrest gave Peisistratus his chances for power. The plural is deliberate because his rule was a chequered one. First becoming tyrant in 560 BC, he was expelled after five years, returned to power temporarily before 550 BC, and finally secured his position in 545 BC with the aid of mercenary troops. Prior to his third attempt at tyranny, Peisistratus had established himself in Thrace, building up wealth from the local silver mines, organizing his invasion force, and making diplomatic contacts with powerful individuals outside Attica. One of his allies was Lygdamis, the future tyrant of Naxos. Peisistratus ruled from 545 until his death in 527 BC and was followed by his son Hippias, whose tyranny lasted down to the Spartan intervention of 510 BC. Although the mercenaries killed or drove into exile his irreconcilable opponents, Peisistratus receives praise from both Herodotus and Aristotle for his government of the Athenians. For the tyrant, once protected from political enemies, chose to rule through Solon's constitution, although always ensuring that his own supporters held the chief offices of state.

The thirty-five years during which the constitution operated, as it were, under the supervision of a tyranny, represent a key period of transition in Athens. There was no possibility of a straightforward return to aristocratic ways after 510 BC. The growing prosperity and political experience of the demos could not stomach a narrow oligarchy, so Cleisthenes' democratic programme won popular support. The reactionary nobles, led by Isagoras, tried ineffectively to put the clock back a century, not least by the disfranchisement of citizens enrolled since the time of Solon. In 508 BC they called in the Spartans to block the reforms and demand that Athens be governed by an oligarchy of 300 of Isagoras' followers. The Athenians rose, besieged Isagoras and the Spartan king Cleomenes on the acropolis, and after seeing them safely out of Attica, adopted the constitutional proposals of Cleisthenes.

The strength of this democratic feeling owes a lot, paradoxically, to Peisistratus. Apart from allowing Solon's constitution to work, the tyrant as a matter of policy fostered civic pride. Theseus acquired a set of legendary exploits comparable with the labours of Heracles, the Spartan hero. He was thought of as a good king who overcame local differences to unite the Athenians as a people. Athena, the city goddess, received a new temple on the acropolis, known as the hecatompedon because it was 100 long; and her birth-festival, the Panathenaea, enjoyed lavish patronage. Tradition also credits Peisistratus with creating the state festival of Dionysus, whose cult he transferred from Eleutherai, north of Eleusis, to Athens. Beneath the theatre of Dionysus, at the southern foot of the acropolis, there are traces of a building dating from the late sixth century BC. In one of the Great Dionysia under Peisistratus it is believed that Thespis won the prize when tragedy was first performed. Thespis added a story told by a narrator to the choral singing, thus preparing the way for dramatic dialogue between actor and chorus leader. Equally entertaining must have been the slapstick comedy of the komasts, whose behaviour and attire approximated to the satyrs, Dionysus' familiars. These actors and actresses enacted the Dionysiac rout, highlighting the humorous aspects of the god's domain, before their caperings were formally encompassed in the satyr play which followed each tragedy.

Another religious enterprise undertaken in Athens, on this occasion by Peisistratus the younger, Hippias' son, was the Olympieion, a temple dedicated to Zeus which lies south of the acropolis. Construction work was abandoned in 510 BC, when the Peisistratids went into exile, and some of the masonry eventually found its way into the city's defences. Fortifications did not surround Athens before the close of the Archaic Period. The Olympieion itself was only finished in AD 132 as part of the redevelopment of the city by the Roman emperor Hadrian. A work Peisistratus saw completed was the magnificent telesterion, a square hall with rock-cut seats like a theatre, with which he adorned the sanctuary of Demeter and Persephone at Eleusis. The fame of the mysterious rites practised here attracted visitors from many Greek states, a source of pride for Athenians and tyrant alike. In general tyrants enhanced state cults and festivals, to the detriment of the local shrines in the hands of the nobility, but the Peisistratids outdid their peers in the spate of propaganda they advanced to glorify the unity of Attica. By the deposition in 510 BC the Athenians were conscious of their heritage, proud of their state, and willing to defend its independence against both Persia and Sparta.

The assassination of Hipparchus, Peisistratus' second son, at the Panathenaea in 514 BC was looked upon by later Athenians as a blow struck for freedom. The murder in fact was motivated by personal hatred, and the lack of response from the demos shows that for all his harshness Hippias was not universally disliked. However, the shadow of the Persian threat was already darkening the political landscape and making the peace at home and abroad under the tyrants seem a very fragile commodity. Everywhere tyranny was patently accommodating itself to the Persians, who in 516 BC crossed to Europe and campaigned in Thrace against the Scythians. At the Athenian colony of Sigeum on the southern side of the Hellespont, Peisistratus' third son, Hegesistratus, was quite satisfied to rule under Persian authority. Even more worrying was the marriage of Hippias' daughter to the son of the pro-Persian tyrant of neighbouring Lampsacus. Sparta's successful intervention at Athens, as against tyrants in Phocis, Thessaly, Thasos, Naxos and Miletus, is therefore best understood as preliminary resistance to Persia. The era of tyranny was over, except where Persian arms prevailed, and the poleis of mainland Greece had a short breathing space in which to gather their strength.

Chapter Eight

THE EXPANSION OF THE GREEK WORLD

Not the least striking effect of geographical dispersion on the ancient Greeks was a sense of belonging to a single civilization: their penetration into distant waters and their contacts with the variety of peoples living along the Mediterranean shore confirmed a deep-rooted consciousness of the value of the polis as a system of government. No matter how small was the initial foundation of a colony, the settlers conducted themselves as the citizens of an independent city-state.

Unlike later Roman colonies, the new Greek settlements owed no political allegiance to their mother-states, for the founders had set out as pioneers blessed by the gods themselves. Divine approval was always sought for an expedition, very often from the oracle at Delphi. The Ionians in Asia Minor were sanctified by Apollo at his shrine in Didyma, some dozen kilometres south of Miletus. The temple of this important sanctuary was destroyed during the Ionian revolt by the Persians, who sacked both Miletus and Didyma in 494 BC. Its cult statue was taken by Darius, the Persian king, to his palace at Ecbatana, where it remained as a trophy until the arrival of Alexander the Great in 330 BC.

After the fall of Lydia to king Cyrus of Persia in 546 BC, the Milesians had enjoyed special privileges because the conqueror continued the treaty of friendship which existed between them and the Lydians: Cyrus the Great realized that he needed a grateful and busy seaport for his newly won province. Trouble with Persia came only in the reign of Darius, who succeeded Cambyses, Cyrus' son, in 522 BC. Internal strife and the machinations of Histiaeus, the tyrant appointed by Persia, caused the Milesians to revolt in 500 or 499 BC, but the fierceness with which other Greek cities followed this lead indicates the resentment they all felt towards the pro-Persian tyrannies imposed on them. Prior to the coming of Persian forces to the Anatolian seaboard, the Greek colonists had flourished as traders with the Lydians, the first people, Herodotus claims, to have used coinage. The drawing eastwards of the wealth of the area, into Persian treasuries sited well beyond the Euphrates River, may have undermined economic enterprise too. The early prosperity of Miletus was famous, as were the colonies she sponsored. The Milesians had already planted Sinope on the southern coast of the Black Sea and Cyzicus on the Asiatic coast of the Sea of Marmara by 750 BC. According to the Roman historian Pliny, there were seventy-five Milesian colonies alone in these north-eastern waters, including a number in the remote Crimea.

163

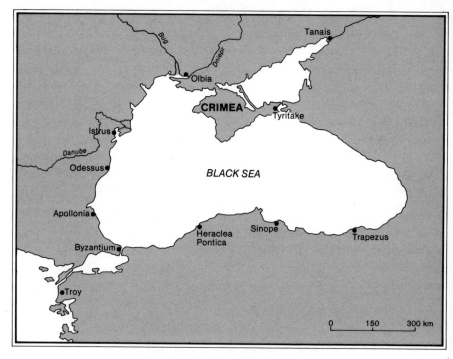

SOME OF THE GREEK COLONIES
ON THE BLACK SEA

Whilst the city-states of the Aeolian and Ionian Greeks in the east were less powerful than those on the Greek mainland, they prospered greatly from the growth of overseas commerce and obtained intellectual stimulation through close relations with the older civilizations of West Asia. These poleis were less exclusive in attitude and in blood, though their belief in the supremacy of Greek culture was by no means diluted. For a late Archaic Greek living in a city-state, the issue of contemporary politics seemed to revolve around the law. He would have regarded almost as barbarians Greek-speaking peoples like the Macedonians who still remained at a tribal stage of development. As a citizen of a self-governing community, tyrants notwithstanding, he found the acceptance of heredi-tary monarchy demeaning. The point was forcibly made by Demaratus, the exiled Spartan king in Xerxes' suite. At the very outset of the invasion of Greece, Herodotus tells us how Demaratus warned the Persian king that in the Spartan phalanx he would encounter an unmovable force, which to Xerxes' bewilderment he did at the defence of the pass at Thermopylae in 480 BC. Speaking of the courage of his fellow citizens, while the Persian expeditionary forces were in Thrace, Demaratus said:

Fighting singly, the Spartans are as good as any, but fighting in formation they are the best soldiers in the world. They are free men, but not altogether free, because the law is their master. This they fear as much as your subjects fear you. They always obey what the law commands; the order is always the same - stand firm, conquer or die however numerous the enemy may be.

Although Xerxes laughed, Demaratus was politely pointing out the gulf which separated Persian and Greek political thought. The Spartan reverence for law and order, as we have seen, was dictated by military considerations. Whereas the Athenians trained themselves in the arguments of the agora, the Spartans preferred the orders of the drill sergeant. Eschewing lengthy speeches and disputation, they acknowledged the effectiveness of fear in gaining citizen obedience rather than persuasion.

It is ironical that Herodotus expresses his own faith in a constitution via the mouth of a Spartan king, one of the last vestiges of Greek feudalism. Even more fascinating is the fact that law-codes appear to be one of the benefits derived from colonization. The earliest known legislation, dating from about 650 BC, belongs to Zaleucus of Locri, a settlement on the sole of Italy. Notorious for its severity, the code is said to have resolved civil disputes and left the Locrians with an aristocratic system of government. Other city-states in Italy and Sicily adopted the laws of Zaleucus, just as later they took advice from Charondas of Catania. Possibly the establishment of a colony tended to encourage the formulation of a law-code, especially where the colonists came from more than one mother-city, like Locri.

The fullest account we have of the sending out of any colony, that of Cyrene from Thera, does not specifically mention legal arrangements, but we are told that the colonists were sent out on terms of complete equality. About 640 BC a drought struck Thera; it lasted for seven years and the Therans were informed by the oracle at Delphi that relief would be obtained only if they set up a colony in Libya. Therefore, they conscripted on pain of death 200 young men from those families with more than one son, and dispatched them in two vessels under the leadership of a young nobleman by the name of Aristoteles. It was understood that if the colony failed and Thera could not offer further assistance, then after five years the colonists would be allowed to return with impunity to their homes and resume their civil rights. In the event the venture succeeded, once they moved inland to the well-watered site of Cyrene, where with Libyan cooperation a city was built. Yet the Therans still had to drive off with stones a small group of colonists who lost heart during the first two trying years of the enterprise. After the sixth year of its foundation, Cyrene opened its citizenship to any Greeks who might wish to settle.

The city grew prosperous on the export of corn, fruit and horses; silver coins were minted on the standard used by Athens, Corinth and Samos; and, not least, the population became sufficient to form further settlements at Barce, an inland site to the west, and on the coast at Euhesperides, present-day Benghazi.

The Cyrenaeans managed to fend off the Egyptians but they could not preserve their independence after the Persian conquest of Egypt. In 525 BC they submitted to Cambyses and remained within the Persian empire until around 475 BC. Twenty years later they were able to shelter the survivors of the ill fated Athenian expedition to Egypt. The Athenians and their allies had intervened in support of a local rising against Persian rule and, though at first victorious, a powerful Persian counterattack annihilated both the expeditionary army and a fleet of 200 ships.

Surviving coins of Cyrene often bear the head of Zeus Ammon and represent the supreme Greek deity with the curling ram's horns of Ammon, an Egyptian sky god. This is a compliment to the respected oracle at the oasis of Siwa, 500 kilometres to the south-east in the Libyan desert, whose fame in the Greek world came to rival that of Delphi. When Herodotus inquired about the history of Siwa, he was told by the priests at Thebes, the former Egyptian capital and the city sacred to Ammon, that two priestesses had been abducted by Phoenicians, who sold one in Libya and the other in Greece. These women, the priests asserted, were the founders of divination in these countries, setting up the original oracles.

Ingenious as the answer is, the chief centre of cultural relations between the Greeks and the Egyptians during the Archaic Period was Naucratis, a trading station in the Nile Delta. One tradition of its origin in the early part of the sixth century BC records that thirty Milesian ships founded a fort at the mouth of the Nile, before sailing upriver to defeat an Egyptian squadron and establish a permanent base at Naucratis. But Herodotus says that it was pharaoh Amasis, a strong philhelline, who gave the site to the Greeks some time after 570 BC. Presumably this refers to a new charter, since Greeks are known to have been active in Egypt from the reign of Psammetichus I. The elevation of this monarch to the throne in 664 BC was accomplished with the aid of Ionian and Carian adventurers, whom Psammetichus had engaged as mercenaries in order to capture Memphis. Their accidental arrival on the Egyptian coast through a storm seemed to fulfil an oracle so that he was delighted to welcome the 'brazen men', clearly a reference to hoplite armour. Another pharaoh who used large numbers of Greek mercenaries was Psammetichus II, who campaigned with them against the Nubians in 591 BC. On the colossal rock-cut statues at Abu Simbel, over 900 kilometres up the Nile, some of these soldiers of fortune carved their names: Elesibios of Teos, Pabis of Colophon and Telephos from Ialysos on Rhodes.

Naucratis, like Al Mina in northern Syria, was a commercial settlement rather than a colony. The eastern Greeks dominated the concession, and in particular the Milesians and the Samians, though from the Greek mainland the Aeginetans also received a large measure of royal favour. Excavation of Naucratis has revealed a mass of finds, including a temple built for Hera by Samian merchants and one for Apollo, which apparently dates from the Milesian foundation. Another deity who received worship was Aphrodite; the Chians are credited with the construction of her sanctuary but, as she was the protectress of sailors and the giver of calm weather, her devotees would have come from every Greek state trading there. A story of her powers over the sea actually concerns Naucratis. *En route* to Egypt a merchant is said to have bought a statuette of the goddess at Paphos in Cyprus, from which his crew begged for succour when a violent storm suddenly blew up near the end of the voyage. Responding to their urgent entreaties amid towering seas and swirling foam, Aphrodite bedecked her own statue and the superstructure of the vessel with sweet-scented myrtle, one of her favourite plants. Soon the sun came out, and they made harbour. In gratitude the merchant took his Aphrodite and her myrtle branches off to the goddess' temple in Naucratis, dedicated them to her, and then invited his friends and family to a feast in the temple precincts, crowning each of them with a myrtle wreath. The association of myrtle, its pungent leaves and flowers, with love and fertility in the worship of Aphrodite serves to remind us of sacral prostitution. At Naucratis it is impossible to be sure that her cult was so served, though Herodotus notes that the prostitutes there seemed particularly attractive. The famous Rhodopis was redeemed at great expense from slavery in Naucratis by Charaxus of Mytilene, brother of the poetess Sappho. Rhodopis decided not to follow her admirer home, much to the annoyance of Sappho; instead, she continued as a courtesan and because of her beauty amassed a fortune, one-tenth of which was presented to Apollo at Delphi. Herodotus saw her offerings and in recent years an inscription relating to Rhodopis' dedication has come to light.

Life in Naucratis must have been hectic in its heyday, before the Persians defeated the Egyptians in 525 BC at the battle of Pelusium. Greek merchants brought wine, olive oil and silver; they may have shipped timber too, an Egyptian import from the Aegean since Minoan times: what they sought in exchange was linen, papyrus and, above all, corn. The population boom behind the colonization movement of the Archaic Period encouraged trade in basic foodstuffs, with Greek merchantmen plying the seas between colonies, cities on the Greek mainland and foreign countries. Naucratis, an earlier version of Alexandria, was well placed as an entrepôt for this expanded world of commerce, and its various public buildings are proof of a development beyond the stage of a simple

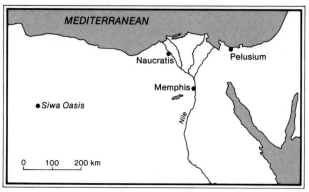

EGYPT, SHOWING THE GREEK ENTREPOT
OF NAUCRATIS

trading-post, which Al Mina essentially remained. To Naucratis came not only merchants and sailors but also poets, philosophers, artists, historians and statesmen. Here they became conscious of the immense antiquity of a sophisticated civilization and observed the relics of a once mighty empire – colossal statues, temples, shrines, tombs, pyramids and cities.

Tradition says that the Milesian sage Thales visited Naucratis in order to study Egyptian methods of land measurement. Because of the annual inundation of the Nile, which disordered the boundaries of agricultural holdings, the pharaohs employed surveyors to ensure that for taxation purposes any significant changes were recorded. 'Perhaps,' Herodotus remarks, 'this was the way in which geometry was invented, and passed afterwards to Greece.' Thales was regarded as a practical astronomer and geometer, hence his inclusion amongst the Seven Sages, whose contributions to the world the Greeks praised for their usefulness. His prediction of the eclipse in 585 BC probably owes something to Babylonian records, which he may have obtained at Sardis; his theory of winds causing the overflow of the Nile suggests a close interest in the river and the Egyptian response to its ways. Even more indicative of borrowing is Thales' view of the universe. He thought that water was the first principle from which everything is fashioned and from which it takes its life-giving force. Specifically, Thales said the earth floated like a raft on the primal waters, an idea common to both Egyptian and Mesopotamian cosmologies.

In Miletus, Thales initiated the entire history of philosophical speculation as it is known in Europe. He and his disciple Anaximander set the pattern of Greek rationalism with their attempts to explain the perceptible world in the light of observation and reasoned theories rather than inherited assumptions. The impact of oriental knowledge upon them was

168

obviously decisive, but their reliance on the intellect determined that they were never uncritical recipients. To the question of how the physical universe evolved, Anaximander gave a more complex answer when he wrote that primal matter was boundless, infinite and everlasting. He argued that our world is produced by the interaction of opposite elements – hot and cold, wet and dry. In one fragment of his treatise, the first philosophical prose, written about 546 BC, he claims that the earth is drying up, thereby implying that it may disintegrate in accordance with the rule of time and return to the state of original undifferentiated matter.

As we possess only parts of his writings, there is no certainty that Anaximander did not envisage this alteration as one aspect of a cyclical process. Such a view was held by Xenophanes of Colophon, who left Ionia for Sicily on the fall of his native city to the Persians in 546 or 545 BC. Xenophanes was impressed by fossils of plant and animal life embedded in rocks far from the sea, and deduced that the earth was once mud. Following Anaximander, who thought that mankind derived ultimately from mud, he argued that destruction resulted not from drought but flood, perhaps recalling the deluge sent by Zeus as a punishment during the lifetime of Deucalion, the Greek Noah. Living things die, then the waters recede and the cycle of creation starts anew. The divergence between the two philosophers turns on their observation of natural phenomena; for Anaximander the earth was being dried up by the sun, for Xenophanes it was already reverting into sea or mud.

While the third great Milesian, Anaximenes, agreed with Xenophanes about the perpetual changes through which the universe moves, he thought the primal matter was air and its alteration was the motive force, as the air became denser or more rarefied. The earth itself was flat, floating on air. Anaximenes explained the existence of the heavenly bodies as exhalations arising from its surface; when the vapour rose it was converted high above the earth into the fire of the sun and the stars. Milesian speculation was never merely theoretical, however; the archaic Greeks failed to distinguish clearly between science and philosophy, and in this lay their strength as original thinkers. Thales devised a method for measuring the distance of ships at sea; and Anaximander was the first to draw 'an outline of land and sea', an exercise later refined into a map of the known world by the geographer Hecataeus, another citizen of Miletus.

An extensive traveller in West Asia and in consequence an expert on the resources of the Persian empire, Hecataeus advised in vain the Milesians against starting a rebellion in 500 BC. His realism was shared by Delphi, since the oracle appreciated the might necessary to subdue Lydia under king Croesus. When in 545 BC the people of Cnidos inquired about the construction of a defensive canal against the Persians the priestess bluntly replied that Apollo would have made Cnidus an island if he had wished it so. The flowering of Ionian philosophy occurred against a background of severe political upheaval. Some communities emigrated on the Persian approach, others were decimated in the Ionian revolt, not least splendid Miletus. It was Ionia's tragedy, and the good fortune of the Greek mainland, that half a century elapsed before Persia was ready to resume its advance westwards.

At the end of the sixth century BC there flourished at Ephesus one of the most enigmatic of all Greek philosophers, Heraclitus. He was no less disturbing to the traditionalist than Xenophanes, though he did not follow the ruthless assaults of the latter on social convention and myth. Tilting at the blatant human attributes of the Olympian gods, Xenophanes had said that if cattle could draw, they would make their own gods in the likeness of cattle. Heraclitus also believed in a single non-anthropomorphic deity or an underlying cosmic principle, which he identified as logos and fire, but he advanced philosophy by considering the structure and behaviour of the natural world. He grasped that its coherence depended more on how matter behaved than on what it was made of. He may even have thought an apparently solid object like a stone was undergoing unseen changes of substance. A key image in Heraclitus is the

Recontruction of Hecataeus' world map, which was compiled in the late sixth century BC.

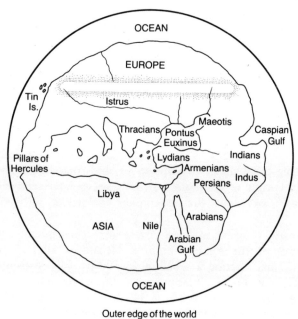

Outer edge of the world

river, which looks the same but is in reality a stream of different water. The river image seems to illustrate best his notion of the natural order of the world as a fiery balance of opposites, persisting through and governing the endless alterations of things. As Heraclitus wrote: 'This world no god or man has made; it was, is now, and ever shall be an everlasting fire, with some parts kindling and other parts going out.' Such independence of mind was a spur to the individualism that the Greeks first made a salient feature of European civilization. It was, moreover, a conscious contribution to the sum of human knowledge because Heraclitus deposited his book in the temple of Artemis at Ephesus. Even though his disconcertingly original style of thought and expression later caused him to be called the riddler, Heraclitus wished to make his ideas the common property of his fellow citizens, and part of the new literate culture of the polis.

The last great thinker of the Archaic Age was Pythagoras, who was born on the island of Samos but left around 531 BC in order to escape from the tyranny of Polycrates. Westwards he travelled like Xenophanes and in southern Italy founded a famous school at Croton. The followers of Pythagoras appear to have been a mystical society held together by common beliefs and practices. They considered the soul immortal, accepted its transmigration through animals and plants as well as men, and as a result professed the kinship of all living things. The late commentator Diogenes Laertius says that Pythagoras could remember the details of his own four previous incarnations because Hermes, the messenger of the gods, had granted him a miraculous memory. Diogenes Laertius also records how the Pythagoreans refrained from eating certain foods, such as red mullet, the hearts of animals and pulses. Indeed, 'windy' beans were thought to be dangerous 'wasters of the breath of life'. Amusing as the Pythagorean prohibition may now seem to us, it was once part of a philosophy which reverenced the unity of life and envisaged the progress of the soul through its diverse forms until the attainment of final release, in some pure realm of existence. Another ancient commentator preserves not only a total ban on the eating of flesh but association with either hunters or butchers. For a while the Pythagoreans exercised a strong political influence in Megale Hellas or Greater Greece, as Italy was then called, but after the Crotoniates expelled Pythagoras the fortunes of the society began to decline. The philosopher died in retirement at Metapontum, an Achaean colony just west of Tarus.

Pythagoras' interest in numbers seems essentially mystical. Yet his attempt to find a mathematical structure in the natural world did represent an important development in scientific thinking, namely the formulation of quantitative method. Perhaps this preoccupation with mathematics owes something to his Samian upbringing, for Herodotus credits the Samians with 'three of the greatest building and engineering feats in the Greek world'. The first was a tunnel nearly one kilometre long cut through living rock by Eupalinos about 530 BC so as to supply the chief settlement on the island with water. It relied on gravity to ensure a steady flow, a circumstance making the calculation of the slope critical. Eupalinos hailed from Megara, where a century earlier the tyrant who had backed Cylon's attempted seizure of power in Athens installed an underground conduit system. Public works and tyranny went hand in hand during the Archaic Period, if only for the reason that the tyrants were the first individuals since the Mycenaean princes who commanded sufficient power and resources to undertake major projects. Self-glorification was naturally involved, though in contrast to non-Greek rulers it must be said that they tended to build for themselves neither lavish palaces nor imposing tombs.

The second great work, according to Herodotus, was 'the artificial harbour enclosed by a breakwater, which ran into twenty fathoms of water and had a total length of one-third of a kilometre'. Again the hand of Polycrates may be correctly seen in its building. Although Thucydides states that the Corinthians first achieved notable advances in shipbuilding, there is more than a distinct possibility that the dazzling successes Polycrates enjoyed also rested on an improved design for the warship. The tyrant had a fleet of 100 penteconters, or fifty-oared galleys, but evidently turned to the construction of more efficient and powerful triremes, possibly in response to the new sea power of Persia. It was after all the acquisition of the Phoenician navy which allowed Persian arms to threaten the Aegean islands, and so Polycrates' shipbuilding programme may have owed something to Phoenician prototypes. We cannot be sure about his technological debt. His domination of the Aegean, however, is quite apparent from the writings of both Herodotus and Thucydides. The new triremes Polycrates deployed were able to sink other warships by ramming them amidships. They achieved the speed necessary for an effective ram by increasing the number of rowers without loss of stability, through an ingenious seating arrangement. At the battle of Salamis in 480 BC, the Greek triremes each had a crew of 200 men, who left on shore masts and sails so as to convert their vessels into deadly projectiles.

Herodotus names as the third wonder on Samos the Heraeum, 'the biggest of all known Greek temples'. Polycrates embarked on this temple of Hera about 530 BC with the expressed intention of surpassing all its predecessors in size and splendour. Measuring 111 by 55 metres, it stood on a platform ten steps high and possessed 123 columns. The vast project was only begun during Polycrates' ascendancy and, with the decline of Samian fortunes after his death in 521 BC, it remained under construction for centuries, work still being in progress under the Romans.

172

From the outset of Ionian settlement of the island the sanctuary of Hera had received special attention. As the cult legend claimed that the goddess was born beneath a tree, and was wedded to Zeus there as well, the initial arrangement of the precinct comprised a sacred tree with a stone altar and, a little way off, a thatched shrine of wood housing the goddess' effigy. About 800 BC a long, narrow temple, thirty-two by six metres, was built, of mud brick laid on stone foundations, with a row of wooden posts down the centre supporting a roof of thatch or clay. Then in 570 BC, a decision was taken to enlarge the Heraeum to colossal proportions. Of the motive we know almost nothing, except that Samos was growing very wealthy on maritime trade and at the time maintained extremely close links with Egypt, whence the idea for large multi-columned stone temples could have come. The new temple was erected in stone, roofed with terracotta tiles of Corinthian type, and adorned with sculpture: its accidental destruction by fire just before 530 BC presented Polycrates with his opportunity to outdo everyone else.

Competition in temple building was stimulated by the generosity of Croesus, who came to the Lydian throne in 560 BC. He financed the new temple at Ephesus for the goddess Artemis as part of a propaganda campaign to demonstrate how Greeks living within his territories could equal the achievements of the offshore islanders. In the process evolved the Ionic order of architecture, which differs from the Doric style favoured on the Greek mainland in having far more carved ornament, because marble was used as soon as the switch from wood occurred. The friezes on Ionic temples raised during the Archaic Age would have been achievements well worthy of Herodotus' praise.

Plan of the temple of Artemis at Ephesus. Heraclitus left his writings here.

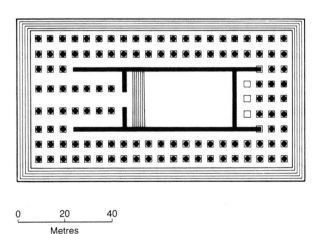

0   20   40

Metres

Underlying the upsurge of activity amongst the eastern Greeks was an increase in population. Several attempts to estimate the numbers of inhabitants in the main settlements have been made, and tentatively based as they are on the few sites explored, the figures do provide a picture of populous city-states. Miletus is credited with 64,000 inhabitants; Samos may have supported slightly under 50,000 people, while the larger island of Chios some 80,000. The rise of slavery may have pushed up the Chian total, for we are aware that these islanders were the first Greeks to acquire non-Greek slaves on a large scale. As Chios lacked any very developed industry, they would have employed the majority of their foreign slaves on the land. Some of them would have toiled for Thales on the occasion he is said to have secured a monopoly by hiring all the olive presses of Miletus and Chios, when he correctly foresaw a bumper crop.

The occasional involvement of the philosopher in commerce, as Sappho's brother Charaxus in the wine trade with Egypt, indicates the importance of economic activity towards the close of the Archaic Age. Neither the Milesian sage nor the Lesbian nobleman regarded business as something beneath their dignity, and both were pleased to reap a handsome profit. Whether Charaxus deliberately transported his wine to Naucratis in order to enrich himself, or simply used it as a means of financing a visit to Egypt, there is no way of telling. The event was remembered because of Charaxus' infatuation for the prostitute Rhodopis, on whom he vainly squandered everything he had gained. This was the folly that angered his sister so much.

Ionia flourished on trade, Miletus in particular. Milesian ships plied northern, western, and eastern waters: they traded with the Greek colonists settled on the Black Sea as well as the Scythian tribesmen who lived on the steppelands of the interior, carrying mostly luxury goods such as bronze vessels, painted pottery, jewellery, perfume and woollen cloth; they exported to Italy both pottery and wool – at Sybaris the demand for finespun Milesian wool was apparently insatiable; and they traded silver, pottery, wood and wine in Egypt and Syria. On their return journeys they invariably carried corn for the hungry cities of the Aegean.

Another important food import was salted fish. At the settlement near Tyritake, in the eastern Crimea, archeologists have uncovered twenty-four reservoirs for pickling, with the bones of fish on their floors. Similar facilities would have existed at the Milesian colony of Olbia, sited close to the Bug, a few kilometres before that river joins the great Dniepr. According to Herodotus the Dniepr was

> the most valuable and productive not only of the rivers in this part of the world, but everywhere else, with the sole exception of the Nile ... It provides the finest and most abundant pasture, by far the richest supply

of the best sorts of fish, and the most excellent water for drinking ... No better crops grow anywhere than along its banks ... An unlimited supply of salt is formed by natural processes at the mouth of the river, which also furnishes a large boneless fish, good for pickling.

Olbia was fortified and possessed a gridiron street plan. Its attractiveness as a city is also recorded by Herodotus, who mentions the house built there by the Scythian king Scylas. Literate in Greek through the education he received from his Milesian mother, Scylas enjoyed entering the town alone and behaving like a colonist. He was able to sustain this double life only as long as the fiercely traditional Scythians were kept in ignorance. Scylas' deposition was inevitable when an Olbian secretly allowed his chiefs to observe him taking part in a Dionysian festival. Excavation of Scythian royal burials this century has shown how interested its members were in things Greek; objects recovered include vases and jewellery either of Aegean or colonial origin.

The horizons of the culture Scylas found so irresistible in Olbia were of course expanding both geographically and intellectually. While the Samians excelled in practical applications of scientific and technological advance and the Milesians concentrated on understanding natural phenomena, eastern Greek poets also reflected the growing emancipation from traditional attitudes and ways. The new critical outlook on the world is already plain in the surviving work of Archilochus, who deserves the title of the first cynical poet in European literature. Discoveries of inscriptions on his native Paros since World War II have confirmed the tradition that this master of invective was as much honoured as Homer in antiquity.

Though his dates remain a matter of dispute, Archilochus appears to have flourished some time after 650 BC. The bastard son of an aristocrat, he managed to combine a disregard for the accepted code of military honour with a contempt for his social inferiors. He spent a considerable period of his life outside Paros, fighting; he was a mercenary who felt 'the lovely gift of the Muses'. He died in an engagement, probably in Thrace, opposite the Parian colony of Thasos. 'We were the scum of Greece that went to Thasos,' Archilochus admits with utter frankness. Scandalizing the Spartan notion of heroism, he adds that he lost his shield 'somewhere in the bushes' during an early campaign against the Thracians. The terseness and vigour of Archilochus' verse can be seen from the few fragments we are lucky enough to possess. His voice comes straight across the millennia in this curse on an unfaithful friend: 'May they pull him frozen stiff and hung with seaweed from the waves, his teeth chattering, his lips vomiting brine, his body sprawling face down like a dog on the sand.' Then the Thracians can haul the wretch off to 'eat the bread of slavery'. Cursing, fighting, drinking and loving – these topics fill Archilochus' poems; a remarkable description of a sexual encounter, thirty-five lines in all, was discovered on a papyrus quite recently.

A younger contemporary of Archilochus and a Samian by birth was Semonides, a poet famous for his satire on the evil propensities of women, whom he compared to sows, vixens and bitches. Less accomplished in style, Semonides did express by implication the overwhelmingly masculine ethos of the period. The ideal woman, like a busy bee, looked after the home. In the growing acceptance of homosexuality, which was complete by the sixth century BC, can perhaps be discerned a further reduction in the status of women.

Yet in the verses of Sappho, the outstanding Archaic poetess, there is no word of any bitterness in relations between the sexes. She speaks of her own feelings, often jealous and frustrated affections, but these invariably concern girls, who were fellow members of a circle dedicated to the service of Aphrodite and the Muses. Sappho appears to have composed a number of ephithalamia, songs celebrating their marriages, besides a fine range of love poems. One charming lyric which has come down to us celebrates the joy she took in the company of her own young daughter. Born on Lesbos about 610 BC, Sappho belonged to the extraordinarily creative Aeolian school of poetry, founded on the island by Terpander fifty years earlier. Tradition attributed to Terpander the invention of the seven-stringed lyre, which he used to such good effect during his sojourn in Sparta that he persuaded his listeners to settle their differences amicably after the Second Messenian war.

Terpander's other renowned successor was Alcaeus, whose life roughly corresponds with that of Sappho. Alcaeus could not avoid political conflict, since when he was still a boy his brothers overthrew Melanchros, tyrant of Mytilene, the greatest of the Aeolian cities. Alcaeus records his struggles against the equally unsatisfactory successors of the tyrant, including Pittacus. Neither in exile nor at home was the poet reconciled to the decision of the Mytilenaeans to invite Pittacus to rule them for ten years. In Alcaeus' eyes this limited tyranny was as bad as a permanent despotism, though Pittacus seems to have forgiven the poet for the abuse he heaped on him even before he resigned his powers in 580 BC. The sentiment would have been shared by Archilochus who, no admirer of the demos, was nevertheless a political realist when he said, 'Gyges and all his wealth are of no interest to me ... I've no desire for a great tyranny'. For Alcaeus the strength of the polis was its citizens, not any mighty fortifications raised by a tyrant. The Melesian poet Phocylides, writing in the second half of the sixth century BC, gives the clearest expression of Greek independence in the Archaic Age. When he states 'a small, well-ordered city ... is better than senseless Nineveh'.

Preference for life in the city-state did not prevent a brother of Alcaeus seeking employment as a soldier of fortune in West Asia. A poem welcomes him back from a term in the army of Nebuchadnezzar, king of Babylon. After a three-month siege in 612 BC, the Babylonians with the aid of the Medes had captured Nineveh, broken Assyrian power, and then gone on to successfully dispute with Egypt control of Syria at the battle of Carchemish in 605 BC. Following the Egyptian example, or possibly because garrisons of Greek mercenaries were left behind after the Egyptian retreat, the Babylonians recruited hoplites for their own campaigns, though after Carchemish they chose not to invade Egypt. This conquest occurred only in 525 BC, at the hands of the Persians: they were led on this occasion by Cambyses, whose father Cyrus the Great had subjugated the Medes in 550 BC and captured Babylon in 539 BC. But great events abroad were not for the Melesian Phocylides. He preferred to have 'a middle rank in the city', ignoring the ostentation of the rich and the clamour of the poor. He doubtless derided the socially mobile, who aped aristocratic manners. His delight in citizenship may be regarded as a perfect testimonial for the polis, yet even in his native Miletus tyranny and Persian pressure were accepted facts of daily life. Despite Phocylides' earnest wish for tranquillity, the power of Persia was about to place the Aegean at the centre of international affairs.

At the other extreme of the Greek world, in Sicily, another conflict was developing with a powerful neighbour. The enemy here was Kart-Hadasht, New City, the Phoenician colony of Carthage. The cause of the conflict was Greek penetration of areas long under Carthaginian influence. As early as 600 BC, we know that an armed struggle existed, for Thucydides says that 'the Phocaeans, when they were founding Massilia, defeated the Carthaginians in a naval engagement'. The reverse was quite serious. The energetic Phocaeans soon moved on from what is now Marseilles to Spain, where they put down a number of settlements and tapped the valuable metal trade. Their cordial relations with the native inhabitants of Tartessus, which we noticed in Chapter Six, ended the monopoly of Carthage over the wealth of the Iberian Peninsula. A combined operation by the Etruscans and the Carthaginians about 535 BC expelled Phocaean colonists from Atalia, a city established thirty years earlier on the eastern coast of Corsica. The island, which fell under the influence of the Etruscan cities of Italy for some time, later became a Carthaginian possession. The Greeks apparently never tried to colonize neighbouring Sardinia, leaving the Carthaginians with no opposition other than the fierce hillsmen of the island's rugged interior, who may have been only partially subdued.

Where the Greeks and the Carthaginians found themselves locked in earnest combat was on Sicily, first settled in 735 or 734 BC by Greek colonists at Naxos, situated on a low peninsula on the coast north of Etna. The rather poor location led within a decade to the foundation of a second city at Leontini, which possessed a commanding hillside position at the southern edge of the plain of Catania, the largest stretch of fertile lowland in eastern Sicily. According to one tradition, the Chalcidian settlers made an agreement on oath to live in peace with the indigenous people, the Sicels, who were supposed to have arrived shortly before from the Italian mainland. The amity at Leontini was unusual; elsewhere, the natives were ejected from colonized sites, and at Syracuse the Corinthians reduced those they captured to serfdom. The colonies built by Syracuse at Acrae in 663 BC and at Casmenae in 643 BC were intended to consolidate the power of the city over its hinterland. That both colonies stood on easily defended hilltops should suggest a military function, an important role in maintaining the subjection of the Sicel serfs, even without the enormous deposit of weapons unearthed in the temple precinct of Casmenae.

Syracuse, destined to become the greatest Greek city in the western Mediterranean, was founded in 734 BC on an outstanding harbour site. The wide bay was sheltered by the island of Ortygia, which nearly joins the mainland at its north-western corner. On Ortygia have been discovered the earliest Greek houses; they were erected directly on top of huts belonging to Sicels, whom Thucydides tells us the Corinthians drove from the island. Quickly the colony spread onto the mainland, where a cemetery has provided evidence of Corinthian occupation in the form of stone sarcophagi and painted pottery. A second source of early sherds is the site of the temple dedicated to Athena on Ortygia. The first temple appears to have been constructed with timber and bricks, but in the fifth century BC, when the prosperity of Syracuse was climbing to a new height, a magnificent stone building arose in its stead. Today its fine Doric columns support the roof of the cathedral of Syracuse, because in the seventh century AD, the building was transformed into a Christian place of worship.

Sicily remains full of churches which incorporate elements of Greek and Roman temples, but nowhere is the original more evident than at Syracuse. Another remarkable temple started during the Archaic period on Ortygia must have rivalled the enormous dimensions of the temples of Ionian Ephesus and Samos, but like Polycrates' Heraeum, the unidentified structure was never finished. In spite of a first-rate harbour and a sizeable urban population, Syracuse financed such construction through agricultural wealth drawn from the extensive area it held inland, as much as 4,000 square kilometres by 500 BC. The fact is reflected in the name taken by its ruling aristocracy, the Gamoroi, literally, 'those who divided the land'. As Sicily lacked metals, colonization rested on farming from the outset. At least two ancient commentators attribute the wealth of Acragas in the fifth century BC to its olive and wine exports to Carthage. The splendid ruins of its temples, especially the one to Zeus Olympios, still impress the modern visitor to Agrigento, the name by which Acragas is now called. Allowing for some exaggeration about the luxurious tastes of the Carthaginians, the volume of trade must have been very considerable in order to support the building of the great temple terrace, at the southern end of the city, just inside the defences. Founded in 580 BC by Rhodian and Cretan Gela, Acragas was planned on a grand scale, its initial circuit wall enclosing over two square kilometres.

The main export of Syracuse would seem to have been grain. We can deduce this from the aid which the Syracusans gave to Rome during the Second Punic War. Following the disastrous Roman defeats at Trasimene Lake in 216 BC and Cannae in 215 BC, they dispatched to Rome substantial shipments of wheat and barley. Presumably Hiero, then self-styled king of Syracuse, felt it was better to help the Romans fight Hannibal in Italy than wait for that Carthaginian general's inevitable attack on Sicily, once Rome had fallen. After Hiero's death relations between the Romans and the Syracusans rapidly deteriorated until, after a two-year siege, Syracuse was sacked in 211 BC.

The quarrel between the Greeks and the Carthaginians in Sicily may be dated to 580 BC. The capture that year of the Carthaginian city of Lilybaeum, at the western end of the island, inaugurated serious hostilities. The Carthaginians and their indigenous allies, the Elymites, were obliged to expel the Cnidian conquerors, who withdrew in disorder to colonize the Lipari Islands. Within fifty years Carthaginian armies were crossing regularly from Africa to campaign in Sicily. Radical though this change of policy was on the part of Carthage, it was Greek pressure that brought about the offensive. Prior to the arrival of Greek colonists, the Carthaginians settled 'all round Sicily, occupying headlands and offshore islands for the sake of trade with the Sicels. But when the Greeks began to sail there in large numbers,' Thucydides continues, 'they abandoned most of these and concentrated at Motya, Solveis and Panormos, in the neighbourhood of the Elymites, partly because of their alliance with these people, and partly because from here the sea crossing from Sicily to Carthage is the shortest.'

The activities of the Phocaeans in the western Mediterranean stiffened the Carthaginian resolve to hold back the Greeks in Sicily. The combined Carthaginian and Etruscan attack on Atalia can be interpreted as a pre-emptive strike against troublemakers: there is strong evidence to suggest the Phocaeans, like the Cnidians at Lipari, were ready to turn to piracy whenever the opportunity occurred. In order to mobilize adequate resources for the struggle with the Greeks the city of Carthage formed a league, which included her powerful neighbour of Utica. Although this Phoenician colony was a no more willing partner than any other member of the Spartan league, the need for mutual defence was pressing. In 514 BC, for example, the Carthaginians had to prevent an attempt led by a Spartan named Dorieus to found a settlement at the mouth of the Cinyps River in Libya not far from existing Phoenician cities at Sabratha and Leptis. In Spain as well Carthaginian soldiers rolled back the Phocaeans, destroying the westernmost outpost of Massalia near Malaga. The frustration of Greek expansion in the west, principally by Carthage but also by Etruria, forms the background of Hamilcar's attack on Syracuse in 480 BC. After this disaster Carthage stood aloof from politics in Sicily, though because of the bitter rivalries among the Greek cities it was inevitable that from time to time conflicts should occur into which Carthage was occasionally drawn.

In Sicily and Italy the Greeks destroyed their own settlements: Syracuse wiped out in 553 BC, and again in 484 BC, its colony of Camarina: the Ionian city of Siris on the instep of Italy fell to an assault by neighbouring Sybaris and Metapontum some time before 520 BC, and Sybaris itself, proverbial for the riches enjoyed by its citizens, let internal dissension bring about a Crotoniate sack in 510 BC. The River Crathis was diverted by the Crotoniates from its course to flow over ruined Sybaris, so that Sybarite exiles could never rebuild on the site.

Friction between the Greek colonists in eastern Sicily marked the saga of Megara Hyblaea, whose foundation in 728 BC we know was fraught with difficulties. Thucydides records the sequence of events: he writes that

> Lamis arrived in Sicily with a group of colonists from Megara. He founded a place called Trotilus on the river Pantacyas, and then left there in order to join up with the Chalcidians at Leontini. After being expelled by them, he founded Thapsus, where he died. His followers were forced to leave Thapsus and found the place called Hyblaean Megara. Hyblon, a Sicel king, gave them the land and invited them to settle. For two hundred and forty-five years they lived here, after which they were driven out of the city by Gelon, tyrant of Syracuse. Before this happened though, they sent out Pamillus and founded Selinus. He had come from their mother-city of Megara in order to assist with the new foundation.

Pamillus may have arrived with reinforcements, especially if Megara Hyblaea was already overshadowed by the Syracusans. The original leader Lamis appears a reckless amateur in the narrative. Trotilus, a rocky headland with a small harbour, lacked adequate farmland, while Thapsus was a low-lying and waterless peninsula, suitable for little more than a temporary trading post. An eighth-century burial in a reused Bronze Age chamber tomb at Thapsus could well be that of Lamis and a companion. In conflict with the neighbouring Leontinians the hapless Megarans were only saved by the intervention of a Sicel ruler, whose name may be commemorated in that of the colony. Hyblon's motives are unexplained, though not entirely obscured. His own stronghold was barely twenty kilometres inland from Syracuse: its abandonment about 700 BC must have been a result of Syracusan activity. Having seen his subjects thrown off the island of Ortygia and heard of the quarrel at Leontini, Hyblon probably hoped to obtain effective Greek allies through his generosity. The site of Megara Hyblaea is quite defenceless and could only have been occupied by permission of the local people. His plan failed and in retaliation the Syracusans set out to subdue all the Sicels in the immediate area. Another political consideration might have been alliances in mainland Greece, where the Lelantine war divided states according to their support for the contestants, Chalcis and Eretria. Whereas the Corinthians sided with the Chalcidians, the Eretrians received help from the Megarans, whose own holdings in the Isthmus were already threatened by Corinthian ambitions.

Gelon's destruction of Megara Hyblaea was part of the tyrant's plans for making Syracuse the most populous and powerful city-state in the Greek world. Having transferred his base from Gela in 485 BC, where he left his brother in charge, Gelon fortified Syracuse, expanded its territories, and built up an imposing army and navy. As his military strength was so great, the mainland Greeks, who were preparing to resist Persia, sought his aid in 481 BC. But in vain, for Gelon asked in return for participation in the war that he be made commander-in-chief of the Greek forces, or at least commander of the navy. Aware that the Carthaginians were planning to attack the Greek portion of Sicily, while Greece itself was embroiled with the Persian invaders, the tyrant demanded impossible terms so as to be free to defend his own position in the west. The actual attack on Megara Hyblaea in 483 BC was provoked by its oligarchs, who foolishly tried to oppose Gelon. Herodotus says that after the surrender, the tyrant 'brought to Syracuse men of substance, who had started the war and therefore expected to be put to death, and made them citizens; the common people, who imagined they would be treated well because they had had no share of responsibility for the war, he also took to Syracuse and then sold as slaves abroad ... He did this because he thought ordinary people were disagreeable to live with.'

Recent excavation of Megara Hyblaea has revealed an extensive, if somewhat underpopulated, settlement. About thirty-six hectares in area, the city possessed a defensive wall, a definite street plan and an agora. Houses were well spaced, rarely faced onto a street, but did align with

N

0   10   20
Metres

The archaic agora of Megara Hyblaea, the only Megarian colony to be founded
in Sicily. The Syracusans destroyed this city in 483 BC.

main thoroughfares. The first houses comprised a single room, usually
five or six metres square and built of stone. A space was reserved from
the beginning for an agora, which by 600 BC had a stoa or roofed colonnade on its northern and eastern sides, two small temples near its southern edge, and on the eastern side a number of unidentified public buildings. The southern section of the city may not have been occupied at all
prior to 650 BC.

Zancle, as Messina was originally called, and Rhegium, modern Reggio,
are exceptions to the rule that in Sicily and Italy Greek colonies were
always sited in notably fertile places. These two Chalcidian cities were
dependent on trade, together controlling the key route through the Straits
of Messina. Zancle was supplied with food by its dependency Mylae,
situated twenty-five kilometres to the west, facing the Lipari Islands.
Rhegium, founded before 700 BC by Chalcidians from Zancle and Mes-

senian refugees from the Peloponnese as well as a group from Chalcis, prospered despite opposition from the Bruttii, the native inhabitants living in the interior. Although Syracusan intervention in Italy led to its destruction in 386 BC, the city was soon rebuilt and Rhegium survived Hannibal's attentions to become a municipality in recognition of loyal service to Rome in 90 BC. Except for Taras, which maintained its wealth and importance down to the Roman period, the majority of the Greek cities on Italian soil succumbed to the increasing pressure of the indigenous peoples. Even Cumae, whose citizens defeated the powerful Etruscans, with aid from the Syracusans in 474 BC, was conquered by the Sabelli and lost its purely Greek character.

Cumae, Italy's earliest Greek colony, is dated on archeological evidence to slightly before 725 BC. Its sheltered beach and good acropolis presented the Chalcidian traders on the nearby island of Ischia with a welcome opportunity to separate from their rivals, the Eretrians. Excavation of Cumae has brought to light a number of native pre-Greek graves, early burials of Greek warriors which echo Homeric rites, and plenty of pottery, later including examples of Etruscan types. Relations between the Etruscans and the Greeks were close: the Etruscans borrowed heavily from Greek culture, yet in 524 BC they attacked Cumae. By adopting the equipment and tactics of the hoplite they were able not only to stand up to the Greek colonists but also briefly to dominate Rome. At least three Roman kings had Etruscan blood in their veins, as did many upper-class families in republican times.

Just south of the Etruscan cities of Campania lay Poseidonia, known as Paestum in Latin. The prosperity of this Sybarite colony is attested today by the ruins of two great Doric temples, one of which was erected for the goddess Hera in the fifth century BC. Arguably this partially reconstructed Heraeum is now one of the most remarkable surviving pieces of Greek architecture. Some of its decorative sculpture has been recovered and can be viewed at the museum on the site. The city itself stood quite close to the shore, with strong fortifications. According to Strabo, who collected historical and geographical information at the time of Christ, the Sybarites first established a fort by the sea, before moving inland to found Poseidonia. Given the archeological data currently available, this seems unlikely unless the rocky headland six kilometres to the south was used as an initial strongpoint. It has been pointed out how suggestive the name of the present-day town there is: Agropoli. Whatever the truth, the foundation date of Poseidonia is close to 600 BC, according to pottery finds. The site was continuously occupied into the Roman period, only being evacuated under the empire when encroaching marshes rendered life intolerable. One unusual recent discovery is a cenotaph dated 520 BC. It consists of a small stone chamber whose roof alone is visible above ground level. Inside were found a bench, bronze jars containing honey and a painted Athenian vase. Another impressive tomb, this time made of stone slabs like a cist-grave, features scenes painted from life. These show various stages of a feast as well as a man diving from a platform into the sea.

Although the intellectual contribution of the western colonists to the Greek world was small during the Archaic Age, its first luminaries were about to appear in Parmenides and Zeno, both citizens of Elea, a Phocaean colony established south of Poseidonia around 540 BC. The older philosopher, Parmenides, is supposed to have been a pupil of Xenophanes, who spent his exile from Ionia at Zancle, Syracuse and Catania. But Strabo was sure that 'both were Pythagoreans' and 'that through them the city of Elea ran well'. Parmenides was born not later than 515 BC. His preference for writing in verse influenced Empedocles, a thinker who the ancient Greeks and Romans marvelled over as much as they did over Pythagoras and Heraclitus. Born at Acragas in the first decade of the fifth century BC, Empedocles was renowned for his success in curing diseases as well as his active support of democratic principles, in addition to his poems and lectures. Legend claims he disappeared in the flames of Mount Etna, his intention being to confirm the report that he had become a god. This apocryphal story doubtless refers to his study of material changes, which informed his view of immortality of the soul. Of himself Empedocles remarked, 'I am a fugitive from the gods and a wanderer'.

In both Sicily and Italy the Greek colonists firmly held onto the territories around their settlements. Unlike the situation in Asia Minor, the western city-states were not usually neighbours of powers belonging to an older tradition of civilization. They tended to give rather than receive: hence the adoption by the Etruscans of the Greek alphabet, mythology, pottery and metallurgy. Whilst the Greeks believed the Etruscans had originated in Lydia, they knew the Carthaginians were Phonicians oversea. Their relations with Carthage were generally uneasy, and often belligerent, although after the clash in 480 BC, a long period of peaceful trading ensued. As regards the indigenous peoples we have noticed both cooperation and conflict, with the Syracusans emerging as the supremely aggressive settlers. Possibly the significant feature of the western expansion of the Greek world was that each colony formed a new and independent polis from the start, retaining merely formal ties with the mother-city. Thus citizenship continued as fundamental to the ancient Greek way of life.

PART FIVE

THE PERSIAN CHALLENGE

Chapter Nine

THE DEFENCE OF EUROPE

In the first quarter of the fifth century BC, the Greeks were severely tested in the furnace of war. The unexpected, almost miraculous victory over the Persians proved the worth of the polis and its citizen soldiers; the successful defence of Europe was commemorated in art and literature, becoming the Great Event of Greek history, the repulse of barbarians who were content to live under a despotic king. It was readily forgotten that more Greeks had fought for or sympathized with the Persians than had taken the field against them. Even Herodotus, whose invention of western history was an attempt to explain the conflict, had to admit at the battle of Plataea in 479 BC that, 'The Thebans who took the Persian side displayed no small enthusiasm for the fight and were certainly not lukewarm in their commitment. In fact, three hundred of their finest men died fighting the Athenians.' For him, the issue at stake was despotism versus liberty, and his readers in the Classical Age believed this to be true, although Athens turned her anti-Persian league into an empire and Sparta was prepared to abandon the Greek cities of Ionia in exchange for Persian gold to build and man its fleets. The years after the Persian defeat lie beyond the scope of this book, not least because effective resistance marked the turning point between the Archaic and the Classical periods of Greek history, but we should bear in mind the tendency of later generations to mythologize the stirring events. This was a quite natural thing to do as long as Persia still posed an active threat to the Greek cities of Asia Minor and even of the Aegean.

For us the Persian invasion of Greece, as well as the smaller Carthaginian campaign in Sicily, appears in a different perspective. Victory was crucial for the future development of European civilization as we know it. Had the Athenians, for instance, carried out their intention of sailing to Italy when they learned that the Isthmus was to form the line of defence, the history of the ancient world would have been very different indeed. That Themistocles was able to use this threat to bring about the decisive naval engagement at Salamis shows how critical the situation was. The Spartan commander of the Greek fleet, a nobleman called Eurybiades, realized as much. According to Herodotus, 'it was enough to make him change his mind. His chief motive was apprehension of losing Athenian support, if he withdrew to the Isthmus; for without the Athenian ships his strength would not have been sufficient to offer battle. So he took the decision to stay where they were and fight it out at Salamis.'

The stunning Greek triumph at Salamis in 480 BC panicked Xerxes, the Persian king: immediately he laid his plans for escape. News of it

186

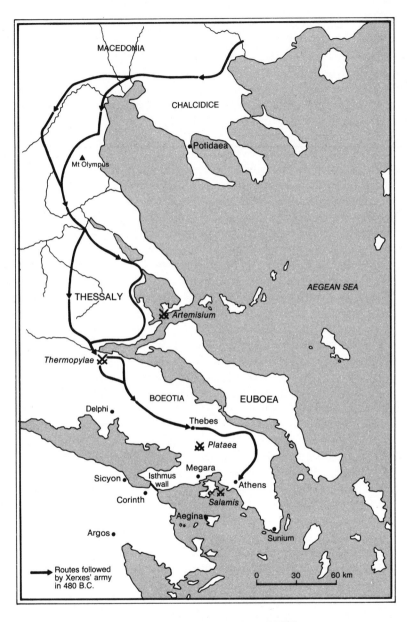

XERXES' INVASION OF GREECE

must have amazed another despot, Gelon the tyrant of Syracuse, who was also certain of Persian success. Herodotus says Gelon deposited a large sum at Delphi with the instructions to his representative that, 'If the Persians won, he was to give the money to Xerxes together with the earth and water of his dominions. If the Greeks won, he was to bring the money back again.' The victories at Salamis, Plataea and Mycale, in Asia Minor, secured Greek freedom; they allowed European civilization to progress from its original phase to the first maturity of the Classical Age. We shall be looking in this chapter at the context of that military achievement, at the poleis which stood together against the might of Persia.

Yet it is necessary to remind ourselves that from the Persian viewpoint the events down to 479 BC did not constitute a colossal reverse. From the palace-city of Persepolis the unsuccessful campaign in Europe seemed little more than a border problem. Apparently Xerxes lost interest in the west and sank deeper into the comforts of royal life at home, until he was assassinated through a harem intrigue in 465 BC. Even his father, the energetic Darius, could hardly be expected to regard the Athenian victory at Marathon in 490 BC as anything more than a pinprick. In the year of his accession to the throne, 522 BC, Darius had had to deal with rebellions in large parts of the Persian empire. His rock-cut inscription at Bisitun, near modern Kermanshah, points out how he fought nineteen battles and took captive nine kings in one and the same year. In the Persian archives, 'the Greeks beyond the sea' receive little attention and those living in Persian territories in Asia Minor are mentioned only for the purposes of taxation. So our source remains Herodotus, whose researches were conducted, 'To preserve the memory of the past by putting on record the astonishing achievements both of our own and of other peoples; and, in particular, to show how they came into conflict.'

First blood was drawn between mainland Greece, 'the Greeks beyond the sea', and Persia in the Ionian revolt of 499–493 BC. An appeal for assistance brought twenty Athenian and five Eretrian vessels across the Aegean to augment the Ionian fleet. Sparta turned down the request on the grounds that any forces sent to the Ionian army would do nothing to improve the chances of beating the Persians on land. Despite this caution, the Persians may have already regarded the Spartans as their enemies because of the attack they launched in 524 BC, along with the Corinthians, on Polycrates, tyrant of Samos. The ships that Polycrates offered to Cambyses for the invasion of Egypt the year before suggests the existence of some kind of formal alliance between Samos and Persia.

From the defeat of the Lydians in 546 BC onwards, the Persians were the real masters of Asia Minor and its offshore islands. Expansion into Europe was started by Darius, after he had completed the conquest of northern India. In 516 BC he led an army across the Hellespont in a campaign against the Scythians, who dominated the lands north of the River Danube. Though the Persians had to retreat, they maintained a bridgehead in Europe, to which they returned after crushing the Ionian revolt. This insurrection spread throughout the Greek cities of Asia Minor as well as Cyprus, and drew in many of the Carians. Nevertheless a Persian counteroffensive had by 495 BC reduced rebel holdings to parts of Ionia and the nearby islands; with the result that the insurgents decided to give up the struggle on land and concentrate all their resources at sea.

The inevitable battle took place in 494 BC at Lade, off Miletus, where the Greeks proved no match for the Phoenician ships in the Persian navy. Disorganized and dispirited, the rebel fleet failed to fight as one, the Samian contingent hoisting sail and fleeing at the earliest opportunity. Whilst the Lesbians soon copied these tactics, the ships belonging to Chios and Miletus faced the enemy bravely, but they had no chance of winning, and so those vessels remaining afloat were obliged to conduct a fighting retreat. The lack of an overall command obviously hampered the Greeks who had assembled more warships than were later engaged at Salamis. Miletus was taken by storm, and the revolt ended in 493 BC.

Reinforced 'with a large army and fleet', Mardonius then reasserted Persian authority in Europe proper. This son-in-law of Darius had been specially sent to the west in order to complete the pacification of Asia Minor, which he accomplished to Herodotus' surprise by replacing tyrants in Ionia with democracies, before he recovered Macedonia and Thrace in 492 BC. His only major setback was the wrecking of the expeditionary fleet in a storm near Mount Athos. Many men were drowned, or 'devoured by sea-monsters', or simply died of exposure. It was a disaster the Persians did not forget, as Xerxes was to have a canal cut on the isthmus where Athos stands in preparation for his own advance on Greece. In 491 BC Darius not only ordered the building of a new fleet but dispatched envoys to the Greek states of the mainland and the islands demanding their submission. If they refused earth and water, they could expect to be attacked.

Persia was now openly looking for further conquest in the Mediterranean. We know from Herodotus that Persian officers had conducted a reconnaissance of the coasts of Greece and Italy prior to the Ionian revolt. Quite likely expansion westwards was halted by this unexpected event, rather than the aid sent to the rebels by Athens and Eretria attracting Darius' displeasure, though the exiled Peisistratids in his court were ever ready to malign all Athenians. Without doubt the Persians intended to punish these two states in 490 BC as a first step towards the conquest of all of Greece. Most of the island states accepted the demand for submission, including the strong naval power of Aegina; many states of the mainland also promised obedience, but Sparta and Athens were among those which refused. The submission of the Aeginetans worried both and, at the request of Athens, the Spartan king Cleomenes intervened to take hostages; ten prominent citizens were held against the possibility of the Persians using the island of Aegina as a naval base. This action caused the enmity between Cleomenes and his co-monarch Demaratus to flare into a public row, which was settled in Cleomenes' favour by the oracle of Delphi. Demaratus took refuge in the Persian court, but his opponent did not long enjoy his victory, for the Spartans discovered that the priestess had been manipulated, and within a year Cleomenes committed suicide.

Relations between the Spartans and the Athenians were made easier by the Persian threat. Though a strong Athens blocked the northern extension of the Peloponnesian league into central Greece, the Spartans wisely realized that they would need reliable allies in the event of an invasion; especially worrying for them because of the helots was a sea-borne blow aimed at Laconia. Whilst Cleomenes' crushing defeat of the Argives in $c. 495$ BC had neutralized pro-Persian forces south of the Isthmus, there was still a long coastline to protect against Persian assault and therefore a place for the Athenians in the allied fleet. The Spartans seem to have learned to stomach Athenian democracy. Even the revelation that Cleisthenes had tricked Cleomenes into deposing the Peisistratids in 510 BC by means of the Delphic oracle failed to cause a breach, though it has to be admitted that opposition to the restoration of ex-tyrant Hippias came chiefly from the Corinthians, who could still remember the worst days of the tyranny they had suffered. So Hippias threw in his lot with the Persians, and Herodotus tells us, 'guided the invaders to Marathon' in 490 BC.

Little is known in detail about Athenian politics during the first decade of the fifth century BC. From the few recorded events we can surmise a struggle between those who wished to appease Persia and those who were prepared to fight. Certainly the anti-Persian party gained in 493 BC a powerful leader, Miltiades, the future victor at Marathon. He had been driven from the Chersonese by Mardonius' operations in Thrace. Originally sent there about 524 BC by Hippias to maintain Athenian interests in the region, Miltiades ruled the natives like a king, but he had encouraged Athenians to settle in some numbers. During the Ionian revolt he decided to renounce his vassalage to Darius and offer assistance to the insurgents, his forces liberating Imbros and Lemnos, islands which had been under Persian control since 509 BC.

Athens' Ionian policy vacillated dramatically. The Athenian squadron was withdrawn from the rebel fleet at the end of the first campaigning season. Miltiades himself was prosecuted by the pro-Persian faction: the charge of tyranny in the Chersonese failed and subsequently he was elected as a strategos, one of the ten generals in command of the Athenian army. He also found a political ally in the younger Themistocles, who advocated the strengthening of the navy. Some time before 490 BC, Themistocles oversaw the fortification of Athens' natural harbours at the Peiraeus, but his vital contribution to the ultimate defence of Europe occurred only in 483 BC, when he persuaded the assembly to apply a large surplus revenue from the state silver mines of Laurium to the construction of 200 triremes. The appeasers were strong enough to have Phrynichus fined in 494 BC for producing a play which lamented the sack of Miletus. Although Herodotus claims that Phrynichus was punished and his play banned because the Athenians were distressed at the reminder of the Ionians' misfortune, the actual reason was most likely a wish to avoid annoying Darius any further. The demand of the Persian king for earth and water in 491 BC wonderfully concentrated minds, in particular when it was understood that submission meant the restoration of Hippias. So it was that, like Sparta, Athens decided to resist.

Dissatisfied with Mardonius' performance in Macedonia and Thrace, Darius appointed a Mede named Datis and his own nephew, Artaphrenes, as commanders of the élite troops to be sent directly against Eretria and Athens. They struck in the summer of 490 BC straight across the Aegean, secured the Cyclades by an attack on Naxos, the sole state in the archepelago to remain uncowed, and landed on Euboea near the small city of Carystus, which yielded under siege. Then Datis and Artaphrenes moved up the coast to invest Eretria, where in spite of an offer of Athenian aid the inhabitants were hopelessly divided about the action they should take. The Persians were able to land unopposed in Eretrian territory and, after a six-day siege, they took the city through treachery. The sack was intended as a dreadful warning to Greeks still defying Darius: buildings were fired and the surviving population deported.

A few days later the Persians crossed to Attica and landed at Marathon, 'the most suitable place for deploying cavalry', the arm in which they excelled. The unopposed landing achieved both a military and political objective. Getting horses ashore in the face of a determined enemy was a risky enterprise, and therefore the guidance of Hippias came in handy. In addition, the spot was at such a distance from the city of Athens that before any battle might take place an opportunity existed for internal discord to weaken the Athenian cause. Neither Hippias' supporters nor any other appeasers managed to deflect the leadership of Miltiades, who marched northwards with his fellow generals to join forces with the Plataeans, longstanding allies of the Athenians. Together they were supposed to contain the Persian invaders, while the Spartans marched up from the Peloponnese. However, Miltiades made up his mind to attack, carried the strategoi with him, and engaged when the heavy-armed Persian cavalry were not in position. Eleven thousand bronze-clad Greeks charged, at the double, a bigger body of infantry which they hit with a single, staggering blow. 'When the Persians saw them coming at such a pace,' says Herodotus, 'they got ready to receive them convinced that the Athenians were wholly possessed with a frenzy of self-destruction. They were so few in number, and had no support from cavalry or archers. That was how the Persians imagined it; but when the two armies closed together, then the Athenians fought superbly.' The Persian infantrymen, who were superior in archery, sent a terrible barrage of arrows at their attackers: once through this fire, the Greeks had the advantage, for the Persians were virtually unarmoured in comparison with the hoplites. Herodotus describes the hand-to-hand fighting as fierce

and prolonged. The foreigners were winning through against the middle of the Greek line; they broke the phalanx and pursued the Greeks inland. On the wings it was the Athenians and the Plataeans who prevailed. More important still, they allowed the Persians that they had routed to escape, and instead gathered their wings together against the Persians who had broken through the centre. In the fighting which ensued the Athenians won the day. They chased the Persians in their flight and cut them down, pursuing them right to the sea, where they called for fire and began seizing hold of the ships.

When the Persians finally put out to sea, they left over 6,000 dead behind them. The Athenian fallen, 192 in total, were afterwards cremated and their ashes buried on the battlefield: a mound marks the place today.

The Persians did not retreat immediately. They attempted to sail round to Athens and capture the city, perhaps by means of treachery. A forced march brought the hoplites back in time; then the vanguard of the Spartan army arrived, and there was little for the invaders to do than withdraw. In response Darius decided a more coordinated attack was required to settle the troublesome Greek frontier. Preparations began, but were interrupted by revolt in Egypt and the death of Darius in 486 BC.

Having inspected the Persian dead at Marathon and studied the armour and weapons they had used, the Spartans congratulated the Athenians and started homewards. Doubtless the professional Spartan eye took in the better protection afforded by the bronze panoply of the hoplite in hand-to-hand fighting, for the iron scale-cuirass worn by the Persians had proved less effective against a direct spear thrust. While the Lydians and the Babylonians in Xerxes' invasion force were to be heavy-armed infantry, the standard attire of the Persian soldier comprised a soft felt cap, an embroidered sleeved tunic with iron 'fish scales', trousers, and a wicker shield, his weapons being a short spear, a bow and a dagger. The lesson of Marathon was the superiority of the phalanx as soon as contact was made with Persian footsoldiers, something Herodotus was quick to appreciate. 'The Athenians', he notes, 'were not only the first Greeks to charge an enemy at the run, but they were the first to prove capable of enduring the sight of the Persians and their outlandish costume. Up to that time, their name alone struck fear into the hearts of the Greeks.'

Yet Datis and Artaphrenes had not fallen back without conquests to their credit, even though the eighty-year-old Hippias seems to have died of disappointment recrossing the Aegean. The captured Eretrians had been deported through an anxious Cyclades and the anti-Persian states of mainland Greece knew that the final day of reckoning was still to come. Euphoria, of course, gripped the Athenians, a mood Miltiades sensibly used to take the offensive at sea in order to induce at least some of the island states to rebel against Persia. In 489 BC, Miltiades cruised about the Cyclades and received a mixed reception: the Parians refused to have anything to do with him, probably because of their rivalry with the neighbouring Naxians, so he attacked their city. A long siege, however, was unacceptable to the Athenians manning the fleet and Miltiades had no choice other than return to Athens, where he was put on trial for the conduct of the expedition and sentenced to a large fine. He died shortly afterwards from the effects of a gangrenous wound received on Paros. Ungrateful as this treatment may appear now, the Athenians were never sentimental about their commanders and always apportioned blame when a failure occurred. Miltiades could have raised expectations too high, or the authority he wielded on campaign may have worried the assembly. His political ally, Themistocles, no friend of Persia, is supposed to have said at this time that Miltiades' trophies kept him awake at night, a damaging insinuation about a leader who was once charged with tyranny. Ostracism was used in 483 BC against Aristides, one of the strategoi at Marathon, on the grounds that his influence in state affairs had become too great. Recalled two years later, Aristides rendered distinguished service during Xerxes' invasion and commanded the Athenian army in the campaign of 479 BC.

Themistocles, the leader of the democrats since 493 BC and a general in 490 BC, was the moving spirit behind the build-up of Athenian strength. His recommendation to construct new warships in 483 BC was farsighted, no matter that the outbreak of war between Athens and Aegina immediately persuaded the assembly. As Herodotus remarks, this struggle 'saved Greece by forcing Athens to become a maritime power. In point of fact the 200 triremes were not employed for the purpose they were built, but were ready in the hour of need.' Sensing a less friendly attitude towards Athens in Sparta, the Aeginetans moved to release the hostages whom Cleomenes had handed over to the Athenians by taking prisoner Athenian citizens at sea. Instead of an exchange of people there ensued an exchange of missiles, as each side organized raids and reprisals. On Aegina itself an attempt by a democrat named Nicodromus to assist the Athenians led to a bloody internal struggle, Herodotus tells us, between 'the property-owning class and the ordinary people', once the betrayal was discovered. Some of the democratic revolutionaries escaped to Attica and settled at Sunium, whence they continued to harass the victorious oligarchs on Aegina by surprise landings. A state of war still existed as late as 481 BC but we hear of no more operations, the renewed Persian threat having overshadowed the entire political landscape.

Xerxes had succeeded his father in 486 BC and crushed the rebellion in Egypt by the end of the next year. He then began a new Persian policy of ruthlessly ignoring Egyptian traditions and imposing his will on the rebellious province. An uprising amongst Babylonians drew a similar retribution in 482 BC, when Xerxes underlined his power as conqueror by removing the statue of Marduk, the city god of Babylon. This repression of local beliefs and ways contrasted with the tolerance shown by previous Persian kings and boded ill for the poleis of the Greeks. The latter, in no doubt as to their danger from Xerxes, held a conference at Corinth in the spring of 480 BC and drew up plans for the defence of Europe. The twenty or more states attending looked naturally to Sparta for leadership, for important as control of the Aegean was in repulsing the invaders, all recognized that in the last resort the Persians would have to be defeated on land. It was agreed to abide by the decisions of a defence council, reached by a majority vote of its equal members: in the field all deferred to the expertise of the Spartans. The acceptance of Spartan commanders both on land and sea indicates that the mainland Greeks had learned from the difficulties experienced by their cousins during the Ionian revolt. Obviously the Spartan commanders would have to consult with the leaders of the contingents from the allied states, such as Themistocles on behalf of the Athenians, but once a decision was taken, then full authority and full responsibility was theirs.

Meanwhile Xerxes marched with his invading forces to the Hellespont, where twin pontoon bridges awaited his crossing from Asia to Europe. Mocked, like the Athos canal, these floating bridges of boats did allow the Persian king to transfer his army and its baggage train without mishap, an impressive performance given the vast numbers involved. The story that Xerxes flew into a rage when two earlier bridges were destroyed by a violent storm is patently intended to denigrate his character: although he may have ordered the Hellespont to receive 300 lashes and a pair of fetters to be thrown into the sea, he also commissioned the building of better bridges, securely anchored to the seabed.

The size of the Persian expedition has been a matter of debate ever since the invasion: Herodotus estimated an army of somewhat under 2 million. A more likely figure would be between 300,000 and 400,000 men, plus the sailors and marines of the 800 or more vessels in the Persian fleet. Of these ships the largest and the finest contingent belonged to the Phoenicians, according to Herodotus 300 in number. Whatever the correct total of the invasion forces, the Persian king was personally directing the most serious attack ever launched against Europe. 'No one', Herodotus writes with awe, 'has calculated the exact number of cooking women, concubines and eunuchs; nor the number of transport and baggage animals and Indian dogs that accompanied the host. To me it is no miracle at all that streams ran dry; I find it rather amazing that provisions were found for so many tens of thousands. And from that host of thousands, Xerxes alone possessed the moral stature that was worthy of supreme command.'

The Greek plan of defence was to put to use the mountain ranges, at first holding the Vale of Tempe and denying the Persians access to the Thessalian plain. This was found to be impracticable as there were several other possible routes south and, except for the Thessalian aristocrats, few northerners were committed to active resistance. The next line of defence chosen was the pass of Thermopylae, in central Greece: it was thought that a hoplite force could defend the narrow gap there between rugged hillside and sea, while the allied fleet lay nearby in the channel between the island of Euboea and the mainland. Here the Spartan king Leonidas, the brother and successor of Cleomenes, stationed himself with 300 Spartans and 6,000 allied hoplites. Herodotus claims,

> the Spartans sent an advance guard under Leonidas, the intention being that if the other allies were to see them, they would take the field and not be tempted to join the Persians, as some had. They might well do this, if they learnt of a Spartan delay in arriving. Indeed the Spartans were held up by the celebration of the Carnea, but they fully intended, once this festival was over, to march out with their whole force as fast as possible. The rest of the allies had similar ideas, since an Olympic festival was due to fall at about this time. So they sent out an advance guard, no one imagining that the engagement at Thermopylae would be settled so rapidly.

In the middle of August the Persians made contact with the defenders of the pass. They reconnoitred the Greek position, rested for four days, then in front of Xerxes seated on his throne, stood ready for the order to attack. The Persian king was bemused by the spectacle of such a tiny force remaining where it was, apparently undismayed by the onslaught to come. Xerxes had listened to Demaratus' explanation of Spartan courage, but he still could not grasp the fact that Leonidas' men were prepared to kill to the uttermost and to meet death themselves. 'They dress their hair,' the exiled Spartan king told him, 'because that is what they do whenever they are about to put their lives at risk.' Xerxes signalled for the attack to commence. To his horror the Greeks held firm, inflicting dreadful casualties on his best troops. When similar losses were sustained on a second day of fighting, he was baffled and frightened, until a treacherous Phocian revealed how a mountain track could be followed to turn the pass. When a strong detachment was thus guided behind the Greek line, Leonidas understood the danger and sent off most of his force, staying behind with his Spartans and the Boeotians to cover their escape. He fell with the rest of them, fulfilling the oracle given to the Spartans by Delphi at the outset of the war that either their city would be laid waste or a Spartan king be killed.

Thermopylae was seen in retrospect as an heroic feat of Greek arms, but it remains a Persian victory which cost the allies central Greece, brought Thebes into the Persian camp, and would have destroyed the Athenians if they had not been persuaded to take refuge on the island of Salamis. Its one benefit to the Greek cause was the naval engagement at Artemisium, north-east of Thermopylae. This indecisive action gave the allied navy a chance to measure itself against the Persian fleet, which had already suffered considerable damage in recent storms. Thermistocles became convinced that, if the Ionian and Carian contingents could be detached from it, there was a chance of winning at sea. Accordingly he left a message for the Ionians to find after the Greek withdrawal southwards, urging them to change sides; even if they were unmoved by the appeal, he hoped that their loyalty would be questioned by Xerxes.

Both sides now needed time to refit their ships and the Greek fleet put in for repairs at Salamis. On this island were gathered the bulk of the population of Attica, evacuated on Themistocles' recommendation after a heated debate in the assembly. Only a few diehards had chosen to stay and defend the acropolis, believing the inviolable wooden wall mentioned by the Delphic oracle referred to its barricaded entrance and not the timbers of the navy. In early September Xerxes occupied Athens and reduced these last defenders after a bitter struggle. There followed a lull in the fighting for several weeks. Having obliged Eurybiades, the allied admiral, to await action at Salamis, Themistocles was content to let Xerxes' patience run out as autumn approached and the difficulties of supply began to tell on the invasion forces. At the same time the Spartan king Cleombrotus, Leonidas' brother, mustered an army of 30,000 hoplites to hold the Isthmus, whose defences he improved by demolishing the road from Megara and throwing up an embankment across the narrowest part of the landbridge, where the Corinthian shipway stood.

The Athenian account of the events leading up to the battle of Salamis, which Herodotus accepts, gives the credit to the ingenuity of Themistocles, who sent a personal message to Xerxes that the allies were contemplating flight one night. The Persian king therefore ordered his fleet to block both ends of the straits and land soldiers on the islet of Psyttaleia, in case any shipwrecked Greeks came ashore. In the morning the allies found themselves trapped, but they were rested and fed whereas the enemy had been busy throughout the hours of darkness. 'At daybreak,' according to Plutarch, who wrote his biography of Themistocles towards the end of the first century AD, 'Xerxes took his seat on some high ground, which enabled him to overlook his fleet and its order of battle. ... A golden throne had been set up for him and a crowd of secretaries were in attendance, whose task it was to record the events of the battle.' There occurred on Themistocles' vessel in the straits, Plutarch continues, a sacrifice of three Persian prisoners-of-war. A soothsayer, Euphrantides by name, demanded that these young men be offered to Dionysus in return for success that day. 'Themistocles was appalled by this horrible command ... but his companions, as so often happens at moments of crisis, were ready to find salvation in the miraculous rather than in a rational course of action. And so they ... dragged the prisoners to the altar, and sacrificed them.' However apocryphal the incident, the Greeks were in a state of acute alarm. Persian units were beginning to move towards the Isthmus, where they would be helped to turn the defensive wall by vessels from the Persian fleet, unless the allies won control of the sea. Everything pointed to a decisive naval engagement, as Themistocles prayed it might. So Herodotus recounts:

The Greeks began putting all their ships to sea, but as they were deploying, the enemy promptly attacked. Most of them backed water and started to beach their ships, but Aminias, an Athenian from Pallene, continued out to sea and rammed an enemy vessel. This ship became locked together with his and they could not be forced apart. The rest of the fleet came to Aminias' assistance, and battle was joined ...

The Phoenicians held the western wing towards Eleusis and found themselves drawn up against the Athenians, while the Ionians who held the eastern wing towards Piraeus were facing the Spartans. Very few of them were prepared to fight half-heartedly as Themistocles wished: in fact the vast majority fought well.

The greater part of the Persian fleet was destroyed at Salamis, mostly at the hands of the Athenians and the Aeginetans. The Greeks fought the battle with tight order and discipline, but the enemy had no proper formation and did nothing with any sense of purpose. They could have expected no other outcome than what followed. Even so, on that day, they proved themselves far better fighters than they had off Euboea. All of them fought as hard as they could, and in their fear of Xerxes, each man was convinced that the king's gaze was directly on him.

As regards the performance of individual Greeks or Persians, there are no accurate details. The exception is Artemisia of Caria. She found great favour with the king (though she escaped being sunk herself) ... only through ramming a vessel of her own side. When the captain of the Athenian ship (in pursuit) saw her attack the barbarian ship, he must have thought Artemisia's vessel was a Greek one, or perhaps a deserter from the Persians that was fighting for the Greeks. In any case he turned aside and chased after others. This lucky circumstance not only ensured Artemisia's safety ..., it also happened that this callous act of hers won her considerable favour in the eyes of Xerxes ...

Among those who died in the fierce fighting was Xerxes' brother, the admiral Ariabignes, son of Darius, and with him many other well known Medes, Persians and allies. Casualties among the Greeks, however, were few; being able swimmers, the crews who had lost their ships but had themselves managed to survive the hand-to-hand fighting swam across to Salamis. But most of the barbarians, not knowing how to swim, were drowned in the sea. It was when the ships in their front line were put to flight that the heaviest losses were sustained. The crews of the ships in the rear pressed forward, in their eagerness to impress the king, and ran into the ships as they were trying to make their escape.

A morning swell added to the confusion. The breeze was no disadvantage to the Greek ships, which were less tightly packed and able to manœuvre without difficulty, but it caught the press of Persian vessels, swinging them broadside to their opponents, who swiftly closed to ram. A group of Phoenician captains whose craft had been sunk went to protest to Xerxes, blaming their losses on the conduct of the Ionians. The interview, Herodotus is pleased to relate, did not go as expected, for as the Phoenicians 'were actually speaking, a ship from Samothrace rammed another from Attica. Then, as the Athenian ship was going down, a ship from Aegina drove in and sank the one from Samothrace. But the Samothracians swept aside its marines with a shower of javelins, boarded the vessel that had sunk theirs and took it for themselves. This exploit saved the Ionians; for when Xerxes, who had become very bitter and ready to blame everybody, had witnessed it, he turned on the Phoenicians and ordered them to be beheaded on the grounds that men who behaved like cowards should not slander braver men than themselves.'

Accounts of Salamis that have come down to us provide no clear picture of Greek tactics. Themistocles, who is generally agreed to have brought about the victory, knew that the Persian superiority of numbers would not count in the restricted waters around the island, and his plan from the very start of the campaign could have been to force the issue there. Some Persian squadrons may not have entered the fray at all; the Egyptians, who performed best at Artemisium, are not mentioned in Herodotus' narrative, and it is thought that they were detached to guard the western exit of the straits towards Megara. Themistocles' assessment of the strategic value of naval supremacy was accurate. Once Xerxes realized the extent of the defeat – the butchery of the Persian soldiers stranded on Psyttaleia by a force of Athenian hoplites under Aristides' command must have brought home the vulnerability of his own position in Europe – he sent his battered fleet to protect the bridges across the Hellespont. This changed the whole situation, because without ships the Peloponnese could not be conquered. The impetus of the Persian invasion was blunted. With winter two months away, Xerxes decided to return to Sardis and deal with any unrest arising from the news of Salamis; he left Mardonius behind in Greece with an occupying army and instructions to reopen the campaign in spring 479 BC.

According to tradition, the day on which the battle of Salamis took place the Sicilian Greeks defeated the Carthaginians at Himera. The reason for linking these two decisive victories was the suspicion in the ancient Greek mind of collusion between the Carthaginians and the Persians. The massiveness of Carthaginian intervention was unprecedented, as a fleet of 200 warships and an army of 300,000 men are reputed to have answered a call for aid from Anaxilas, tyrant of Rhegium and Messina, and his father-in-law, Terillus, the deposed tyrant of Himera. The invaders were asked to attack the territories of two powerful men, Gelon of Syracuse and Theron of Acragas; these tyrants were in alliance and together dominated most of Greek Sicily. In order to halt their further expansion and to reinstate Terillus in Himera, the invasion force landed at the Carthaginian settlement of Panormos, modern Palermo, and prepared to advance along the northern coast of the island. Its commander, Hamilcar, a Carthaginian of Syracusan descent on his mother's side, intended to meet up with his Greek allies at Messina, before turning south against Syracuse. *En route* there was also opportunity for an assault on Himera, which was defended by Theron. It came as a rude shock to Hamilcar, when his men were besieging this city, that Gelon arrived with 50,000 infantry and 5,000 cavalry, after a long overland march.

Having lost most of his own cavalry in a storm off the Sicilian coast, the Carthaginian commander was unwilling to risk a pitched battle and he retired into a fortified camp to await Greek reinforcements. Pretending that they were friendly cavalry, a squadron of Gelon's horsemen succeeded in penetrating the defences of the camp and admitting the infantry. In the ensuing conflict Hamilcar was cut down by the altars on which he was sacrificing to the Carthaginian sea god, his army routed, and many of his ships beached near the camp burned. So crippled was Carthage by this defeat that peace had to be purchased with a large indemnity. At the battle of Himera, Gelon secured Greek freedom in Sicily and established Syracuse as the leading city-state. Hieron, his successor, helped Cumae defeat the Etruscans at sea in 474 BC, but after his death the Syracusans turned away from tyranny and embraced democracy. The achievements of these two leaders were not forgotten, however. An ode composed by the Theban aristocrat Pindar about 470 BC is their testimonial; it securely links the triumphs over the Carthaginians and the Etruscans with those over the Persians, for together they 'saved the Greeks from harsh slavery'.

Vital though the action at Salamis was in determining the outcome of the invasion, the independence of European civilization was not assured until the Greeks had mastered the remaining Persian land forces. These were still formidable: slightly under 300,000 men in total, they included 30,000 cavalry, the finest Persian infantry, the hoplites of Thebes, as well as the crack Iranian division with which Artabazus returned after escorting Xerxes to the Hellespont. Subsequently regarded as the Persian empire's expert on western affairs, Artabazus managed to extricate his soldiers from Greece after the battle of Plataea, succeed to a governorship in Phrygia, and conduct negotiations with the Spartans in 476 BC. On his way back from the Hellespont in 479 BC, he protected Mardonius' communications by stamping out a rebellion of the Greek cities of Chalcidice. Only the Potidaeans held out behind a wall they had built right across the peninsula of Pallene. But in the Cyclades the disappearance of the Persian fleet gave the islanders scope for revolt which a number took advantage of. By the spring of 479 BC the allied fleet could reckon on a friendly reception all the way to holy Delos.

Mardonius wintered in Thessaly. Since he was blocked by the Isthmus wall, his strategy for the second campaign season was to entice the allied army out of the Peloponnese and bring it to battle. He did his utmost to exploit rivalries between the Greek states offering the Athenians a separate peace on favourable terms. Alexander, the Macedonian king, told them on Mardonius' behalf that in return for their allegiance to Xerxes they would be granted local self-government, like the Phoenician cities of Tyre and Sidon. When this ploy failed, he invaded Attica and, while the Athenians fled again to Salamis, finished off the work of destruction there. Although the Athenians had announced they would never come to terms with Persia 'so long as the sun stays on his present course', the Spartans were worried enough by summer 479 BC to let the allied army leave the Isthmus and march into Attica under the command of Pausainias, the son of king Cleombrotos. In this force were 5,000 Spartans, nearly two-thirds of the age group capable of bearing arms. The decision of the ephors to risk the lives of these men indicates the effectiveness of Mardonius' diplomacy. An equal number of perioeci, hoplites from Laconian towns, accompanied them, along with 35,000 light-armed helot troops.

Warned by the Argives, Mardonius withdrew from Attica and occupied a strongpoint on the north side of the Asopus River in southern Boeotia, six kilometres away from the city of Thebes. Here he concentrated his supplies and cleared the ground of trees for cavalry action. His fortified encampment, holding the river line and extending some five miles in length, was astride the principal routes leading from both the Isthmus and Attica. The preparations the Persians made for the coming battle are evidence of the esteem they had for Greek infantrymen. Mardonius realized that his chance of victory depended on any mistakes the allies made, especially where his horse could catch formations of hoplites in the open.

The Greeks duly arrived on the scene and halted on the foothills of Mount Cithaeron, near Erythrae. Eight thousand Athenians commanded by Aristides had joined the allied army at Eleusis, its strength in hoplites having now risen to around 40,000. Mardonius gave the Greeks every opportunity to descend onto level ground, but finding them unwilling to expose themselves,

he sent out his entire cavalry, under the command of Masistius. This man was a distinguished officer ... and he rode on a Nisaean charger that was decked out with a bridle of gold and other beautiful trappings. The cavalry rode right up to the Greeks, attacking by squadrons, causing great havoc and calling them women.

Now it turned out that the Megarians found themselves occupying the one spot on the battlefield that was most open to assault, where the enemy cavalry had an easy way through to them. Being under constant pressure, they sent a messenger to the Greek generals with an urgent request for help. In response Pausanias called out for volunteers ... and three hundred Athenians, together with a company of archers, went to their aid. There was considerable fighting, but it ended like this. During one of the cavalry charges, Masistius' horse, which was out ahead of the others, was shot in the side by an arrow. As it reared in agony, it pitched Masistius to the ground and he was immediately set upon by the Athenians. They seized the horse right away, but they only killed its rider after a struggle, since the armour he was wearing prevented them from dispatching him at once. Underneath his outer tunic of purple he was armed with a scaly breastplate of gold, which frustrated all attempts to pierce it. In the end, an Athenian who had carefully watched what was happening, stabbed him through the eye. Masistius fell dead, but the other horsemen were still unaware of it ... When they realized what had happened, they shouted to one another and galloped back to take possession of the body.

The Athenians, seeing that the cavalry was no longer riding at them in squadrons but in full force, called on the rest of the army for support. Now while the infantry was coming up to their assistance, a furious fight ensued around the body. During the time the 300 hoplites stood alone, they got very much the worst of it, and were on the point of abandoning the corpse, but as soon as others arrived in force, the Persian horsemen could no longer hold their ground or find a way to retrieve Masistius' body ...

Once the Persian cavalry had returned to camp, Mardonius and the entire army went into deepest mourning for Masistius. They cut their hair and the hair of the horses and baggage animals. The wailing cry they raised was so loud and immense that the sound of it could be heard all over Boeotia. There had died a man who ranked second only to Mardonius in the high esteem of the Persians and their king.

While the Persians were honouring the dead Masistius according to their custom, Greek confidence was growing from the fact that they had withstood the attacks of the enemy cavalry and had driven them back. As for the corpse, they placed it in a wagon and paraded it up and down the ranks ... Then they decided to march to Plataea, since it appeared to be a more suitable spot to camp than Erythrae because of the better supply of water there.

This inconclusive initial encounter is given here almost in full because for the morale of the allied army the repulse of the dreaded Persian horse was a godsend. Pausanias remained committed to staying on the defensive, as the omens advised, but he ceased worrying about the ability of his men to withstand the cavalry probes Mardonius was continuously making of the line. He could do nothing about the damage the mobile Persians did to his supply line, and there may have been shortages during the ten days the Greeks stood still. Rumblings among the Athenians were swiftly handled by Aristides, who seems to have crushed an anti-democratic conspiracy. Plutarch says the would-be appeasers were 'members of the leading families ... impoverished by the war'. Aristides was firm but merciful, telling those who wavered that they might clear their names through 'the great tribunal of the battlefield'.

On the Persian side, too, there were uncertainties. Artabazus recommended that Mardonius occupy Thebes and employ gold to break up the alliance of Greek states opposing Persia. Although the Thebans acknowledged the wisdom of this scheme, Mardonius refused to countenance any retreat and ordered his officers to make everything ready for a full attack. King Alexander of Macedon warned the Greeks of the impending battle and they were ready when all the Persian horse charged, but were severely pressed and could not stop the enemy from choking with stones the spring from which their water came. Faced with the prospect of thirsty and hungry troops, Pausanias determined to move closer to the city of Plataea at the end of the day's fighting. This redeployment during the night seems to have been badly executed. According to Herodotus, different units became widely separated because a certain Amompharetos, a Spartan battalion commander, refused to compromise his honour by retreating; he was thought after the battle to have met his death in exemplary fashion. As a result, at dawn Mardonius discovered the Spartans isolated on a slope and, thinking his moment had come, at last committed his infantry to the attack.

The Athenians, whom Pausanias ordered to close up on his left flank, were already battling with Greek troops who had sided with the Persians. These Thebans prevented the Athenians from joining the Spartans, who with 3,000 Tegeans had to face the flower of the Persian army. Everything depended on how Pausanias met this challenge: if he faltered, then the Peloponnesian hoplites moving to fill the yawning gap between the Spartans and the Athenians would hold themselves back. His nerve and timing were perfect. Allowing the Persian infantry to advance within bowshot, Pausanias held his ranks steady under an intense fire of arrows until he perceived that other enemy soldiers crowded behind them. 'These men', notes Herodotus, 'had no formation or discipline; each person simply ran as fast as he could. So with a great deal of shouting they surged forward in a crowd expecting to annihilate the Greeks completely.' Once it was clear to Pausanias that the Persians had no room for further manoeuvre, he led the Spartan phalanx forward.

The fighting at first centred on a hedge of wicker shields. This breached, desperate hand-to-hand combat was the order of the day as Persian infantrymen were reduced to snapping the Spartan spears with their hands. Lacking proper armour, they were no match for the finest hoplites in Greece, despite showing the courage that had made them masters of a great empire.

Not so the Greeks opposing the Athenians. With consummate skill, the Thebans reluctantly disengaged and, covered by cavalry, fell back on the defences of their city. The Theban cavalry-commander, Asopodorus, also accounted for 600 Peloponnesian hoplites who carelessly poured onto the plain at the news of Pausanias' victory. Out of formation they were easy prey and some compensation for the 300 Thebans who died fighting the Athenians.

The fortified camp was stormed, its occupants slaughtered, and the booty divided among the victors. Herodotus puts the allied losses at an amazingly low figure: besides the 600 Peloponnesians, the Spartans took ninety-one casualties, the Athenians fifty-two and the Tegeans sixteen. On the Persian side he believed 260,000 perished. Artabazus appears to have made off with his division of 40,000 men as soon as Mardonius fell. Seeing the rout as he was moving up towards the Greeks, Artabazus turned and headed for Phocis, then travelled up through Thessaly, Macedon and Thrace, crossing to Asia at Byzantium. 'He reached the city', Herodotus says, 'not without severe losses; for many of his men were ambushed by the Thracians, and many succumbed to hunger and exhaustion.'

The hoplite charge of the Spartans cleared Europe of the Persian threat on land: the steady judgement of Pausanias had kept the allied army safe from the Persian cavalry and at the final moment thrown the phalanx at Mardonius' choicest troops. The death of the commander of the invasion force turned the defeat into disaster – for Persia, the chance of conquest had passed. Yet in the Aegean the issue of foreign domination was by no means settled, and it was to the Athenians, who were ready to sacrifice everything for the sake of freedom, that the islanders and colonists in Thrace and Asia Minor owed their independence. The immediate problem for the allies was of course Thebes. Although they had sworn to punish every state which assisted the invader, it now became evident that this would necessitate a protracted war in central and northern Greece, which few of the citizen-soldiers wanted on the eve of autumn rains and the ploughing season. Thebes itself was also no mean city-state. So it was decided to besiege the Thebans in order to force them to surrender the leaders responsible for pro-Persian policies. When of their own accord most of these men gave themselves up, Pausanias declared the land campaign over for the year and returned to the Isthmus, where he executed the collaborators.

While these events were taking place on the Greek mainland, another victory over the Persians was gained in Asia Minor. The Spartan king Latychidas, who was now in command of the allied fleet at Delos, accepted a request from the Samians for aid. The Persian fleet, stationed at Samos since Xerxes' return to Sardis, fell back to the Anatolian shore and hauled their ships onto the beach near Mount Mycale, where a Persian army could protect them. Apparently provided with a strong force of marines, Latychidas landed nearby and made an attack. Though the Persians were hindered by Ionian desertions, they fought well and were overcome only at a considerable cost in allied lives. Mycale was a relatively small battle, but it cleared the Aegean of the Persian navy and encouraged a second Ionian revolt.

The Spartans, however, were still loathe to be committed to land operations in Asia Minor and the initiative slipped to the Athenians. In 478 BC Pausanias undertook two strategically valuable campaigns with the allied fleet: he liberated the Greek cities of Cyprus, thus giving the Phoenician fleet an enemy closer to home, and then captured Byzantium, the crossingpoint between Persian holdings in Europe and Asia. After his recall to Sparta, the Ionian and Aeolian captains in the allied navy insisted that Aristides, the Athenian admiral, assume command.

The unity of purpose caused by the Persian menace was beginning to break down. At the prompting of Corinth and Aegina, the Spartans had objected to the rebuilding of the city walls of Athens in case the Persians should return and use the site as a base. The Peloponnese, they contended, was the true citadel of Greece. Themistocles hoodwinked the ephors while the rebuilding was accomplished, and, the work done, there could be little achieved by further argument. Although his sweep through northern Greece with Latychidas in 478–477 BC restored mutual confidence, the days of the united action were passed.

From 476 BC, the Athenians and their allies conducted independent campaigns; under the leadership of Athens, the Delian league they formed soon succeeded in reducing the last Persian possessions in the Aegean. Thucydides tells us that Sparta 'no longer wanted to be burdened with the war against Persia and therefore was pleased to let the capable Athenians exercise command, at that time being on friendly relations with them.' Aristides fixed the annual contribution of the member states of the Delian league to the satisfaction of all, and the large fund that was raised paid for the expensive naval operations. A major Persian offensive was met in 467 BC and a year later Cimon, son of Miltiades, ejected the last Persians from Europe. Even the disastrous intervention of 460–459 BC in Egypt failed to weaken resistance to Persia, though 200 ships were lost on the Nile. The Delian league continued in existence after the conclusion of a formal peace with the Persians in 449 BC, gradually turning into itself an Athenian empire, but not until its collapse in 412 BC were any of the successors of Xerxes able to assert themselves in the Aegean.

Together the Spartans and the Athenians had defended European civilization. Their fight wrought something of the way in which we live. Their bravery and sacrifice set our history on its present course. The later internecine conflicts of the Classical Age cannot sully their achievements at Salamis and Plataea. They fought so hard in these engagements because they did not question the idea that the proper medium for a civilized life was citizenship in one of the many city-states of Greece. The polis was being defended. Nor should we overlook the contribution made by the small poleis themselves: Plataea sent 600 hoplites to join Pausanias, Mycenae and Tiryns combined 400, and neighbouring Hermione 300. The Great Event belonged to all who had refused the Persian kings earth and water.

CHRONOLOGY

Timescale	Western Mediterranean	AEGEAN (inc. mainland Greece)
3000 —		
2000 —		House of Tiles destroyed (c.2100) Palaces at Knossos, Phaestos and Mallia built (c.2000)
		New Minoan palaces constructed, following earthquakes (c.1700)
1500 —		Thera eruption (c.1500) Mycenaean invasion of Crete (c.1450)
		Destruction at Pylos and Mycenae (c.1200)
1000 —	Carthage, the earliest Phoenician colony (814) Pithecusae founded on Ischia (c.750) Syracuse established by Corinth (734)	Lycurgus begins reforms at Sparta (c.804)
700 —	Cumae, first Greek colony on the Italian mainland, founded (c.725)	Spartans annex Messenia (c.720) Lelantine War (c.700) Argives defeat Spartans at Hysiae (669) Death of Pheidon of Corinth (657) Second Messenian War (650–620)
600 —	Poseidonia founded (600) Lilybaeum temporarily captured by Greeks (580) Birth of Parmenides (c.515) Roman republic comes into	Spartans defeat Argives at Thyreae (546) Death of Polycrates, tyrant of Samos (522) Cleisthenes reforms Athenian
500 —	existence (c.507) Greek colonists defeat Carthaginians at Himera (480) Etruscans defeated by Greeks at Cumae (474)	constitution (507) Battle of Marathon (490) Battles of Salamis and Plataea (480–479)
450 —		

WEST ASIA	EGYPT (inc. Libya)	Timescale
	The pharoah Menes becomes first ruler of unified country (c.3100)	—— 3000
Men-barage-si, king of Kishi, first known Sumerian ruler (2630–2600) First dynasty of Ur (2480) Sargon, king of Akkad (2340–2315)	End of Old Kingdom (c.2258)	—— 2000
Hammurabi ascends throne of Babylon (1792) Hittites dominant in Asia Minor (c.1750) Miletus first founded (c.1600) Mycenaean traders replace Minoans in Cyprus (c.1400)	Hyksos, Asian rulers, assume power (c.1652) Expulsion of Hyksos (c.1567)	—— 1500
Fall of Troy (c.1220) Ugarit, in northern Syria, destroyed (c.1190) Greek settlement of Asia Minor starts (c.1120) Tiglath-pileser I, king of Assyria (1114–1076) Solomon (c.960–922) Euboeans trading in Syria at Al Mina (800)	Merenptah repulses Sea Peoples (c.1218)) Ramesses III successfully defends Egypt against a determined attack by the Sea Peoples (c.1182)	—— 1000
Sargon II of Assyria annexes Israel (721) Sennacherib, king of Assyria, sacks Tarsus (696) Assyrians reduce Tyre (666)	Nubians seize power in Egypt (c.715) Assyrians overrun Delta (663)	—— 700
Fall of Assyrian capital, Nineveh (612) Persians conquer Lydia (546)	Egyptians defeated by Babylonians at battle of Carchemish (605) Greeks given charter at Naucratis (c.570) Persian army, under Cambyses, occupies Egypt (525)	—— 600
		—— 500
Ionian revolt (499–493) Xerxes becomes Persian king (486) Battle of Mycale (479)		—— 450

GLOSSARY

agora   originally the market-place, but by the late Dark Age the civic centre of a Greek city-state.

apella   the popular assembly of the Spartans. It remained, however, subservient to the gerousia, or council of elders.

autarkia   self-sufficiency, the ideal condition for the city-state according to Aristotle.

basileus   the word for king after the collapse of Mycenaean civilization.

cist   a boxlike depression in the ground: common for burials in the Aegean, but also used for storage purposes in Bronze Age palaces.

damos   in Linear B the term probably meant community. In its later form of *demos* the meaning was enlarged to include the people collectively.

demos   the people, or merely the lower classes.

diolkos   the shipway built across the Isthmus by the Corinthians about 580 BC.

double axe   the *labrys*, the supreme symbol of Minoan religion, associated by Evans with the mother-goddess.

dromos (pl *dromoi*)   the passage way leading to a chamber or tholos-tomb.

ecclesia   the popular assembly of the Athenians. An increase in its influence occurred under the Solonian reform of the constitution, but not until after the radical changes introduced by Cleisthenes in 507 BC did the assembly seriously challenge the council of the Areopagus, the Athenian equivalent of the Spartan *gerousia*.

ephor   one of the five annually elected magistrates, or overseers, at Sparta. Their relationship to the monarchy suggests an origin in some early dispute between the kings and the nobles. They had the authority to prosecute a king before the *gerousia*.

ethnos (pl *ethne*)   the alternative form of political organization to the polis. Essentially survivals of tribal federations, ethne provided the basis for a new system of government after the decline of the city-state in the fourth century BC.

frying pans   vases of Cycladic provenance, whose function remains a mystery.

gerousia   the Spartan council of elders. This select body largely controlled Sparta, from the Second Messenian War onwards (which ended in 620 BC). It claimed the right to make laws and to decide policies as long as unanimity prevailed. The *apella* was only consulted when more than one course of action had been suggested.

helots   the oppressed rural slaves of Laconia and Messenia. They outnumbered the Spartans to such an extent that their control determined the conduct of the Spartan state. Without helots working the land, however, the Spartans would not have been able to concentrate on military affairs.

hequetai   in Linear B, followers. These members of the ruling class were the immediate companions of the king and dwelt close to his palace.

hippeis   cavalry, and initially cavalry-riding aristocrats. In Athens it was one of the names for the uppermost class, the Eupatrids.

hoplites   the heavy-armed infantry of the city-states.

hoplon   the round shield from which the hoplite took his name.

horns of consecration Evans' name for the clay or stone symbols used by the Minoans on altars and house decoration.

klawiphoros literally key-bearer. From the Linear B tablets found in the palace archive at Pylos it would appear that key-bearers performed religious duties.

koreter a Mycenaean provincial governor, whose deputy was a prokoreter.

kleroi allotments of land first given equally to Spartan citizens by Lycurgus. Concentration of holdings in the classical period greatly reduced the manpower of Sparta.

krypteia the Spartan secret police, the dagger of the ephors.

lawagetas a title discovered in Linear B inscriptions at both Pylos and Knossos. Although the meaning can be rendered as leader of the people, Chadwick is uncertain as to whether this implies the command of the war-host.

megaron (pl *megara*) literally great room. Usually the megaron comprised in the Mycenaean period a threefold building, with a covered porch, an antechamber, and the inner megaron; the latter was often a throne room.

metic resident alien, especially in Athens. Such people were important chiefly in trade and industry. They were taxed and called-up for military service like ordinary citizens.

perioeci literally neighbours, in fact the subjugated allies of the Spartans. In Thessaly and Crete similar arrangements are known to have existed, the perioeci enjoying only a limited form of self-government.

phalanx the close-packed formation of the hoplites.

pithos (pl *pithoi*) a large storage jar, usually of clay; sometimes used for interments.

polis (pl *poleis*) the Greek city-state. For Aristotle it represented the only rational system of government.

relieving triangle the triangular hollow space above a lintel of a Mycenaean entrance, such as a tholos-tomb.

stele (pl *stelai*) any marker standing over a tomb, particularly the carved ones above the shaft graves at Mycenae.

stomion entrance passage of a tholos-tomb.

strategos (pl *strategoi*) military commanders. In Athens from 501 BC the assembly elected ten strategoi each year, one for each of the regiments in which the citizens served.

telestai in Linear B local magnates, who may have stood in the same relationship to the Koreter, the provincial governor, as the hequetai did to the king.

thetes the humblest class in the polis, whom Solon admitted to the Athenian ecclesia.

tumulus a mound raised over a tomb.

tyrannos (pl *tyrannoi*) the title given to individuals in many poleis of the seventh and sixth centuries BC who assumed personal power. Few tyrannies lasted more than a couple of generations.

wanax king during the Mycenaean period.

zeugitai the farmers, citizens of moderate means in Athens.

FURTHER READING

The following list is not intended to be a complete bibliography, merely a note of some of the books on the period down to the Persian Wars that the reader might find helpful. As many contain detailed bibliographies, specific interests can be pursued through them.

TRANSITION FROM THE NEOLITHIC

ANGEL, J.L.   *The People of Lerna. Analysis of a Prehistoric Aegean Population*, New Jersey and Washington, 1971.

MELLAART. J.   *Catal Hüyük, a neolithic town in Anatolia*, London, 1967.

RENFREW, C.   *The Emergence of Civilization. The Cyclades and the Aegean in the Third Millennium B.C.*, London, 1972.

TRUMP, D.H.   *The Prehistory of the Mediterranean*, London, 1980.

THE BRONZE AGE

BLEGEN, C.W.   *Troy and the Trojans*, New York, 1963.

BRANIGAN, K.   *The Foundations of Palatial Crete*, London, 1970.

BURNEY, C.   *The Ancient Near East*, Ithaca, N.Y., 1977.

CHADWICK, J.   *The Decipherment of Linear B*, Cambridge, 1967.

CHADWICK, J.   *The Mycenaean World*, Cambridge, 1976.

CHADWICK, J.   *The Mycenaean Dorians*, Institute of Classical Studies, Mycenaean Seminar, London, 1975.

COLES, J.M. and HARDING, A.F.   *The Bronze Age in Europe*, London, 1979.

COTTERELL, A.B.   *The Minoan World*, London, 1979.

DOUMAS, C.G.   *Thera, Pompeii of the ancient Aegean*, London, 1983.

EVANS, Sir Arthur.   *The Palace of Minos*, London, 1921–35.

GEORGIEV, V.   "The Decipherment of the Inscriptive of the Phaestos Disc," *Balkan Linguistics (Balkanskoto Yezikozmanie)*, XIX, 2, Sophia, 1976.

GRAHAM, J.W.   *The Palaces of Crete*, Princeton, 1962.

GURNEY, O.R.   *The Hittites*, London, 1952.

HOOD, S.   *The Minoans. Crete in the Bronze Age*, London, 1971.

HOOD, S.   *The Home of the Heroes. The Aegean before the Greeks*, London, 1967.

HOOKER, J.T.   *Mycenaean Greece*, London, 1976.

HUXLEY, G.L.   *Crete and the Luwians*, Oxford, 1961.

KARAGEORGHIS, V.   *Cyprus. From the Stone Age to the Romans*, London, 1982.

KERENYI, C.   *Dionysos. Archetypal Image of Indestructible Life*, Princeton, 1976.

LUCE, J.V.   *Homer and the Heroic Age*, London, 1975.

MacQUEEN, J.G.   *The Hittites and their contemporaries in Asia Minor*, London, 1975.

MARINATOS, S.   *Excavations at Thera*, Athens, 1967–73.

MARINATOS, S.   *Life and Art in Prehistoric Thera*, London, 1971.

MYLONAS, G.E.   *Mycenae and the Mycenaean Age*, Princeton, 1966.

NILSSON, M.P.   *Minoan–Mycenaean Religion*, Lund, 1950.

PALMER, L.   *Mycenaeans and Minoans*, London, 1965.

PENDLEBURY, J.D.S.   *The Archaeology of Crete*, London, 1939.

PLATON, N.   *Zakros, the Discovery of a Lost Palace of Ancient Crete*, New York, 1971.

SANDARS, N.K.   *Sea Peoples. Visitors to the ancient Mediterranean*, London, 1978.

TAYLOUR, Lord William.   *The Mycenaeans*, revised edition, London, 1979.

VERMEULE, E.   *Greece in the Bronze Age*, Chicago, 1964.
WACE, A.J.B.   *Chamber Tombs at Mycenae*, Oxford, 1932.
Mycenae. An Archaeological History and Guide, Princeton, 1949.
WILLETTS, R.F.   *The Civilization of Ancient Crete*, London, 1977.

THE DARK AGE

Cambridge Ancient History, volume III, part I, The Prehistory of the Balkans; and the Middle East and the Aegean World, Tenth to Eighth Centuries B.C. ed. J. Boardman *et al.*, revised edition, Cambridge, 1982.
COLDSTREAM, J.N.   *Geometric Greece*, London, 1977.
DESBOROUGH, V.R.d'A.   *The Last Mycenaeans and their Successors. An Archaeological Survey c.1200 – c.1000 B.C.*, Oxford, 1964.
The Greek Dark Ages, London, 1972.
FINLEY, M.I.   *The World of Odysseus*, revised edition, London, 1978.
HAMMOND, N.G.L.   *Migrations and Invasions in Greece and Adjacent Areas*, Park Ridge, N.J., 1976.
SNODGRASS, A.M.   *The Dark Age of Greece*, Edinburgh, 1971.
STARR, C.G.   *The Origins of Greek Civilization, 1000 – 650 B.C.*, New York, 1961.

ARCHAIC GREECE

ANDREWES, A.   *The Greek Tyrants*, London, 1956.
BEAN, G.E.   *Aegean Turkey*, London, 1966.
BOARDMAN, J.   *The Greek Overseas. Their Early Colonies and their Trade*, revised edition, London, 1980.
BOARDMAN, J.   *Greek Art*, London, 1973.
BURNETT, A.P.   *Three Archaic Poets. Archilochus, Alcaeus, Sappho*, London, 1983.
Cambridge Ancient History, volume III, part III, The Expansion of the Greek World, Eighth to Sixth Centuries B.C. ed. J. Boardman and N.G.L. Hammond, Cambridge, 1982.

COOK, J.M.   *The Greeks in Ionia and the East*, London, 1962.
DUNBABIN, T.J.   *The Greeks and their Eastern Neighbours*, London, 1957; reprinted, Chicago, 1980.
FINLEY, M.I.   *Ancient Sicily*, revised edition, London, 1979.
FINLEY, M.I.   *Economy and Society in Ancient Greece*, London, 1-81.
FITZHARDINGE, L.F.   *The Spartans*, London, 1980.
FORREST, W.G.   *A History of Sparta*, London, 1968.
FORREST, W.G.   *The Emergence of Greek Democracy*, London, 1966.
GERNET, L.   *The Anthropology of Ancient Greece*, trans. J. Hamilton and B. Nagy, Baltimore and London, 1981.
GRIFFIN, A.   *Sikyon*, Oxford, 1982.
HOOKER, J.T.   *The Ancient Spartans*, London, 1980.
JEFFERY, L.H.   *Archaic Greece, The City-States c.700 – 500 B.C.*, London, 1976.
KIRK, G.S. and RAVEN, J.E.   *The Presocratic Philosophers*, Cambridge, 1957.
LLOYD, G.E.R.   *Early Greek Science. Thales* to Aristotle, London, 1970.
Melas, E.   *Temples and Sanctuaries of Ancient Greece. A Companion Guide*, trans. F.M. Brownjohn, London, 1973.
SNODGRASS, A.M.   *Arms and Armour of the Greeks*, London, 1967.
SNODGRASS, A.M.   *Archaic Greece. The Age of Experiment*, London, 1980.
TOMLINSON, R.A.   *Greek Sanctuaries*, London, 1976.
VERNANT, J.P.   *The Origins of Greek Thought*, London, 1982.
VERNANT, J.P.   *Myth and Society in Ancient Greece*, trans. J. Lloyd, London, 1980.
WHITE, K.D.   *Greek and Roman Technology*, London, 1984.

THE PERSIAN CHALLENGE

BURNS, A.R.   *Persia and the Greeks. The Defence of the West, c. 546 – 478 B.C.*, London, 1962.
COOK, J.M.   *The Persian Empire*, London, 1983.
HUART, C.   *Ancient Persia and Iranian Civilization*, London, 1927.

INDEX

214

START OF BRONZE AGE - 3,000 B.C. —Pg 17